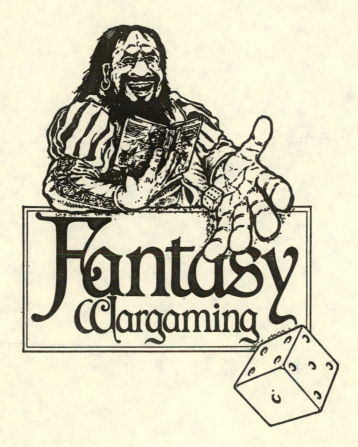

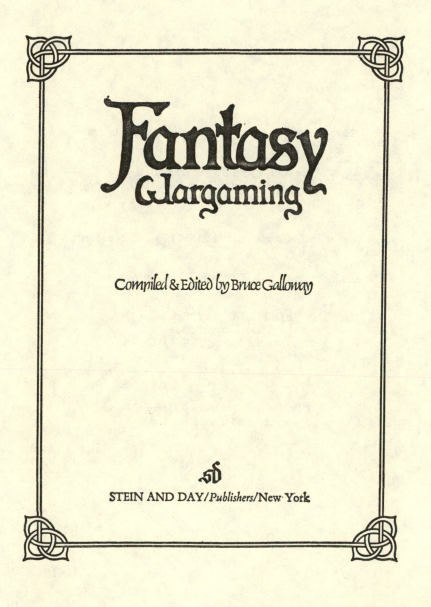

Fantasy Wargaming

Compiled & Edited by Bruce Galloway

sd

STEIN AND DAY/Publishers/New York

First published in the United States of America in 1982

Printed in the United States of America

STEIN AND DAY/Publishers
Scarborough House
Briarcliff Manor, N.Y. 10510

Ingredients

Revelation

(or "In which all is revealed")

So what *is* fantasy wargaming?

If you have picked this book up, the chances are either that you don't know and would like to, but are put off by the sheer complexity and cost of the many commercially imported games and rule books available; or you *do* know and are interested in finding out how anyone can bring a fresh approach to bear on such a well-documented subject.

To begin at the beginning then, fantasy wargaming is a hobby which started in America a few years ago and rapidly mushroomed throughout the English-speaking world, to such an extent that, today, it has virtually supplanted all previous forms of "historical" wargaming. Barely a day can pass without some mention of it in the press; the tables and trade stands at military modelling and wargaming events are thronged with figures of warriors, wizards, naked slave girls and assorted monsters; and still the diehard wargaming "purists" avert their faces, making the sign against the evil eye, hoping it will simply go away.

No chance! For unlike historical wargaming, which requires research, an interest in military history, and the patience of Job in turning out hundreds of identically painted model soldiers, all that fantasy wargaming requires is imagination. Mind you, it does not appeal to everyone, any more than everyone enjoys reading science fiction or fantasy novels. But it is probably true to say that, if you enjoyed reading *Lord of the Rings,* you will also enjoy fantasy wargaming.

In a fantasy game, each player assumes the persona of a particular character, be it witch, warlock, mighty warrior or pious priest, nimble-fingered thief or brazen harlot. This is why it is known as a *role-playing* game. Unlike conventional wargames, in which the troops maneuvered on the table have no personality, in fantasy gaming each little metal figure becomes endowed with life and character. How this is achieved is explained later, but in essence, dice throws are used to determine various aspects of each character—strength, build, agility, intelligence, social status, wealth, psychic ability, etc.—and these determine how he or she will behave during the game. A record of all these characteristics is kept on a card by each player, as they may change during the course of a game.

The game itself can be one of two sorts: it can be a commercially packaged scenario with its own rules and predetermined characters, as in the *Lord of the Rings* game now available. Here, everyone knows how Aragorn or Frodo will behave under given circumstances, so their characteristics are already fixed. Or it can be a "free" game in which the scenario will have been designed by one player (hereinafter referred to as the "Gaming Master," or GM), but in which each of the principal characters will be "designed" by the other players themselves. Nor is there anything to prevent you having more than one character.

The scenario for the game itself is usually set in a fantasy world which can either be based on a Dark Ages or medieval model; in a world of pure fantasy, such as Middle Earth; on another planet entirely; or on an "alternate Earth" in which, somewhere in the past, history has taken a different turn and "magic rules OK." The game can take the form of a quest, in which a band of adventurers set out after a hidden treasure or to rescue a damsel in distress; it can take the form of a foray into an unexplored region, such as a lost city or some mysterious catacombs, in which anything can—and usually does!—happen; or, if you belong to a regular group of players, you can design an ongoing scenario in which you play the part of your character in everyday life, struggling to increase your social status, acquire more wealth, gain promotion in the army or the Church, or study arcane secrets.

Historically, the most popular fantasy scenario is the second of the above options. The venue is usually an underground city comprising a maze of tunnels with various vaults, chambers and rooms leading off them. This city—or castle, or whatever—will be populated by a variety of inimical monsters and non-human races, dotted with various mechanical and magical traps, and filled with assorted chests of gold or jewels, magical swords and other desirable properties which each player is after for himself. This is the type of game usually referred to as "Dungeons and Dragons" (D&D) since it was first popularized under that name by American writer Gary Gygax, and it is still the most prevalent.

In many ways, however, D&D is unsatisfactory. Take a typical "dungeon." Firstly, very few game designers seem to give any thought as to *why* it is there. Secondly, the party of adventurers will usually be an oddball assortment of warriors wearing armor and bearing weapons from a wide variety of cultures and historical periods; Black and White magicians; thieves, clerics and a few slaves to carry any loot discovered. Apart from the sheer unlikelihood of such a motley crew being able to agree on any course of action without coming to blows, *why* should they associate together in the first place?

Then, when you think about the setup of the typical dungeon itself, you will find it is usually populated with a variety of non-human races, such as orcs, dwarfs, skeleton men, Undead beings and others, who would normally be at each others' throats. Yet they exist in separate rooms or caverns bare yards from each other, their only purpose in life seeming to be to lie in wait for your adventuring party. What do they do, what do they eat and live on, the rest of the time? And those assorted treasure chests, etc., scattered around: surely the inhabitants of the dungeon would have sought out and appropriated them long before?

Motive is the key word. D&D scenarios exist in a vacuum, and that is why we call them unsatisfactory. To be satisfying, a fantasy scenario must contain its own intrinsic and consistent logic.

There are a variety of ways of achieving this. One, as outlined later, is to choose a fantasy world which already "exists," complete with its own geography, history, opposing deities and races. These can be found within the covers of dozens of paperback fantasy novels (see Chapter Five). But it is much more challenging, and a great deal more fun, to design your own world—or, if a whole world is too much, at least a continent. And that is precisely what this book has been written to help you do.

Our group grew up a few years ago from a circle of friends whose main interest at the time—other than imbibing ale!—was Napoleonic wargaming. D&D—wash your mouth out! Then, one afternoon, we decided to give it a try. One of our members had obtained a fairly basic set of rules, called "Tunnels and Trolls," and designed a rudimentary "dungeon." Well, we enjoyed it, as an afternoon's pure escapism, but it lacked something, a something which we later resolved to be that internal logic and consistency mentioned above. From this it was inevitable that we should wish to progress, and the result, in time, was a game called "Leigh Cliffs" which will be marketed separately following publication of this book. "Leigh Cliffs" had all the right ingredients for an adventure. It was set in a small coastal town wherein certain mysterious events had been happening of late, and the purpose of the game was for the players to find out who—or what —was behind it. In addition, each player had a personal quest or motive for being in the village, a motive known only to himself unless he chose to reveal it. The game lasted over a complete weekend and we obviously can't reveal the end, except to say that it was out of this world!

Talking afterwards about the weekend's events, and how satisfying the game had been both from the viewpoint of the GMs who had designed it and from that of the participating players, we evolved the basic concept of this book. Our thanks are particularly due here to the encouragement we received from Patrick Stephens Limited who, as publishers of non-fiction books, must have felt a certain trepidation at accepting this project. It has been long in the writing, for it has involved extensive research in bestiaries, grimoires and antique books on myth, magic and religion in Cambridge University Library—whose staff also deserve a vote of thanks. And we hope that you find the result interesting and informative, even if you disagree with any of our conclusions.

This book takes as its basis the real Europe of the Dark and Middle Ages, the world of both the historical King Arthur and the Round Table of medieval romance. Here you will find an outline of the cultures which existed at the time, a sketch of how the feudal system operated, sections on the crafts of the weaponsmith and armorer, on the design of castles and, most importantly, on the beliefs, both religious and magical, of the period. Where we have stepped outside historical fact is in assuming, for fantasy wargaming purposes, that magic actually does work in the ways it was believed to—with all that that implies. We have evolved, after much research and discussion, what we call our "unified field theory" of magic and religion, which owes nothing to the battle between Law and Chaos extracted from the writings of Michael Moorcock and which forms the basis of most existing fantasy systems.

One beneficial result of our "unified field theory" is that there is no need for lengthy lists of spells such as clutter other sets of playing rules. Within our system, you can design any spell you like, constructing it according to the ability of your character and his standing with whichever Higher Power he worships. Whether you succeed in casting your spell is another matter, but all the information you need is here. You may even begin to believe it is true . . .

The playing rules are designed to cater for fantasy adventures at all levels, from those involving a mere half dozen characters to battles between the armies of entire nations. An innovation in the combat section, too, is the development of an infinitely flexible man-to-figure ratio, which permits forces of any size to be pitted together in mortal combat, regardless of how many actual model soldiers you have available. Thus it is not necessary to amass large armies of figures in order to construct a complete fantasy campaign lasting perhaps several weeks or months.

Our aim throughout has been to demonstrate our belief that greater richness and flavor can be introduced into fantasy role-playing games by delving back into our actual historical past, particularly one as well-known and loved as the Dark Ages. We hope that, after reading *Fantasy Wargaming*, you will have acquired some of the "feel" of the period and its beliefs and that your future adventures will benefit therefrom.

Bruce Galloway, Mike Hodson-Smith, Nick Lowe,
  Bruce Quarrie, Paul Sturman
Cambridge, May 1981

Gramercy!

To Adrian Palmer, Pete Tamlyn, Andy Strangeways, Gail Smith, Kevin "Igor" Prior, Ian and Lawrence Heath, Bob Whittaker, "Teddy," Maggie, Margaret, Verity, David Stein and all other High Powers who may have inadvertently helped in compiling this book.

Chapter I

City, Court and Country

(*or "God is Groat"*)

The working of the land

At the bottom of everything—literally—lay the land.

The kings, the nobility, the church, the knights; the master merchants, guild apprentices and journeymen, the lowest town whore; the king's regular soldiery and the mercenaries alike all relied throughout the Dark and Middle Ages on the labors of the peasantry. Medieval scholars described themselves as pigmies on the shoulders of the Greek intellectual giants, Plato and Aristotle; but they, and everybody else not involved in raising food, were more like giants on the shoulders of the hunchbacked peasantry. It was their work which fed the rural community; it was their surplus food which supplied the towns, the court and the army. That surplus was small, precarious, easily wiped out by famine, war or pestilence. A single blow, like the Black Death of 1346, could do more than merely decimate the population; it could remove the very basis of the entire society and economy. Everyone suffered when the peasant suffered. Indeed, society was overwhelmingly rural, the towns merely isolated marks on the countryside. Even in the 15th century, over 90 per cent of the people lived in hamlets and villages, or isolated farms. In the Dark Ages, and on the fringes of Christendom such as Scandinavia, Celtic Britain, or eastern Europe, the proportion was more like 99 per cent. If we wish to understand the period, we must start with the land.

Enormous areas of Christendom were still wastelands; bogs, marshes, fens; windswept upland heaths and moors, rising to snowcapped mountains or dry plateaux: arid deserts and dust-bowls, in Mediterranean areas overgrazed during the Roman and Greek domination. Still more potentially fertile soil lay covered by forests, whose size and density would be unimaginable to any inhabitant of the same area today. These fringe areas might be the size of entire kingdoms, isolated from the rest of Christendom, with their own social and economic systems. More frequently, they lay within or on the borders of a kingdom, owing a nominal allegiance but fiercely suspicious and independent of any "foreign" interference. Here could be found small, tight communities of families, inter-"marrying": shepherds, herders, hunters, fishers, with a little arable land for cultivation. Such hamlets were almost totally cut off from the outside world, frequently the home of pagans, heretics, outlaws—or even Devil worshippers. An excellent place for an adventure, but not for a tax collector!

Wasteland probably covered a third of every country in Christendom, outside Italy, and forest another third. Rural population and production was overwhelmingly (80–85 per cent) in the remaining part. Geographically, settlement was densest in certain areas. Valley bottoms were heavily populated, settlers even attempting to bring flood plains and river fens under their control. Flat, sandy areas like the English Brecklands or the North German Plain similarly attracted early colonization, their slight covering of scrubby woodland being more easily cleared by primitive tools, their light soil more easily tilled by scratch ploughs. Such areas were usually not abandoned even in the height of the Roman collapse after 350 AD. From here, the new inhabitants of the land—in England, the Anglo-Saxons and later Norsemen—gradually advanced into the heavily forested areas, often undulating claylands like East Anglia. The pattern of deforestation was clear. At first, the edges of the forest would be raided for firewood, and then used as grazing for pigs. Eventually, it became possible to clear the area and plough it, using the heavy, wheeled plough developed by the Slavs in the 7th century and quickly extended throughout Europe. The need to eat into the forests became greater because of the relative poverty of the farmer's soil; overplanted and under-manured, its crop yields were too low to sustain an expanding population. Frequently, villagers would plant "colonies" inside the forest, a few miles away—a daughter hamlet to open up new areas of the country to cultivation.

This slow deforestation of the country, and gradual expansion in the rural population, is the real revolution of the Dark and Middle Ages; but it has relatively little effect on adventuring, except to GMs drawing up their landscape maps. Much more important is the nature of the rural society itself.

"Fringe" peasants were often free, outside the law. In more settled areas, throughout the period, the peasantry were bound to serfdom, and to the law. The majority lived together in villages, their size varying from 30 to 300 people depending on the date, the place and, above all, the fertility of the soil. Earlier villages (Dark Age) or settlements on the borders of Christendom tended to be at the lower end of the scale. Farming was a mixture of communal and individual effort. Around the village were commons, meadows and areas of woodland used for common grazing of cattle, sheep and pigs—the individual's right to graze here being closely regulated by the community of peasants itself. Also here were the grain-producing areas: two (or, exceptionally and usually after 1300, three) enormous open fields, ploughed in gently curving strips up to a furlong or more long, each strip (or furrow) being separated from its neighbor by a ridge of earth thrown up over centuries by the act of ploughing. At the end of each strip was the headland, where the plough was turned round. The ploughing was often communal; one family might own only a part of a plough team, or pay another with a team for its use. The strips were distributed communally—one family being given different strips each year by decision of all the community. Different families, however, had different numbers of strips, and therefore different "wealth." Each had differing numbers of poultry and beasts, larger or smaller cottage gardens where extra crops might be produced. The peasantry were not a class, but a range of classes.

They were united, however, by two things: their poverty, and subjection to greater men.

There is no doubting their poverty, even during the latter part of the Middle Ages. In the early Dark Ages, the peasantry seem to have lived at worst in covered pits, at best in crude wattle-and-daub huts covered with thatch, with a single room. The descendants of the same huts can be found also in the Middle Ages. Some peasants' houses had a second room, or even rose to two stories; but the extra space was frequently used to house the cattle, neatly solving the problems of heating and rustling at the expense of smell! There were hearths, but no chimneys—and certainly no kitchens, bedrooms or bathrooms. Natural functions

would be undertaken in a midden outside the hut, and go forward
with animal manure for use on the fields. Diet was monotonous,
almost entirely cereal: barley, rye or oat bread, meal-based por-
ridges and gruels, with ale as the principal alternative to disease-
bearing water. The diet was supplemented by peas and beans
from the cottage garden, fish on Fridays and perhaps half a
pound of meat a week. The total calorie consumption was between 2,000 and 4,000 a day—just enough for heavy manual
laboring, probably six rather than five days a week. Celebrations,
predictably, centered on feasts. 30 per cent of infants died by the
age of ten, and life expectation even for those who had survived
childhood was short—40–45 for a man, 30–35 for a woman.
Malaria, dysentery, etc., were endemic. So were illiteracy, ignorance, and superstition—peasant folklore being a major source of
material for the myth, magic, monsters and religion of *FW!*

The subjection of the peasantry to great landowners is equally
patent: although its terms and severity varied from class to class
within the peasantry. At the very top of the manorial pyramid
were the "free peasantry"—equivalent to the Yeomanry of Tudor
England. Some of these worked their own farms, usually of 50
acres or more; some were millers, innkeepers, blacksmiths,
foresters, etc., working for the village community on an independent basis, or for the lord of the manor. These owed only judicial
obedience to the lord—i.e., attended his court, and were bound by
his decisions and verdicts. Their land was their own, and they
might move on as they chose. Immediately beneath these were the
rent-paying free peasantry—known in the English Domesday
Book (1086) as "sokemen." These paid rent for their land,
which belonged to the lord. They owed judicial obedience too,
but were free to give up (or sell) their lease and move on. Both
of these classes were very small, and the sokemen often paid for
their nominal freedom with poverty and small landed estates.

At the other end of the scale were the slaves. Separating slaves
from the "unfree" classes immediately above them is very
difficult, from the historical divide of centuries. Nevertheless,
there always were slaves, even in countries like England where
the law did not recognize a separate slave class. A man might become a slave through a judicial decision, outlawry, or capture in
war; his children and children's children would probably remain
non-people within the feudal system, working on their owners'

fields or as servants in their houses, for nothing more than up-keep. Their only hope of advancement was manumission, or escape.

Between these two extremes lay the "unfree," or serfs (*servi*). The mass of the peasantry were serfs, and variations between them were a matter of wealth and terms of service. At the higher end of the serfs were the villeins. These owed judicial service to the lord, together with certain financial and other dues. Financial dues included the obligation to pay *heriot,* for the inheritance of their land, *merchet,* for the marriage of their eldest daughters, and *tallage*—the last being an arbitrary tax taken at the lord's pleasure. Heriot would be equal to the family's best beast, merchet rather less stiff a price. Additionally, they owed three days' work a week on the lord's own manor farm, which might either be a part of the open fields or a separate group about the manor house. Villein holdings varied from 15 to 40 acres; they could not be sold, nor could the villein leave the area without the lord's permission. Below the villeins lay the rich and poor cottagers—cottars and bordars, respectively, in Domesday terms. These held only smallholdings of 1–5 acres; they owed correspondingly less labor on the home farm (*demesne:* usually one day a week), but were otherwise subject to the same impositions. Most cottagers in fact worked as virtually landless laborers, on the farms of the lord or of the richer peasantry, for a subsistence wage.

How absolute was the manorial system? Certainly, subjection was never total. Mobility upwards and downwards within the peasantry was common; a sokeman might sink in hard times into serfdom, a serf might acquire more land or even break out of the system entirely. There were certain difficult, but possible channels of escape. The army and the Church were two—unfree villeins proving their worth in a peasant militia might surreptitiously find their way into the free soldiery. The richer villein might buy his freedom, and possibly even the land which he had been farming. Adventurous and hot-headed villeins could simply run away—into the forests and outlawry, or to the nearest town. If he was not caught within a year and a day in the town, he was automatically a free man. In *FW,* these "escape routes" are of vital importance, for they explain how a character with low social class can still participate in an adventure. Historically, they were much less common than the slow transformation of the unfree, labor-paying tenantry into a semi-free, rent-paying one. This process, "commutation," was greatly speeded after 1350 by the Black Death. As the population plummeted, the price of labor shot up; the great lords found it difficult to compel labor services, or prevent the flight of villeins to other lords willing to offer wages or cheap land. By the last years of the Middle Ages, the manorial system was practically dead. Social class was equated in the country with the size of your landholding—and nothing more.

The growth of the towns

"Civilization" came from towns.

That is linguistically undeniable—the word literally does arise from the Latin for "city." Historically, it is not the whole truth, at least in the Dark and Middle Ages. "Civilized behavior," for example, was influenced as much by the habits of the Court and the teachings of the Church as by the urban bourgeois. Nobility, Church and towns were three legs of a tripod, standing on the solid base of rural peasantry, supporting the Crown. But of the three, the towns were numerically and economically the most important.

To talk glibly of "the towns" is perhaps misleading. A small center like Saffron Walden in 1400 cannot meaningfully be comprehended in the same breath as Winchester or London. Similarly, the London of 1400 was vastly different from that of a millenium before. Generally, the same rule of thumb applies as with rural settlement; the earlier the date, the more isolated the position, the smaller the size. This alone cannot explain differences in size, however. Towns served different functions—not merely economic, but political. For convenience, they can be divided into four types: the market town, the county town, the city and the metropolis.

The market town in a fairly fertile area might have as many as 600 inhabitants in the High Middle Ages—under half that in the Dark Ages. It would serve an area of countryside about the town up to eight or ten miles in radius—sufficient for a farmer to come into town, sell his agricultural produce at the market, purchase other goods there, and return home within a day. Frequently, the town would be the head of an "honor"—a group of neighboring estates all held by the same noble. In such a case, it would also be the center of his court, with a fine manor house and perhaps a small castle. The market itself, if not controlled by the lord's courts, would come under specially convened courts of "pie-powder" ("dusty-feet"), covering all crimes of burglary, fraud, false weights or coinage, etc. Agricultural produce would be traded for salt, manufactured necessities like ploughshares, cloths or candles and spices. The market town would have its own miller, blacksmith, candlemaker, etc., but probably no guild merchant and no powers of self-government.

The county towns of the same period would be 800–2,000 in size, and a full day's journey—about 30 miles—apart. In many respects, they resemble an overgrown market town. There would be the weekly market, serving the agricultural neighborhood. The goods would, however, be more varied, with many more luxury items. These would serve not only the peasantry, whose wants were small, but also other towns, the local nobility and churchmen, passing travellers on trade or expeditions of war. A county town—by Dark Age standards a proper city—would be conveniently situated for regional trade, almost invariably possessing its own royal charter, king's law court and powers of self-government. Frequently, it would also possess a large castle, and occasionally complete city walls. Many county towns had a mint, producing local money for the king or the leading noble of the area. Most also possessed a guild merchant, and an annual week-long trade fair for the wider region.

Cities and metropolises occur in a nation unpredictably, wherever the dictates of politics marry happily with a good trading situation. Many were at the lowest fordable point on major river trade routes—London and Paris being good examples. Others stood on the few surviving Roman roads still in use, in a strategic point where two roads crossed or a road crossed a major river. Some lay on the coast itself—like Genoa, Bruges and Venice. The difference between them was only one of size; a medieval city before the Black Death would normally be between 20,000 and 50,000 people—a metropolis, like Florence, might have over 100,000. Cities and metropolises invariably attracted the courts of the highest aristocracy, if not the king's court itself. Paradoxically, they also had formidable powers of self-government, and acted as political and judicial institutions in their own right. Each city had its own courts, not under royal, noble or ecclesiastical control. Each had a multiplicity of guilds, each with its own internal structure and regulatory systems. Besides the market place or square, the law courts, pillory and fountain of the county town, cities would have many other street markets, and possibly three or four fairs in a year. Most were ports, by sea or river. Here, above all, was carried out the large-scale international trade and industry upon which the activities of the Court and Church relied. Many cities generated intense local pride, some creating false histories of their greatness, or laying out their streets to recall the pattern of the Biblical New Jerusalem. The encouragement of universities, as marks of their greatness, was another frequent factor.

The differences seem almost greater than the similarities; yet all lived off the same narrow agricultural surplus of the peasantry, which fed the town dwellers and allowed trade and industry to build up. Similarly, all had much the same class structure, and form of government.

"The poor we will have with us always." Certainly, there were many in the towns and cities as breathtakingly poor as the peasantry outside their walls. Some of these were, of course, former peasantry themselves, fled to the towns to find freedom and a better life. Most were not. There was a hereditary lower working class of servants (9–18 per cent of the population), sluts and beggars, to say nothing of criminals, whores and the unemployed —all lumped together in the suspicious mind of the respectable urban burgess. The living conditions of these classes were appalling. Most towns and cities, outside the public areas and the suburbs of the rich burgesses, simply stank. "The streets were ill-paved and had no sidewalks; the crown of the causeway sloped down on both sides to the 'kennels,' into which the filth ran . . . householders and tradesmen threw their garbage, litter and offal into the streets from doors and windows." The poor lived in rickety timber tenements, paying rent, subject to fire and endemic disease.

Above the poor lay laborers—skilled or unskilled—in full time employment. Their living conditions were little better, their chances of advancement still relatively few. The average laborer worked a five-day week, with Saturdays at work but a large number of odd Saints' Days to add to his leisure. His working day, however, might be as long as 12 or 14 hours. "The medieval town patriciate wrenched the peasant from servitude to the land to tie him to servitude in the workshop." With the poor, these founded the basis of the urban mob, of which City Fathers were so scared.

The difference between a laborer and a guild journeyman was very small. Within towns, certain occupations quickly became noted as having a status. This did not just apply to obviously skilled jobs such as goldsmith, glassblower, armorer or clothier, but also to carpenters, bakers, cobblers, butchers, cartwrights, and so forth. Which occupations did and did not qualify for guild status varied enormously from place to place. In many towns and small cities, there would be only one guild, the guild merchant, of all qualified craftsmen. In large cities, each occupation had its own guild, with a master, master craftsmen (known in *FW* as Guild Members, to avoid confusion), journeymen and apprentices. Apprentices were boys sold to Guild Members to learn a trade; paid nothing, expected to act as personal servants and workers at all hours of day or night, they were little better than slaves and could be sold to another Member at will. Sons of Members and journeymen did not normally go through this stage. Journeymen were the basic laborers of the Guild Member, their status in the town varying with the importance and wealth-making capacities of the trade. Most Guild Members were self-employed small businessmen, employing a handful of journeymen and apprentices in a workshop by or part of their own homes. The benefits they got from the guild, besides a sense of status, were mainly financial: a Member could call upon his brothers/competitors for credit, in time of need. By his arguments at guild meetings and before the master, he could seek to regulate the trade in the town to his own advantage.

There were frequent explosions of tension within guilds, particularly between the workforce and the Members. Equally, guilds might themselves clash, especially where their interests were involved. Attempts to restrict working hours by richer guilds sure of a market for their goods would always provoke opposition from poorer guilds, with a smaller profit margin—and, of course, from the candle-makers. Despite the differences between them, however, the guilds did form the effective government of most large towns and cities. The towns and cities were formally and legally set up under a charter, setting out their privileges. These included self-government by a corporation, under a mayor. The corporation was almost invariably dominated by representatives of the different guilds, the mayor being from one of the richer ones. The corporation can in some ways be seen as a force for change, in resisting the demands of the local aristocracy and (occasionally) the monarchy. In many respects, however, it could be relied on to be (highly) conservative. It formed a self-perpetuating craft oligarchy, levying unequal taxes upon the urban poor, selling justice, and driving prices up by restrictive practices on foreign merchants seeking to trade in the town.

The full development of the guild system only came in the High Middle Ages; adventures in the Dark Ages should substitute a much looser domination of the laboring and poor classes by skilled craftsmen, working generally in much smaller towns. Only Winchester, York, London and a handful of cathedral centers really qualify as "cities" in the Anglo-Saxon period. In the Dark Ages, too, the impact of trade and industry at anything but a local scale was very limited. There was no equivalent for the sophisticated commercial, financial and industrial arrangements which we shall examine in the next section. Trade items were produced locally, or hawked about the country in small quantities by persons more akin to peddlers than master merchants.

Medieval trade and industry

In the last section, the scale of local trade and manufacturing became clear. For most towns and cities, commercial and industrial activities were essentially small-scale. The local nobility and Church apart, there were few customers for expensive, luxury goods, or bulk orders for necessities. Even other townsfolk did not earn sufficiently more than the villein to make major trading ventures feasible. The great merchants visited the area perhaps once a year, during the fair: otherwise, goods were produced locally, or trickled down to the towns via lesser traders.

In a few areas, however, much more intensive manufacturing, mining and trading was possible. Medieval Christendom was criss-crossed by a pattern of well-known international trading routes, connecting major centers of population. The men who traded along these routes were mainly master merchants from the bigger cities, and the scale of their operations after 1200 became increasingly international. Frequently, the merchants within the cities became the new aristocracy, over and above the other guilds. Instead of merely buying manufactured goods from other guilds and trading them, the merchants would order goods in advance. From here, they would advance into moneylending and banking—previously reserved for the despised Jews, of which nation there was a ghetto in every leading city. The age of the merchant bankers had arrived by about 1300—and gave rise to some of the most famous names in medieval history. The Peruzzi, Frescobaldi and Fuggers of Christendom were not of the nobility: but they could buy out most dukes many times over, and frequently were the support for kings. Their financial power, with branches of the banks in every city, became enormous. Some gave up mere trading altogether. Others, however, made their money specifically by the long-distance haulage of goods, investing great amounts of money for greater returns.

Where were the raw materials of this trade—and which the cities that profited most? One source of desperately-wanted goods was the exotic east. In the Middle Ages, trade routes were opened up with India, the Moluccas, Java and even China; land routes, by year-long caravan through Byzantium, Persia, Bokhara and Samarkand; sea routes, by Arab dhow to Levantine ports like Damascus and Tripoli. Silk and spices were the main trade goods here. In return went gold, grain—and slaves. The greatest beneficiaries of this trade were the capital of the Greek Empire, Byzantium; its Genoese colony, Pera; and the leading Italian ports, Genoa—and Venice. Venice in particular established itself as a maritime republic of enormous opulence and power. From these ports, wealth and enterprise spread inland. Florence became the greatest of all banking and manufacturing cities, under the able and ruthless de Medicis. Milan, at the southern end of the transalpine trade route, prospered as an entrepot. Other Mediterranean seaports suffered from Genoese and Venetian competition; but most Italian ports, together with French cities like Marseilles and Spanish ports at Barcelona and in the Majorcas, did well.

The south produced luxuries: Oriental goods, spices; manufactured items; and wine. Northern Europe paid for these with necessities: fish, grain, salt—and, above all, woollen cloth. The scale of the wool and cloth industry in England and the Low Countries was spectacular. Whole counties in England were enclosed to serve sheep, English merchants helping to finance the development and then shipping the raw wool to Bruges and Brabant. There, it was made into fine cloth, and moved south. At first, it tended to move by land, the goods of north and south meeting in enormous open-air fairs throughout the year in the region of Champagne. After 1300, when the Genoese began to trade by sea to La Rochelle and Bruges, the Champagne fairs declined in importance. Still later, the English took over much of their own cloth production, merchants again encouraging weavers in small towns and rural villages with loans to buy looms and other equipment. A regular wine trade was opened up between La Rochelle and London, again cutting out the great international markets at Bruges and Antwerp.

This was very far from the only trade route of importance. Southern and central Germany in the High Middle Ages became a major center of mining and metallurgy. Throughout the period, Christendon suffered from enormous metal poverty. Despite the suits of plate armor and gleaming weaponry characteristic of the period, there were only a few pounds of worked metal per person in any part of Europe. Gold and silver were in particularly short supply. The output of the German mines was therefore the basis of great local wealth. Technologically advanced industries developed: armory, artillery, clock-making, even spectacle manufacture. Cities like Nuremburg, Augsburg and Munich came almost to rival the Lombard centers as commercial and banking areas. North Germany had its trading importance and, even in the Dark Ages, the Vikings had succeeded as traders (as well as conquerors!) between Normandy, the Low Countries, London, Denmark, the Baltic and Russian cities like Novgorod. This trade continued throughout the High Middle Ages, dominated by the German Hanseatic League cities of Bremen, Lubeck, Hamburg, Danzig and Visby. The Hanse had its center in every north European port, with wide privileges often resented by the local mercantile community—like the Jews, a foreign ghetto vulnerable to intense medieval fear of the different.

The later Middle Ages were more than the age of artillery, or nobility, or advanced and sophisticated sorcery. They were the age of the master merchant and merchant banker: top dog in his own city, with international financial tentacles spreading deep into national life. The nobility, the Church and the Court itself all felt the drag. As authorities, they naturally sought to exploit these trading operations. Merchants were highly taxed, especially if foreigners. The best trading routes—established roads, convenient rivers—were subject to tolls, imposed by kings or dominant local nobles. Customs were placed on goods landed by sea, and purchase tax on the same goods sold at market. Merchant bankers, like the Jews before them, were "asked" to make enormous loans to the powerful, at low rates of interest. Yet these debts, and the indispensability of the master merchant's revenues to the operation of the court, gave the merchant some power over the king—if he dared to use it.

The nobility and the Court

Medieval thought divided society into three classes: those who worked, those who prayed and those who fought. So far, we have been concerned mainly with the workers. In Chapter Two, we will look at the men and women who prayed. Later still, our attention will turn to warfare. Must we then invent a new class, to cover the aristocracy? Not really; for in origin, and in a great deal of their attitudes, the Dark Age and medieval nobility belonged to the class of those who fought. They were, overwhelmingly, nobles in arms.

This is one of the few generalizations that can be made about "the nobility and the Court" during the whole of the period covered by *Fantasy Wargaming*. The higher up the social scale one goes, the greater differences appear between individual times and places. Peasants were—more or less—the same at the start of the Dark Ages and the end of the Middle Ages, in Yorkshire or Spain. Towns showed greater change, but can still be meaningfully considered as a unit. It is with the mercantile class—the "barons of trade and industry"—that we must start drawing a line between time and place. This line becomes a gigantic maze of divisions and qualifications, when one looks at the ruling classes. To consider all the variations would require a book several times the size of this; readers wishing to site an adventure in a particular nation, at a particular time—rather than in their own universe conceived according to these medieval guidelines—would do well to carry out some background reading before they start.

Take, for example, Dark Age Britain. The "social class" table on page 128 shows a neat division of the nobility into dukes, marquises, earls, etc. Anglo-Saxon England had earls, but none of these other ranks: and the "eorls" or "ealdormann" varied in power from rulers of a county to over-mighty princes, like the Godwins under Edward the Confessor, challenging and dominating the monarchy. A historical universe would have to take account of this situation. In many cases, the entire notion of kings, nobles, knights and commoners needs revision. A Viking war band was not the collection of equal freebooters under a popularly-selected leader that Hollywood would have us believe. Equipping a band cost money, and therefore was restricted to the Norse and Danish aristocracy. Each leader had lieutenants. Nevertheless, the leader was not usually of truly royal rank. Even "kings" might descend in terms of real power and status to the ranks of mere nobility. The Celtic kings in Wales, Strathclyde and Pictish Scotland were rulers over tiny kingdoms, more like medieval earldoms or (sometimes) baronies. Again, fewer ranks separated the ruler from his people. The Celtic practice of inheritance through the female line, and of divided inheritance equally between all sons, simply confuses the picture further.

Equally, there is much variation in the structure of the ruling classes during the Middle Ages, between different parts of Christendom. One simple (?) illustration is between the position of kings and nobility in England, France and Germany. Each had all the ranks of nobility included in our Social Classes table—sometimes more—but differed considerably in the real balance of power. English kings were relatively strong, except during times of royal minorities and disputed succession. They held wide personal estates, and maintained the nucleus of their own standing army. A network of royal officials exercised justice and administration even within the lands of their nobles. By contrast, the French kings were weak, little more than *primi inter pares* ("first among equals") in comparison with strong dukes and counts. Germany had what might be considered impossible—a strong monarchy, but also dukes and margraves (marquises) akin to kings themselves. Many of the German nobles ruled large areas of land, such as Saxony, with little interference from the Emperor or his officials. On the other hand, the Emperor's enormous personal holding of lands in Germany, and particularly in his dominion of Austria, gave him power to intervene if necessary, and authority over the nobility. Italy, with its pattern of city states and rural duchies owing little or no allegiance to any monarch, needs different treatment again.

In constructing a feudal universe, the Gaming Master must decide for himself whether to use a historical or imaginary scenario. If he decides on the former, he must do a little research; if the latter, he must consider carefully himself how strong and centralized he wishes the kingdom(s) to be. In either case, he can rely on certain principles—"the feudal system."

The feudal system in one form or another dominated the nobility and monarchy throughout the period. Its basis was simple, and military. The king owned all the land, and therefore the production of all wealth. But the king needed service as much as wealth. He therefore entered into bonds with lesser mortals—known as homage and fealty. The homager ("Vassal") vowed to serve the king faithfully in all things, and—above all—to put his sword at the king's disposal. In return, the king promised protection, and maintenance—either by the feeding of the homager at court, or more normally by the gift of estates (the "fief") which the vassal's peasantry might farm. The larger the estate, the greater the service required. A grant of large estates would be coupled with demands for service with 20, 100 or several thousand soldiers. The noble thus endowed ("enfeoffed") would then have to enter into similar bonds of personal obligation with lesser men—granting them either maintenance at the lord's court, or estates of his own. Such estates were in return for service; if the service could not be given by that person, they reverted to the lord. Fiefs were therefore, originally, uninheritable.

This neat feudal pyramid of king, lords and knights superimposed over a bound manorial peasantry can be applied to any historical scenario within the Dark and Middle Ages. It was an arrangement born of conquest and settlement, and made necessary by defense of the kingdom. The basic unit was the king and his warband—the Welsh *teulu,* the Anglo-Saxon *huscarles,* the continental *comitati.* The terms of protection/maintenance/service might vary (surprisingly little), but the exchange remained the same. Viking raids, when not occasioned purely by a desire for plunder and escape, followed the same rules.

Like all systems, feudalism quickly started engaging in contradictions. The essential keynotes of the system were personal loyalty and obligation, personal service: the unbreakable and unique bond between the lord and the man. Yet, very soon, we find compromises: vassals holding land by homage from *two* lords, owing each personal service and obligation. What if they should come to blows? The vassal there invariably supported the lord from whom he held most land—which was "legalized" into the system as the doctrine of the "liege lord." Lords are found holding land of each other, even lands by homage owed to lords of lesser rank than themselves. In a clash of arms between the king and one of his nobles ("tenants-in-chief"), the barons and knights of the rebellious noble had to choose between their loyalty to the king and their personal obligations to the noble. Usually, they chose the second. In England, the monarchy cut across the skein of interacting personal obligations, demanding personal oaths of loyalty from vassals of their nobility ("vavassours").

Finally, and inevitably, the connection between personal service and personal obligation progressively weakened. Very quickly, the principle of inheritance by primogeniture (i.e., the eldest son) was established. The eldest son of a vassal almost always succeeded in his estate. Primogeniture of course supported the idea of military service—who else might fight better than the eldest son? But what if the eldest son were four years old, or if there were no sons? Inheritance of fiefs quickly introduced the idea of service by money; instead of owing personal service (usually 40 days unpaid, and any paid days after that) on the field of combat or in military duties about the lord in peacetime (e.g., escort or castleguard), the vassal paid "shield money," *scutage,* to be quit of the obligation (see Chapter Four). This was by no means the only financial or non-military obligation that came in time to be laid upon the vassal. Since inheritance was not a legal right at first, the heirs of the vassal had to pay for it: this *Relief* (anything up to 50 per cent of the vassal's annual income) entered the feudal system as a major feature. Lords similarly started to demand proofs of their vassals' loyal devotion, in the form of hospitality for the lord and his entourage once or more each year, and gifts (*aids*) on special occasions. The latter were eventually narrowed down to three occasions: ransoming the lord, knighting his eldest son, and marrying his eldest daughter. Up to 20 per cent of the vassal's annual income could be demanded for any of these.

Besides these financial obligations, there grew up throughout the feudal pyramid certain traditional rights and duties. Some, again, came from the increasing inheritability of fiefs. If the eldest son was to take over from his father the personal service and obligation owed to the lord, it was obviously in the lord's interest that he should be brought up correctly—able to bear arms, and aware of his debt to the lord. In many cases, this meant education of the child at the lord's court, as a page and later squire—often a useful hostage, against the disobedience of a treacherous vassal! Where the child actually inherited the fief, the lord had the power of wardship. This covered not only education of the minor but also administration of the fief, very often to the financial advantage of the lord or someone to whom he had granted the wardship, and also the right to approve or veto the marriage of the heir. Marriage alliances were as potent weapons in the battles for power within the feudal aristocracy as within the monarchical class of Christendom; by refusing to allow marriages of his vassals to his enemies—a reasonable request, one might feel—the lord effectively opened up a "right" which he could and did exploit for cash or other concessions. It is impossible to put limits to the degree of exploitation acceptable to the vassals.

The major remaining right of the lord was, of course, judicial. The lord had the right to expect loyalty and service from his tenants. If this were not forthcoming, without good reason for the failure, he could judge the tenant guilty of disloyalty (usually by the advice of a jury of fellow tenants) and "escheat" (take back) the fief. Similarly, the holder of any estate, from knight's fee upwards, had powers of jurisdiction and judgement over all its inhabitants and those who entered the area. Knights, lords, earls, dukes, etc., all exercised justice over their own lands, and over the persons of those who held other lands from them. All the usual crimes could be dealt with here: murder, assault, perjury, arson; theft of all kinds of property from horses and cattle to purses and pins; rebellion and fraud. Private justice is in *Fantasy Wargaming* the major source of justice. (It is not the only one. Archdeacons and other high Christian clerics can personally try characters in canon law courts, for a range of offenses including witchcraft, usury, blasphemy, heresy, bigamy, sexual perversion—including adultery and fornication—breach of promise, breach of contract, etc. *Fantasy Wargaming* also allows for exercise of royal justice throughout the kingdom, by itinerant judges [justices-at-eyre] and by town- and shire-reeves holding courts in every incorporated borough and every shire. In every case, justice was normally by judgement of a jury of peers, although defendants might opt for alternatives such as Ordeal—e.g., carrying a burning iron ten paces—or, if of the nobility, combat with their accusers.) GMs must be sure of designing their universe to include means by which wilful and wayward characters—such as most adventure parties'!—can be brought to book.

The system above is of course "a hitchhikers' guide": vastly simplified, yet by no means comprehensive. The same must be said of the pattern of classes implied by the Social Class table. Leaving the king aside for a bit, let us look at the remaining ranks of the nobility. "Duke," "marquis," "count" (in England, "earl") were all originally military titles rather than marks of social status. The duke was the provincial commander of military forces in a large area. The marquis or margrave similarly covered a troublesome "March," or border district where raiders and invading armies might strike. The count (*comes*) was essentially a deputy, member or leader of the *comitati* serving the king or great noble as bodyguard and army nucleus. Very quickly, however, these military duties took on real social and economic meaning. An *FW* duke will normally have several palaces and major castles scattered throughout the kingdom, with at least three castles and a palace in the area where his estates are most concentrated. He will exercise authority and influence over a considerable tract of territory—e.g., Saxony, Normandy, Brittany, Wessex. A king with more than two dukes is normally a weak king. A marquis is very close to the duke in power, but his holdings and sphere of influence are more concentrated, and more peripheral. A typical *FW* marquis will hold perhaps three castles *and* a major fortified palace in an isolated area of danger and invasion—Brandenburg, the Welsh or Scots Marches, etc. An earl or count will again hold perhaps three castles—but only two of these in the "central" area of his influence (the third being on a more isolated estate elsewhere in the kingdom), and one of those two being the site also of his main residence. All these nobles will normally hold their estates directly from the king, and pay homage to no other.

Below these ranks are the baronage and knights. The barons

(Lords) varied enormously in wealth and power. A rich baron might almost be the equal of an earl, and spend his time like the upper nobility travelling from estate to estate with an entourage, living off the agricultural surplus stockpiled in each location. He might have two castles, one containing his main residence, and a rather smaller number of lesser manor houses than the earl. His lands would usually be held of a greater noble, exceptionally of the king himself. A lesser baron would have only one castle, also his main residence, and perhaps two manor houses on other estates; again, he would usually be a vavassour.

Below the baronage lay the knights. These were originally of no great eminence—just the soldiers (*milites*) which the nobles agreed to bring to the king's aid at the time of homage. The English name came from *cnihtas,* meaning "serving youths"! Originally maintained as the bodyguard of men about the lord, knights were increasingly settled on estates and thus admitted to the landed feudal aristocracy. A rich knight might have all the appurtenances of the poorer baron except the title. A poor knight might be reduced to the single five-hide village or manor, with a semi-fortified manor house, which was reckoned in Domesday as the minimum estate needed to support a mounted warrior with his equipment. Some might even fall into serjeanties—a semi-feudal class, holding half a knight's fee, and normally serving on foot. The difference between a serjeant and a common man-at-arms, hired for money, was only one of gentility and command—for the serjeant was often used as the commander of the men-at-arms.

This pattern conceals enormous mobility. Families might rise and fall in wealth and influence from century to century, or even year to year. Primogeniture maintained the family estates, but left younger sons (Lords and knights) with small or no estates, a destabilizing influence in conservative feudal society. The complex interplay of family holdings, marriage alliances, feuds, old loyalties and present debts influenced the operation of the ruling classes quite as much as any simple counting of ranks and power. It is these intangibles which the GM must build into his universe.

At the top of the feudal pyramid was the king: ordained by God for the rulership of the people, to curb their waywardness and lead them out of original sin into a state of grace. The medieval king was in theological and political thought a quasi-divine figure; and yet, at the same time we have seen how weak his real power could be. Like the dukes and lesser nobles, the king had his own personal estate, including castles and palaces, between which he travelled and off which he lived. The size of these personal holdings largely determined his power. His feudal rights over tenants-in-chief were precisely the same as those of his nobles over the vavassours—and exploited, wherever possible, in full. At the same time, the king's power was also imperial; feudal system aside, he had a right to obedience and loyalty from every inhabitant in the kingdom, and to exercise justice (and taxation) over the same. The tension that resulted between local officials of the king and the feudal nobility was considerable.

The king ruled his lands through institutions with which his immediate inferiors were very familiar. The major branches of the court were the Treasury, Chapel, Hall, Chamber and Council. The Hall was simply the baronial Great Hall writ large—a place where the king and his family sat to receive guests, make judgements, eat, drink and be seen with the attendance of as many of his vassals as had been summoned to the place. It was ruled by the Butler and Master Steward, responsible for drink and food respectively. The Chapel, ruled by the Chancellor, was the bureaucratic powerhouse. From its writing office were issued the commands or (in England) writs by which the kingdom was governed and justice exercised. The Chamber, under the High Chamberlain, was the private departments of the king, where he slept, dressed and performed other functions not conducive to public places. It also housed the Treasury, under its own Treasurer—a development from the Dark Age days when every noble kept his treasures in a chest, and slept next to it. Only in the High Middle Ages were the Chapel (Chancery) and certain parts of the Treasury hived off into permanent residence at the capital, to handle difficult duties like the taxation of the kingdom. The leading officials of the Court—including the Justiciar, responsible for justice, and the Marshall and Constable, who kept order at Court and developed wider martial functions as a result—were usually great nobles, whose actual duties were normally deputed to nominees of the king. The noble tenants of the offices only exercised them on great Occasions of State.

The last institution of the court was the Council. Every feudal lord had the right to summon any or all of his vassals about him, for their advice on difficult matters. The king was no exception.

However, both at the royal and baronial level, this duty of counsel was one which the vassal also could exploit. Increasingly, it was accepted that the lord *should* listen to the advice of his vassals before taking major decisions, such as the waging of war, that affected them. The lord did not have to take that advice, especially if a king answerable only to the divine: but the moral and political pressure that could be put on a monarch or magnate by a combination of his lessers was considerable. King John signed Magna Carta after a "Council."

Where in all this lies the idea of chivalry? Everybody knows the idea, because it is part of their mental baggage. Where is the "gentil knight," sworn to defend the Church, the poor, widows and the helpless, to rescue the victims of evil, to support his lord and king faithfully to the very best of his abilities? The ideal existed. It was partly Dark Age in origin. The ideas of dauntless courage, enormous free-spending generosity, total loyalty and heroic strength recall the Anglo-Saxon *thegns* of *Beowulf*. On to these martial virtues were grafted Christianity—just as the original legends of Arthur were given Christian gilding with the Holy Grail and True Cross. With the Middle Ages too came the allied ideal of romantic, or courtly love—of the chaste maiden, human image of the Virgin Mary, to be worshipped and championed by all good knights, saved from her perils, courted in a stately and thoroughly chaste manner. Courtly love was, in an age of infant marriage alliances conducted for financial or power-profit, the nearest approach to true sexual liaison possible.

It is really up to the GM to decide how "chivalrous" he wishes his universe to be. If he desires a historical adventure, then the chivalric gloss is small. Christendom in the High Middle Ages did adopt some of the trappings of the literary tradition—with tournaments, "Round Tables," knights being ritually purified and subjected to night-long vigils in church before dubbing, massive oaths to protect the weak and oppress the strong. In practical terms, however, the effect was small. Knights and their feudal superiors were not the high-minded Companions of the Arthurian legends. They were landholders, politicians, and fighters—the last above all. Some were pious; more were ruthless. Much as people of today!

Chapter II

Myth, magic and religion

(or "Mana maketh Man")

At the heart of fantasy gaming lies the supernatural.

Feel free to contradict that statement. The elements of a successful adventure are danger and mystery. Both can be achieved without supernatural intervention. Danger can arise from combat, from ingenious tricks and traps, from a bestiary of monsters. Mystery can lie in the theme of the adventure itself—the mission, the "secret." Supernatural powers? Useful as long-range artillery to "zap" an enemy, as instant technology to escape a perilous situation. Often no more.

At the heart of fantasy gaming *should* lie the supernatural. Fantasy cultures are steeped in Otherness. Magic works, is practiced by men. Gods exist, in another place where men too may find themselves on occasions, e.g., after death. Bardic tales are the best journals, myths carry the secret to understanding and survival in an adventure. But in most universes, the connections made are superficial; natural and supernatural worlds are kept firmly separate.

Fantasy Wargaming tries to bridge that gap—to bring the supernatural into everyday adventuring, and to show how adventurers' behavior influences and is influenced by ethereal forces whose nature they only partly comprehend. Involvement is one keynote of the system. Gameability is obviously another. The rules are designed to allow for a multiplicity of effects, and situations. They can be used in conventional, Earthly "dungeons," in specialized magical duels, and indeed in adventures sited entirely within the Otherworld of spirits, gods and demons. Spells can be invented, and any person may attempt any effects; but the range of influences upon the use of supernatural powers ensures also that the most powerful Mage can fail, in the simplest spell. Complexity, flexibility and uncertainty are the names of the game.

A system could have all these factors, and yet still lack cohesion and flavor. For a distinctive atmosphere, more is needed. The supernatural must be true to its culture—and to itself. These two goals of historical and self-consistency often clash. The historical record shows a vast complexity of individual effects; folklore, myth, theology, the arcane texts amplify, reinterpret, contradict each other. Only the underlying themes can wholly be relied on. From these, and from cross-cultural studies of the supernatural like Frazer's *Golden Bough,* must be created a set of basic assumptions about the workings of the Otherworld and Other powers: an "occult philosophy," tying together myth, magic and religion in one overall picture of the supernatural. In the next section, we will briefly outline this "unified field theory" —the assumptions on which the system is based, and which ensure self-consistency. Then we will look at the historical record, and the details of the system.

If that sounds daunting, it shouldn't. For the purposes of *Fantasy Wargaming,* this section can be boiled down to just three questions: What *is* the Supernatural? Where does the Power come from? How does the Power operate? The questions are fairly simple, the answers not too complicated.

What IS the Supernatural?

A 50,000-"Gold Piece" question! One definition saw magic as "using invisible and incomprehensible means to achieve visible and comprehensible effects." We accept this. How, then, does magic differ from science, medicine, or technology—or from religion? *Fantasy Wargaming* makes no separation. The medieval scholar made no distinction between "scientific" chemistry and astronomy, "magical" alchemy and astrology. The same persons practiced both, saw them as part of one universal system. The physician mixed "medical" techniques (surgery, herbs, bleeding) with "magical" (astrology, charms). Only after 1500 have we distilled from these disciplines whatever didn't work, and labelled it arbitrarily as "magic." In contrast, the distinction between magic and religion was much clearer to medieval than modern eyes. Both involve arcane forces to achieve Earthly ends. In detail, the two overlap. The Celtic cross started life as a religious symbol—but not a Christian one. In the Dark Ages, it was used as a pantacle of protection for magicians. Their incantations frequently included Christian prayers, or appeals to Teutonic gods. Tarot, a magical divination system, contains cards full of pagan symbolism. Christian objects and ceremonies were considered to have magical properties. Conversion to Christianity in Ireland followed St. Patrick's trial of supernatural power with the Mages; his "miracles" were more powerful than their "spells." In the later Middle Ages, the theologian and magician accepted the same view of the universe. The distinction was theological, not technical. Religious and magical power were of the same type—but had different origins. Many Christian Mages questioned even the latter separation.

Where does the Power come from?

This is the most important question of all—for unless you know the origin of supernatural power, you cannot understand how to tap or use it. At first sight, there is no answer. Almost *everything* has been considered "magical," in at least one culture. The most common source of supernatural power restores in part the distinction between magic and religion: Higher and Lower Powers. All cultures have gods, demons, beings in the Otherworld—wielders of supernatural power, bestowers of power upon their worshippers. In effect, gods are no more than magical beings of enormous might and majesty. But using their magical power requires worship, and appeals; magic "proper" is an activity done by yourself, controlling and dominating the arcane forces.

In this activity, you can call on innumerable sources of power. In most cultures, nature itself is magical. Plants, trees, animals, rocks, metals, gems, etc., are unhesitatingly considered reservoirs of power. The stars, planets and the Sun are another potent magical area—where they are not themselves gods or the homes of gods. Time too is supernaturally significant: days, dates and times of day having their own special "virtues" and meanings, to religious and magical beliefs alike. Places may concentrate power. This is often religious, too, locations like the Dome of the Rock of Jerusalem (sacred to three religions) being an example. But there are many cultures where magical power is associated indiscriminately with individual woods, mountains, springs, waterfalls, etc., or indeed with *all* such spots. A whole island, or indeed continent, may be thought Enchanted.

The works of Man himself have likewise been given "inhuman" power—an important clue to the real source of magic, in *Fantasy Wargaming*. Objects of all kinds have been labelled magical, from purpose-built talismans, fetishes, totem poles, staffs and seals to everyday equipment like broomsticks and doorposts. The abstractions used by Man to make sense of his world—words, letters, numbers, symbols—are also invoked. By words, you can start or stop a storm, halt an enemy, command spirits. A man's knowledge of your name gives him power over you. Symbols carved on a staff or rock can be commands or help in divination—whether in Celtic ogham, Viking runes or Cabalistic letters.

We are moving rapidly to a conclusion. There *is* a magical power—which we call *mana,* although not using it strictly in its Polynesian sense. An enormous range of things possess mana; but in terms of detail, cultures are as divided about the sources of power as is physically possible. The same object may be highly magical in one culture, and powerless in another—or magical, but with a different effect. Even in the same culture, the magical significance of a thing may change with time. The power of gods and other supernatural creatures varies accordingly with date and place. Gods decline into water sprites—or rise from nowhere to claim dominion over Otherworld and Earth alike.

How can such anarchy be reduced to a system? The key is simple, and deserves to be spelt out in capital letters:

THEIR POWER COMES FROM *YOUR* BELIEF. THE GREATEST SOURCE OF MANA IS YOURSELF.

It is the person's worship of the gods that gives them power. It is his belief in the magical efficacy of certain objects (a belief very close to veneration) that determines their power and effects. One man's belief is but a drop in the ocean, however. For an object or being to take on a significant supernatural role, the support of whole populations is essential. Outside that time or area, the role diminishes or is lost: disbelief exceeds belief.

This neat assumption has the advantage of support from scholars and occultists alike. Storms, historian of Anglo-Saxon magic, concludes flatly that "The success of magic will largely depend on the personality and force of the magician and only to a small extent on technical knowledge . . . No amount of knowledge will make a man into a magician and the smallest smattering will do, if he is born with certain personal qualities." The Renaissance Mage Paracelsus agrees. Ceremonies, conjurations, equipment, etc., are at best secondary; meditation, faith and imagination are the essential qualities for success. Kors and Peters, in their history of witchcraft, also spoke of "the witches' belief that 'the power' resides within themselves, and that their rites serve to bring it out."

How does the Power operate?

This question follows directly from the first. If mana came solely from men, Man could rival the gods. All men would be magicians. A little more thought is necessary.

The quotation of Kors and Peters is a clue. Magic operates by the accumulation and expenditure of mana. It is built up by certain kinds of rite—incantation, meditation, shamanistic dancing etc.—and expended by spells. The religious accumulate mana in their ceremonies, but transfer it to their gods through an act of worship. In return, the worshipper obtains access through appeal to the enormous reserves of magical power stored up by the god. The cleric is thus potentially more powerful than any Mage. But gods are sometimes fickle, and always self-interested. Mana is the god's magical being; in casting a miracle, he loses part of himself. For an appeal to be successful, you must have the goodwill of the deity. Some gods require standards of personal behavior. *All* demand action that will maintain their power—frequent ceremonies, conversions to increase the number of mana-giving worshippers. The Christian God seeks a monopoly of power and worship. "Thou shalt have no other god but me. Thou shalt not bow down to them or worship them, for I, the Lord your God, am a jealous god." His jealousy extended beyond other gods to the exercise of *any* supernatural power (such as magic) not dependent on worship of Himself.

Religious power therefore operates by a cooperative agreement between god and worshippers—the terms of the contract varying from god to god. By contrast, the Mage accumulates and spends his mana individually, and is not bound to any standards of behavior. But questions remain. Where is mana accumulated from —and where does it go to? What happens when a spell is cast?

In *Fantasy Wargaming,* a distinction is made between preparations for a spell, and its execution. The former go well beyond gathering mana—they include the means by which the magician establishes contact with his target or victim. Incantations calling on the power of the supernatural and invoking the True Name of the victim are not, as Paracelsus showed, the spells themselves, but the preliminaries establishing a link between Mage and target though another plane. The spell proper follows this link. It is the malevolent thought, the spoken or unspoken command, which takes effect.

The place of magic is therefore in another plane, outside the Earthly sphere with its four Elements of Earth, Air, Fire and Water. The Otherworld—the medieval "Primum Mobile"—is composed of the fifth Element, Ether, and is hence referred to in this book as the Ethereal Plane. At its center lies the Ether Elemental, the ultimate source of Ether and of mana itself, for mana is but another name for this magical essence. The preparations of the Mage accumulate small amounts of Ether/Mana from the Ethereal Plane. It is to this plane that the mana returns, expended during the creation of an Ethereal Link and giving of a magical command.

The Otherworld

The Ethereal Plane is the last element (sic!) in our theory of the Supernatural. The Otherworld has no particular geography, but does contain many different identifiable areas, and populations. It is the home of all the gods—the size of their holding varying directly with their mana, and so with the size of their worship upon Earth. Crusades, schisms, drives to convert the unbeliever and rally the faithful therefore affect the composition of the Ethereal Plane! It is the home of all the spirits—the five Elementals, the angels, demons, valkyries and lesser beings of all religions. Heaven, Hell and Purgatory are here—the last being an area between Heaven and Hell, set aside for the purification of souls. The spirits of dead "Christians" not wicked enough for Hell or pious enough for Heaven are placed at the Hell end of Purgatory, where demons as well as angels operate. As the soul makes its way towards Heaven, shedding sins as it goes, the area becomes more pleasant. The soul's progress is impeded by Higher

Powers checking its spiritual progress—the Sephiroth of Jewish Cabalist philosophy. The various regions of the Teutonic Asgard (see page 38) can also be found in the Ethereal Plane—as, for that matter, can the remnants of the old Celtic underworld and of Olympus, and the flourishing areas of the Moslem Paradise, the Buddhist and Hindu Otherworlds, etc. After death, the spirits of living creatures can be found in the halls of their gods. Before death, these spirits are independent operators in the Ethereal Plane. It is possible to conjure these spirits, or indeed any Ethereal being, on to the Earthly plane. Indeed, it is possible to unite parts of the two planes, by enormous magic. One part of the medieval mythic tradition, Faery, is just such a part.

These are the assumptions on which our system of Supernatural powers is based. The theory is cross-cultural; it can be applied to any culture, accommodate any magical or religious tradition. This is itself useful, especially for the creation of a consistent system. The particular flavor of myth, magic and religion in the Dark and Middle Ages can, however, only be looked at separately.

Religion: the rule of the cross

Far and away the most important factor in the Supernatural life of the Dark and Middle Ages was the dominance of the Christian Church. Any attempt to hold an adventure during this period that does not take account of its power, its teachings and above all its disapproval of magic and other worship, is doomed to failure.

The Church was an enormous institution. In the number of its servants, its resources in money and buildings, it dwarfed any nation in Christendom. Churches and priests could be found in every sizeable community in Western Europe, no matter how remote. To have no church was as bad as having no law, and a new village would as a first priority set about building one. Once built, and the priest installed, the church would still receive financial support from the community, in the form of tithes—in theory, a tenth of the village's income. Above the priest lay a hierarchy or pyramid of ordained clergy. At the center of each province (diocese) was a bishop, with a cathedral and a bureaucracy of lesser clerics including archdeacons and deans. Most bishoprics held vast estates of land, as well as wealth in coin and treasure. They were potent instruments of justice, with their own ecclesiastical courts trying men on a series of "moral" charges. Even the local priest had some judicial powers, e.g., by excommunication.

Beyond the bishops lay archbishops and primates, and above them—well, the Church was the only international institution in Christendom. Beside the occasional Councils of Bishops, there was the authority of the Cardinals and the Pope himself. The Popes' wealth and power were awesome. They ruled the Church, through Papal Bulls and appeals from ecclesiastical courts. They claimed the right to judge, even depose kings and emperors, to lay an entire nation under interdict. They also had ultimate authority over the other main part of the Church—the monastic and quasi-monastic orders.

In the Dark Ages, these comprised monks and monastic canons —either living in abbeys, or wandering at large. In the High Middle Ages, monks were increasingly settled into the reclusive life of the monastery, ruled by priors and abbots under the control of the great Mother Houses like Citeaux and Cluny. Each monastic order—Cistercians, Benedictines, Cluniacs, etc.—was independent, of each other and of the temporal clergy. Each declined steadily from initial austere ideals into wealth, luxury and—as Chaucer's *Canterbury Tales* tells us—vice. The same decline also applied to the friars, who replaced the wandering monks of the Dark Ages as a class of mendicant (begging), travelling preachers.

Here too there were different Orders: the Franciscans, or Grey Friars, founded in 1215 by St. Francis of Assisi; the Carmelites, or White Friars; the Austins; and the more sinister Black Friars, or Dominicans, dedicated to the extirpation—by torture if need be—of atheism, heresy and witchcraft.

Monasteries were, of course, parallelled by nunneries, of particular importance in Anglo-Saxon England where a royal princess might wield great power as Abbess in a House like Ely. There were no female friars, however. The other great contribution added in the High Middle Ages were the religious knights—semi-monastic, semi-celibate, some said semi-Christian, orders of knights who had dedicated their lives and arms to the service of the Church. The main associations were the Knights Templar, the Knights Hospitaller, and in Eastern Europe the Teutonic Knights. Halfway between clerics and warriors, they are an interesting option for players in *Fantasy Wargaming,* in High Medieval adventures!

The relations of Church and state were often difficult. Popes quarrelled with Emperors, especially over royal interference in administration of the national Churches. Kings set up Anti-Popes, to challenge the Pontiff. Great nobles sought to dominate the Church inside the nation. Bishoprics might be left vacant, diverting money into the king's coffers—or filled with creatures of the king instead of zealous clergy. Knights and barons similarly preferred their own men to parish churches, for a share of the tithes often. The Church became the recognized career for younger sons, with no inheritance to hope for. All this compromised ecclesiastical independence—but reinforced its links with the accepted leaders of feudal society.

The power of the Church must be measured in more than money, more than manpower. A more important factor was its enormous hold over hearts and minds. The Church never had anything approaching 100 per cent dedication. Heresies flourished in different parts of Christendom, often infecting whole provinces like the Albigensians in Southern France. Reacting against a remote, alien and often corrupt Catholic Church, the heretics showed enormous zeal and vitality; but the Church struck back with "crusades" and Inquisitions, burnings and devastations. Every burning of a witch or heretic was a sacrifice to God, an act of worship—and a means of creating mana! Yet in *Fantasy Wargaming,* the heretic too must be counted as a Christian, worshipping God—acquiring piety for his tribulations.

Beside heretics, the small pockets of Jews, pagans and devil worshippers in Christendom, there were enormous numbers of nominal Christians in all social classes who simply ignored Christianity. Nevertheless, the Church was an unrivalled instrument of propaganda. The rights and moral teachings of the Church were enshrined in law. The Church had almost exclusive control over the medium of ideas. Books, art, music and other entertainments were laden with Christianity—often produced by and for the Church, its rites and festivals. The Church was literate, in an illiterate society. The only relief for the laborer came on Sundays and Saint days—holy days. The church was in most villages the only meeting place, the only large building. Its rites marked the

significant points in a villager's life, and promised him salvation
in the next.

The hold of Christianity was strengthened by the doctrine itself.
It was an exclusive religion. There was only one god, one acceptable source of Supernatural power. He was Creator of the Universe, of every person and creature in it, knew every hidden
thought and saw everybody: Omnipotent, Omniscient, Omni-
present. He was served by an enormous host of lesser beings,
from Archangels, Apostles and Saints down to cherubim. Men
were absolutely subject to God for good fortune on Earth and
(through the sacrifice of His Son) salvation in Heaven. Souls
were to his whim received into Heaven, banished to Hell or con-
signed to Purgatory. The secret of success was obedience—to the
moral precepts of the Church, to its (fallible) priesthood, to the
service of God.

The Church did not deny the existence of other Supernatural
powers, at least in practice. To do so would have made every illness or misfortune the direct work of God, and raise doubts about
His benevolence! The Church rather accepted that there were
other, malevolent influences, and semi-sanctioned the use of
Christian ceremonies, objects, etc., as protective magic. The other
acceptable Supernatural effect was the appeal (prayer) to God,
for a miracle. Success here depended on the experience of the appellant, his rank (if any) in the Church and his pious service to
the Lord. The cleric, however, had his own "magical" powers,
like benediction, exorcism and pardoning.

These were the only types of Supernatural power allowed. Increasingly, witches, sorcerers, conjurers and even occasionally as-
trologers and alchemists followed atheists, Jews, heretics and ho-
mosexuals ("faggots") into the fires. The Church interpreted the
First Commandment to mean that no other god existed. Independently, theologians like Thomas Aquinas also decided that
"magic" could not exist either. Any supernatural power that was
not of God could only come from one other source.

The specter of the Devil

"I saw an Angel come down from heaven, having the key of the
bottomless pit and a great chain in his hand. And he laid hold on
the dragon, that old serpent, which is the Devil, Satan, and bound

him a thousand years, and cast him into the bottomless pit, and shut him up, and set a seal upon him, that he should deceive the nations no more, till the thousand years should be fulfilled . . . And when the thousand years are expired, Satan shall be loosed from his prison, and shall go out to deceive the nations which are in the four quarters of the Earth. Gog and Magog, to gather them to battle; yea, as countless as the sands of the sea. And they went upon the breadth of the Earth, and compassed the camp of the Saints about, and the beloved city: and fire came down from God out of heaven, and devoured them. And the devil that deceived them was cast into the lake of fire and brimstone, where the Beast and the false prophet are, and shall be tormented day and night for ever and ever." (*Revelation of St. John,* Chap 20, Verses 1–10.)

Satan appears in the Old Testament as a minor figure—God's faithful servant, employed to test the faith of Job. In medieval theology, too, he existed to tempt Man that he might more fully appreciate Divine Grace. By the time of Revelation, however, there was a vital difference. From being a loyal servant, Satan had become the Fallen Archangel, God's Infernal Enemy and would-be rival. All that was ill and evil in the world came from him. To some, like the Catharist heretics, this made him all but God's equal. Like God, he could be in a multitude of places simultaneously, possessed enormous Supernatural power and knew your deepest secrets. He was served by an army of demons and lesser beings scarcely less impressive than the Heavenly Host, which it would meet at Armageddon. If God could inspire you, the Devil could corrupt or possess you. The souls of the impious would be imprisoned after death in Hell, subjected to everlasting torments—a major source of diabolic mana!

Medieval man was thus surrounded in his mind's eye by invisible demons seeking his discomfort, and his soul. A moment's lack of thought or impiety might bring disaster. The circumstances, perils—and rewards—of contacts with the Lower Powers were well known. The Devil or his minions might appear in any of a thousand forms. Favorite diabolic poses were a goat, a dragon, a scholar, a knight, a beautiful young man or woman. Demons were infernally (sic) clever, plausible and potent. For your soul, they would offer rich rewards: knowledge, wealth, revenge, love, power. But Satan went beyond mere Faustian contracts with individuals. He actively encouraged impiety of all kinds on Earth, seeking to build up congregations of worshippers—fuelling both his mana and the number of damned souls.

This is the place of witchcraft in *Fantasy Wargaming*. Few questions in anthropology have raised as much controversy as the nature of witchcraft. There are three quite separate views of the witch—the peasant magician, the pagan, and the devil worshipper. *Fantasy Wargaming* accepts all three as valid. Witches clearly exercised magic, and not just Supernatural powers by appeal. Equally, the theory of a surviving pre-Christian Celtic fertility cult has some force. Some ritual elements, notably the sacred dance and orgy, appear at the very beginning of the period, before diabolism had really taken root. There are echoes of Bacchic revels, and of Diana's Wild Hunt. Some medieval witches strenuously asserted their worship of a "different" god. Yet equally, the evidence for devil worship among medieval covens is overwhelming.

The answer is very simple, and arises directly from the dogma of medieval theology. God and the Devil were opposites. God was the Creator, the inventor, the innovator. Satan was incapable of creation; he was the imitator, perverter, parodier. This "explains" why the Heavenly and Hellish Hosts mirrored each other, and why they operate in the same ways: why the piety system for God is the impiety system for Satan—and so on. It also explains the ceremonies of the genuine diabolic covens. "If the Christians had their creed, their Eucharist, their kiss of peace, the witches formally forswore the faith, confected obscene parodies of the sacrament, and bestowed kisses upon the Devil's fundament." The symbolic flesh and blood of communion became literal flesh and blood—for preference, from a slaughtered innocent. This is the familiar, "Gothick" atmosphere of "Malleus Maleficarum" and Denis Wheatley. The witch was a damned person, marked out by the Devil for his own: a claw slash on the forehead to remove the baptismal mark, a mole or blemish on the skin where the witch's imp familiar sucked blood.

Fantasy Wargaming treats witchcraft as a pagan cult infiltrated and perverted by the Devil, into a foul parody and deadly enemy of Christianity. An underground "Church," persecuted and small, it yet provided sufficient mana for the Devil to maintain his operations; while the practice of magic by the witches gave them power on Earth and an incentive to continue their diabolic association. The Devil might be doomed—but St. John was a Christian, and not an impartial witness. Who could say what future there might be, for the Satanists?

The Teutonic gods (Dark Ages only)

By the beginning of the period covered in *Fantasy Wargaming*, the Judeo-Christian God had all but ousted his three great rival religions from Western Europe. The classical Olympian religion was dead and forgotten; the old Celtic gods had been expelled or in the most tenacious cases absorbed by a monastic Christianity in Britain and Ireland before the pagan Anglo-Saxons invaded. Only the old native gods of the Germanic peoples held out against Rome, and in England their stand was brief: after Augustine's mission to the Anglo-Saxons about the time our period begins, conversion was rapid and the Teutonic gods survived only underground or in isolated pockets. In Scandinavia, things were different. The Norsemen remained the last great heathen people in Europe up until the end of the millennium, which makes them pagans over the whole Dark Ages period.

The Teutonic religion wasn't a Church: it had no central organization, no doctrine, and no universal texts or liturgies. Instead, its chief mythological personalities like Odin, Thor, Frig and Tyr (the Norse names under which they're best known; the English equivalents are Woden, Thunor, Frig and Tiw) tended to get attached to particular sites, communities and individuals, so the celestial hierarchy was considerably less structured than its Christian counterpart. Which god sat at the top of the Ethereal pyramid could vary from one place to another: in mythology, we find Odin's supremacy undisputed, but in practice his cult was rather less widespread than Thor's. Our vivid, coherent picture of the Norse region of the Ethereal plane is an accident of literature more than a reflection of belief.

Still, the northern gods did enjoy the three basic religious institutions of temples, priesthood and sacraments. Temples varied from the makeshift to the extravagant, usually consecrated to a single god but sometimes shared with one or two others, and were dominated by idols of the patron. Gods were also associated with natural spots, rocks or groves or mounds; sacrifices could be offered at these to a god thought to reside in the place. The temples had a permanent staff of priests or priestesses (both sexes served, irrespective of the divinity's gender) who tended the sanctuary and performed sacrifices for the worshippers—although anyone could sacrifice in practice, in a temple it would tend to be the priestess unless the sacrificer was particularly aristocratic.

Sacrifice was the Teutonic religion's universal form of sacrament, and it was nearly always blood sacrifice. All sorts of domestic animals could be offered, particularly cattle and horses, but the supreme offering was a living man, though this was relatively rare among the Vikings. The manner of execution varied more than with animals: animals were usually butchered and liberal dollops of blood splattered around the altars and congregation, but men could be hanged (particularly in honor of Odin), drowned or pushed over cliffs, as well as simply having their throats cut. Especially nasty was the form of execution called the "blood eagle," where the victim's ribs were cut open at the back and the lungs drawn out; this tended to get reserved for particularly hated enemies. Human victims tended to be prisoners of war rather than one's own kin; it was common practice before a battle to dedicate the enemy army's souls to one of the war gods.

The Asgardian zone of the Ethereal plane had an unusually specific geography. Asgard was the realm of the Aesir, the gods, but was only one of the three astral realms, each of which supported a root of the world tree Yggdrasill. The others were the land of the frost giants and Niflheim (or Hel), land of the dead. Not all dead men went to Hel; warriors slain in battle went instead to the rather more cheerful Valhalla in Asgard to feast, carouse and fight in company with Odin himself, while virgins went to the goddess Gefion and those drowned at sea to the undersea halls of the goddess Ran.

A few striking differences ought to be mentioned between the styles of belief in Christianity and Teutonic religion. First, the old northern gods weren't jealous like the Christian God, and especially during the period of conversion men would cheerfully accept the Christian religion while retaining their ancestral cults, and worship Christ and Thor side by side. Thor didn't mind in the least (although it's reported he once challenged Christ to single combat, an offer our Savior politely declined), though naturally the Christian God wasn't too pleased. A second point to note is that the Norsemen never sought to win converts; their syncretistic religion allowed them to be converted to new gods, but because it had nothing of the one true religion about it didn't impel them to proselytize new worshippers. Finally, the Teutonic gods were acknowledged even by their most ardent votaries to be a touch wilful and perverse, and quite capable of deserting a loyal worshipper in his need if it conflicted with other divine whims.

The challenge of magic

This title has a double meaning. As we have seen, one of the most important facts about medieval magic is the challenge it posed to the dominant, Christian religion. This contributes almost as much to the atmosphere of a *Fantasy Wargaming* adventure as the parallel opposition of God and Satan. Magic is, however, a challenge also to the rule makers, as to generations of historians. Even more than other subjects, it is "seen through a glass, darkly": a scattering of evidence from folklore, myth, Christian antagonists and the very occasional book of magic "spells"— more often than not very late in the period, frequently no more than a list of the "True Names" of Ethereal Powers. Our systematic examination has produced more than 3,000 separate uses of "magic," throughout the Dark and Middle Ages. One conclusion emerged: that there was no evidence to suggest that any effect was impossible, or that there had ever been a simple list of known spells with known effects, to be learned and practiced. There *were* certain standard preparations—but the magical effect was merely whatever the Mage wished to achieve at the time. From an early stage, therefore, we abandoned lists of spells for rules by which a player might easily compute the degree of difficulty in almost any magical effect; and from an early stage, we separated the creation of the Ethereal Link from the execution of the spell.

There remained the fact that divisions between types of magic could be made, and were made by medieval Mages. Equally, distinctions were made at the time between different types of Mage. Unfortunately, the two did not correspond as exactly with each other as might be thought. For example, there was a branch of magic known as Necromancy; but not even John Dee, the greatest Mage in this field at the end of our period, was ever called a "Necromancer" by profession. Professionally, he was a Sorcerer.

He specialized in Necromancy—but no more than in other fields like Astrology. The arbitrary divisions between "Power-Word Magicians," etc., by games like *Chivalry & Sorcery* is not historical; power-word magic existed, but not a specialist cult of magic users.

The basic aim of the authors was therefore to isolate what types of magic there were, what types of magic user (Mage), and how they related to each other. Let us start by saying what is NOT useable.

Chaos, Neutral, Law

Previous fantasy gaming rules have tended to take from Moorcock these nebulous terms as meaningful divisions for magic users. It is, however, impossible to relate these in any useful way to the historical cultures in *Fantasy Wargaming*—although at least one other game has tried. Nor can "Good," "Neutral" and "Evil" quite be made to fit the bill.

"Black" and "White" magic

Black magic and White magic have some call to credibility, and are used for very limited purposes in *Fantasy Wargaming*. The terms themselves only go back to the 16th century, but they do reflect older traditions that certain types of magic were less abhorrent to God than others. "White magic" was, however, still a sin, subject to the overwhelming censure of the Christian religion against magic as a whole. There could not be a "Good" or Christian magic. In this book, there are no Black and White magicians, and no absolute separation between Black and White magic. Some spells are automatically Black magic, such as Conjuration: some, like Divination, are automatically White. Most, however, can be either Black or White or neither, depending on the purpose for which the magic is used. If the purpose is approved by God, and reflects at least some virtuous intention by the Mage, then it is White magic. If the purpose favors the Devil, or is inherently sinful, it is Black magic. Thus a spell of Sudden Death against any of God's favored creatures may be Black magic— but White if used against a servant of the Devil. A spell of Curing may be White if done from mercy, Black if performed upon an enemy of God, and neither if done for cash! Most Mages carry out a mixture of Black, White and "Grey" magic. The only difference made in this book for these categories is therefore in calculation of piety. In cases of doubt, the GM must decide.

Aristocratic, peasant, and ethnic Mages

In a hierarchical society like that of the Dark and Middle Ages, one might not be too surprised to find magicians, too, divided primarily by class. There is a marked difference between, at the one end of the spectrum, the peasant Mage (Wise Woman, Cunning Man) alternately helping and terrorizing his village, and the noble Sorcerer in his castle drawing pantacles and birth charts. Between these extremes can be seen three other traditional types of Mage. One is the Cabalist, the Jewish Sorcerer of the High Middle Ages—magically of great power, alienated from the social system of Christendom. The others are the Witch and Wizard. The witch, male or female, appears in many ways like a Wise Woman —usually peasant-based, and solitary. Traditionally, however, she has been accorded much greater power, and malevolence, a result of diabolic contact. The Wizard (often maligned as a charlatan) is an interim stage between the peasant Mage and the aristocratic High Sorcerer, often developing out of the former and, after study and experience, into the latter.

Types of magic

"Black" and "White" magic apart, the main distinctions drawn in the Middle Ages were between Sorcery and Divination. These terms are parallelled by "Active" and "Passive" magic in *Fantasy Wargaming*. Divination was the main (but not the only) constituent of Passive magic. It was itself divided into different techniques—astrology, tarot, clairvoyance, the study of runic rods/entrails/lines on a hand/bumps on a head, and so on. The aim of the techniques was, however, to obtain answers to certain, normally the same, questions: about the whereabouts of a lost thing or person, about the identity of a thief or a future spouse, about one's own personal character and prospects, about treasure. It did not directly alter the structure of the universe. Active magic *did*. When a Sorcerer cast his spell, something happened—often at a point a great distance away on Earth, made directly contiguous through the Ethereal Plane. The main divisions within Active magic are:

Basic Sorcery. This is a catchall for any use of magic to change a part of the universe by a single spell. Within the catchall lie certain general categories of spell—the types of magic which Sorcerers were most often called upon to use. These include spells of curing, disease and death; of protection, especially against malevolent magic; of illusion, or of absolute command; and finally, spells altering matter itself—shattering of rock wall, parting waves, repairing a broken sword.

Enchantment. The creation of magical items. These objects too could satisfy a multiplicity of purposes: magical enhancement or protection, success in combat or in love, etc. An enchanted item might be primarily magical itself, or merely given the aid of arcane forces to do its job more effectively. The process by which the Sorcerer selected the right objects, combined them into a suitable item and imparted magical power into them is Enchantment —a very potent form of magic, producing objects which could be used by all.

Conjuration. This is the summoning and control of Ethereal beings. It had several branches. Necromancy was the summoning of the spirit of the dead—sometimes for divinatory purposes, occasionally for the sinister purpose of binding the spirit into the dead body to create a Undead servant. Demonology was contact with the Lower Powers, Angelology contact with the Higher. Attempts at control here were fraught with danger. As Paracelsus said, "Nothing can be forced or drawn from the spirits," except with great uncertainty.

The final variety in the use of magic lies in the preparations used. The standard preparation was incantation or ululation—the reciting of names, formulae, etc., to concentrate the mind and open up pathways through the Ethereal Plane. Similar effects could however also be achieved by deep meditation and study, by fasting, or by shamanistic dancing, frenzy, etc.

It remains necessary to relate these preparations and uses of magic to the types of Mage set out above. This is done schematically in the rules, on page 217. The brief descriptions below should, however, give some of the different "flavors" of each type of Mage.

Cunning Man/Wise Woman. By far the most common user of

magic in either the Dark or Middle Ages. The Cunning Man or Wise Woman is a solitary, rural magician, usually situated permanently in a single village or area. He/she is part of the community, and usually accepted until something unfortunate and inexplicable happens which can be fastened upon him/her. The Mage specializes in appropriate kinds of spell: the curing of people and domestic animals, the bringing of disease and death as retribution, and certain kinds of detection (especially thief, lost things, etc.). He/she uses immediately available materials for enchantment, and the basic incantatory preparations for spells. Mainly "White" magic.

Wizard. The Wizard is a mixture of rural/peasant traditions and sophisticated, "intellectual" sorcery. Frequently of middling, urban origins, the Wizard is a professional Mage touring the towns, villages of a region offering a great variety of magical services. Curing, Detection and Illusion—especially tricks involving sleight of hand—are the Wizard's main stock in trade; but he can turn his hand to almost anything, and often (as his Experience grows) becomes interested in High Sorcery. Many Wizards indeed develop into High Sorcerers.

Witch. Member of a Devil-worshipping coven, in which magical skills are taught both by other members and by demons themselves. Witchcraft is an eclectic, powerful type of magic, drawing on as many traditions as the varied membership of the covens allows. The Witch is most effective in magic involving people, and compulsion—Curing, Disease and Death, and Absolute Command being the greatest specialities. Witches may be found in the highest and lowest walks of society, in court, city and countryside alike. Other Mages may join covens and become Witches, without losing their own spell specializations. The Witch is almost always a secretive figure, his/her magical skills either being hidden or practiced in solitude. The Witch is automatically damned, and all his/her magic Black.

High/Runic Sorcerer. The closest Mage to the proud and free Sorcerers of other fantasy games. The High Sorcerer (Runic Sorcerers are their Dark Age equivalents—Norse sorcerers using runes, Celts using ogham, Anglo-Saxons a mixture of the two) is a free man of some position, gained either by birth or the dedicated development of magical skills as a Wizard. He is normally from the urban, clerical or upper warrior and landowning classes; often indulging in Sorcery, Astrology, etc., as an adjunct (often secret) to his main pursuits. His specializations are wide, including Spells of Elemental and Complex Matter. He is interested in the *why* of magic, as well as the *what,* and eagerly seeks information on the Ethereal Plane (Primum Mobile). Many are good Christians, in their own eyes—while others desire power, e.g., through Conjuration. Faust was the Highest of High Sorcerers.

Cabalist (High Middle Ages only). Even the highest High Sorcerer has no access to the magical traditions and insights of the Jewish/Mohammedan Cabalist. Almost entirely restricted in Christendom to the urban ghetto, Cabalists have a very clear picture of the Ethereal Plane and how it works. They seek both personal salvation and power, using rigorous mental and physical exercises, deep study of arcane texts, and practice. For their high mastery of all types of spell, the Cabalist pays. As a magician, he is abhorred by his own community, while as a Jew or Mohammedan, he is persecuted by the Christians. Unable to attend any religious ceremonies, his piety will be low—and Appeals usually unheard.

These general types of Mage remain much the same throughout the Dark and Middle Ages. The Cunning Man in 1500 operated on much the same types of magic as in 700, using the same balance of incantation and herbs. The Witch too is found throughout the period, her powers of mayhem only strengthening after about 1200. The Wizard in Dark Age times would have been less likely to have come from the few towns, more likely to be an experienced Cunning Man who has left home to become a professional Mage. The only major differences within a category come with High Sorcery. The Anglo-Saxon, Norse or, above all, Celtic Sorcerer did differ in some distinct ways from his medieval successor. Dark Age Runic sorcerers seem to have specialized in spells of illusion, inscribed (runic) command, water breathing, combat and, in particular, shape changing. Battles between Celtic shape changing Sorcerers form a major mythological element, as we shall see. By contrast, the medieval High Sorcerer appears better at curing, and at "sophisticated" spells such as psychic disruption, time stoppage, etc. These are accounted for in the rules.

Otherwise, the keynotes are unity and continuity. At the end of the High Middle Ages, magic was becoming increasingly systematized, almost scientific. Alchemy, Palmistry and Physiognomy are examples. So is Astrology, and the great medieval System of Correspondencies. That system occupies a central place in medieval magical thought, and so in *Fantasy Wargaming*. It reflected Platonic ideas about the microcosm and the macrocosm. "What is below is similar to that which is above." The microcosm was Man, or Earth; the macrocosm was the Universe, the Ethereal Plane. There were invisible, magical links between different Star Signs, planets, colors, jewels, metals, parts of the body, plants, animals, times, places, etc. A man who correctly understood these Correspondencies (see page 180) knew himself to be surrounded at all times by astrological influences, which he could read, foretelling the future and manipulating the Ethereal forces. The system was used in basic Sorcery, Enchantment, Divination and Conjuration alike. Every person, creature, being on Earth or in the Ethereal Plane had a Birth Sign, a Controller—and an opposite sign, known as the Diminisher. They too were therefore tied into and part of the great System. Altering one part of the System —e.g., by constructing a magical item binding together several correspondencies under one Star Sign—could affect every other part, and so act as a map of the Ethereal Plane. These ideas reached their fullest elaboration in the High Middle Ages; but the System was constructed from beliefs already existing about the magical "virtues" of different herbs, metals, Star Signs, etc. We therefore had no hesitation in linking Dark Age sorcery too into the System.

And yet, throughout, came the clear message. Even at the most sophisticated level of magic, the most intellectual discipline, it was the Mage's intuitive imagination and understanding of the Otherworld which mattered most. For magic came from within you, from your Faith—in yourself, and in the forces you were seeking to control.

Myth: The Bard's Tale

Different cultures view the Supernatural in different ways. Up until now we have described how magic and higher powers operate in principle, and outlined some universal characteristics of the Supernatural beliefs of Christian and pagan peoples in the *Fantasy Wargaming* world. We have aimed to be as true to historical authenticity as gameability will allow; but in granting a real existence to Supernatural forces we naturally have to improve on history a bit. Social systems, religious activity and combat can all be drawn from life, and so to a point can spells and magicians. But fantasy games insist on more than bland reality has to offer: they demand fantastic creatures, Sorcerers actually wielding powers beyond nature, and preposterous adventures such as never were dared on this earth. Other games have more or less copped out at this point and abandoned history for atrocious pulp fiction: "as the devouring jelly advanced, Merlin made a mystic gesture and a bolt of green fire stabbed from his finger . . ."

But a game can be both imaginative and authentic together. All medieval cultures had their distinctive mythologies, their own bodies of legend expressing their own favored style of fabulous adventure and Supernatural events; and this mythological tradition is no less real than concrete historical data, and no less simulable in gaming. The monsters and magical beasts in *Fantasy Wargaming* never walked, swam or flitted this earth, but all derive from real mythological, literary and artistic traditions; and we have similarly fleshed out our magic system not only from real spell texts and beliefs about Sorcery, but from literary sources as well. We hope, too, that we can inspire fantasy game enthusiasts to try casting their adventures in the style of real medieval epics, legends and romances. Aside from the challenge of authenticity, you can have enough of blundering up and down tunnels.

This section, accordingly, will try to convey the flavor of the different mythological traditions drawn on in this book, and describe the chief elements of the mythological style of each. By "mythology" here we mean two fields of fabulous invention: ideas about the Supernatural, and patterns of adventure. Faithfulness to medieval tradition here is largely a matter of dungeoneering stylistics, so how much of the following you choose to regard or discard will be up to the GM's discretion. Only be it said that the medieval imagination is a joy to experience, and we hope you will savor its variegated delights for yourself.

First, a handful of general points. All the legendary traditions concerned, with the single exception of the Christian "mythology" of Saints' lives and miracles, are *heroic*. That is to say, they are all set in a mythical past with the general features of the heroic age, chiefly a premium regard for martial prowess in the individual and a strongly aristocratic bias in the heroic ideal. On the whole, though, every society tends to dress its heroic age in contemporary colors, and the heroes' arms, religion and social setup will reflect those of the storytelling society. Non-aristocracy can enter the heroic ranks in Arthurian and Norse mythology, but only by a striking demonstration of heroic prowess.

The elements that make a mythology distinctive are diverse, but the following accounts deal with about half-a-dozen main headings, which aren't formally set out and might consequently be useful to have listed here. First, *landscape:* perhaps the most powerful impression of a mythology's distinctive style is made by the kind of scenery against which the action is set. An Arthurian adventure set in a terrain of snow and mist would be as unthinkable as an Anglo-Saxon game spent chasing round catacombs. Second, *magic:* the forms most commonly taken by enchantment, the types of spell you tend to encounter and the situations they appear in. *Monsters* are covered elsewhere. *Heroes* have their own specially regarded ethos and abilities, and where there is a recognizable culture stereotype we will try and define it. *Imagery* is a rather more nebulous category: each mythology tends to have its peculiar repertoire of objects, qualities, organisms that get used in magical, symbolic or otherwise significant ways, of which service as magical items is the most important. Three important sources of medieval imagery are sacramental symbols (like the Christian cross, chalice, etc., or the hammer of Thor), weapons, and art objects. Finally, *patterns of adventure:* your typical Norse sea raider would be most startled to encounter a Moorish knight under a rock festooned with the heads of maidens, while your typical dragon will have little to fear from a Norse sea raider but will know his number is up if he is confronted with an Irish Saint.

Dark Ages

Literature, and consequently mythological ideas, were much less cosmopolitan in the Dark Ages than in the High Middle Ages, and the three main cultures involved in *Fantasy Wargaming* in this period had three distinctive mythological styles: Anglo-Saxon, Norse, and Celtic, in increasing order of complexity.

Anglo-Saxon mythology is pretty much confined to the solitary epic poem *Beowulf* which, although apparently clerical in origin, remains free of overtly Christian elements. Still, *Beowulf* does present a powerfully distinctive mythological world that can be fleshed out from other Old English poetry. It is a rather bleak, grey world of low hills, rocks and lakes, and the pervasive awareness of the sea owes nothing to the sunny blue Mediterranean—it is cold, grey and stormy, much as the Viking ocean and the North Sea of real life. By and large, it is not a magical world, having been early Christianized and the old Anglo-Saxon magical tradition progressively repressed by the Church. We do have a fair number of spells preserved in manuscripts, and from them we can glean something of the characteristics of historical Anglo-Saxon magic; but it does not feature much in storytelling. It is essentially medicinal, with prescribed chants to aid the charm of herbs and other culinary preparations, and the spells that survive are mainly concerned with protection (from disease, theft, misfortune) and healing. In literature, the only strictly magical event is Beowulf's unexplained ability to breathe underwater; otherwise, the supernatural manifests itself only in monsters. Besides the famous Beowulfian trio of Grendel and his dam and the dragon, we meet also sea and lake monsters and various sorts of Undead.

Old English poetry is tragic and elegiac in outlook, and lacking in the humor one finds in Norse sagas. This means heroes tend to get killed, especially since the most admired qualities in a hero are courage, loyalty, largesse, martial prowess and responsibility to those he is meant to protect. Self-sacrifice for honor, duty to comrades or society is the usual way for an Anglo-Saxon hero to go down; religious considerations rather take second place. Although generous, friendly and appreciative of the arts, the Anglo-Saxon hero tends to be rather serious and fatalistic. The most characteristic adventure pattern is a fight against impossible odds in which the hero acquits himself honorably and then snuffs it.

Anglo-Saxon society is particularly strong on bonds and pledges (between warriors, between a lord and his retainers, between friends), and much of its imagery clusters around symbols of solidarity and community: the hall, feasting, the mead which a lord dispenses to his men and according to which his bounty is measured. Gift items, too, are important, particularly gold artifacts, rings and torques. Wild things (particularly wolves and ravens) and weapons (swords, shields, spears) are also extremely common; a good sword is prized above all else.

Norse legend splits into two sorts, the myths of the gods and the sagas of men; and unlike (say) Greek mythology, the two categories do not intersect much. Stories with divine protagonists tend to be much more magical, with a good deal of comedy; tales of mortal men still admit a good deal of magical creatures and performance, but take place in a more naturalistic setting, often quite specific about places, historical characters and families. Sea, mist, mountains and snow are, of course, the backdrop against which we generally envisage the sagas, but in fact a great deal of action takes place indoors (usually for meteorological considerations), in homestead farms in valleys or in aristocratic halls. But although the gods do occasionally walk in Midgard—particularly Odin, in his familiar aspect of a one-eyed stranger in a wide-brimmed blue hat—most of their adventures are located in other compartments of the Ethereal plane, such as Asgard, Hel and especially the lands of the frost and fire giants. These are vast places with vast inhabitants (some literally mountainous in scale), and the magic tends to be on a similar scale, usually in the form of illusion, shape shifting and other transformations.

Midgard magic is less extravagant, and the mythical beasties rather less awesome, though both still show a bewildering diversity. Historically, magic took two main forms: the active runic magic of symbols and chants, which features strongly in myth as well, and the passive divinatory magic of the shamanic *seidhr,* which could also on occasion be turned to active command, sometimes with deadly power. Runic magic was used for a wide range of purposes: spells of protection against specific dangers (wounds, poison, the elements, and so forth), control of weather and the outcome of combat, increased intelligence or volubility, healing, curses, inducing madness, making the dead speak, and a good deal more besides. Sorcerous skill was particularly associated with the Finns, who were believed to produce the most powerful magicians and were regarded with mingled respect, hatred and dread. Terrestrial giants were less prodigious than their Ethereal counterparts, but still formidable; they dwelt mainly in hills, caves and forests.

Like Anglo-Saxon heroes, the protagonists of the sagas tend to be fairly short on magical skills and extraordinary talents, although they are powerful warriors and still a bit larger than life. They are not the most powerful fighters, though; this honor belongs to the berserks in the war band, who rarely have much identity of their own. Once again, loyalty between friends and retainers and lords is highly prized, and adventures are generally undertaken in company and treasure duly distributed by the leader with generosity and fairness. Family ties were strong, and many sagas deal with the long-term relations of rival clans. But these tend not to have much of a Supernatural element. Women have rather more opportunities for distinction in Norse legend than elsewhere in the period; in character, martial prowess and magical skill they can sometimes rival men. There are not really any typical forms of adventure, but the sagas, though tragic when they feel like it, are generally rather optimistic in contrast with the tone of Anglo-Saxon heroic poetry, and happy endings are common enough.

Weapons and domestic livestock (especially horses and cattle) feature large in the sagas as prized items and as gifts. All runic writing, whether or not inscribed with magical intent, is highly symbolic; mead is used with mystical significance as well as the social implications it bears in Anglo-Saxon society; and other common images are staffs, wild animals (bears, elks) and treasures.

Celtic mythology is unabashedly bizarre and extravagant, intensely magical and idiosyncratic, and much the most fantastic of the cultures we are concerned with. Many of its individual personages, particularly the Supernatural ones, appear to be the degenerate remnants of pre-Christian religion, gods lapsed into fairies and even mortal men. The complexities of the Celtic Otherworld are too many and diffuse, and the interrelations of Welsh and Irish conceptions too difficult, to be worked into our system; but we hope to offer some guidelines to the general flavor of Celtic magic and adventure.

Celtic heroes are powerful characters. In the *Táin Bó Cuailnge,* for example, which is probably the most preposterous celebration of the Irish martial ideal, heroic feats include leaping over oak trees in chariots, standing erect on the point of a lance in flight, and slaying 130 kings (not to mention their armies) without sustaining a scratch. This is exceptional, though, and in the Welsh *Culhwch and Olwen* each member of Arthur's band has a single gift known as his "peculiarity," most of which simply express a special gift of strength, swiftness, agility or stature by the usual Celtic means of a striking illustration, such as being able to flatten mountains by standing on the summit, or being able to hit a wren between the legs from the opposite side of the Irish Sea. But some are more magical, like gifts of invisibility or altering one's height at will; while other peculiarities serve no profound practical purpose at all, like being able to stand all day on one foot, or being able to make the soles of one's feet red hot.

In order to keep heroes' skills within the normal range of characteristics in *Fantasy Wargaming,* we advise GMs to use discretion and ingenuity in parcelling out peculiarities! They might be either rather tame but poetically described (e.g., "he could shave the pubes off a man without nicking the flesh," which could be managed with an agility of 16 or so), or better still rather remarkable but entirely useless (e.g., "he could turn his eyeballs around in their sockets," or "he could describe the weather to a gnat").

Celtic magic is pervasive in the mythology, and cannot really be reduced to its methods or principles of operation. There are no real limitations to its form, its use, its effect or its power except those dictated by the plot, which makes it peculiarly difficult to quantify for gaming. Spells of transformation, especially shape shifting, are commonest, followed by various kinds of binding (magical imprisonment, paralysis, sleep, weakness) and illusion (specific, or merely general befuddlement of the wits). Celtic mythology delights in wonders for their own sake, so not all magic is purposive; the world is full of mysteries, magical happenings with no overt point. Perhaps the most famous instance is the river in the Welsh tale *Peredur* with on one side a field of white sheep and on the other a field of black sheep, and by its banks a tree with one half in flames from root to summit and the other half green and unconsumed; and now and again a sheep jumps the river and changes color accordingly as it does so.

Celtic adventures take many fabulous forms, but there are a few recurrent types. One such is the quest for magical items, which may be required for fulfilment of a promise of an agreement. Another is the *Imram* marvellous sea voyage, in which a hero or heroes (or a Saint, in the case of St. Brendan) sail away on a slender pretext and pass all sorts of strange islands harboring fantastic adventures. A third is the revenge story, the pursuit and reprisal of an enemy after a raid, usually culminating in an all-out battle between the opposing hosts.

Monsters are treated relatively conservatively in Celtic myth; they are nearly always enlarged and souped-up versions of naturally occurring creatures, giants and monster birds, ants, horses and what have you. A special category are the "venomous" animals: venomous hounds, venomous sheep, venomous editions and any normally harmless species. Animals play a large part, too, in the diverse and colorful imagery of Celtic imagination, being both valued and frequently enchanted. In addition to the usual weapons and objets d'art, we find music highly regarded (harps are a common symbol), as well as birds (particularly crows and ravens) and domestic items (notably cauldrons).

High Middle Ages

In the 11th century, the mythmaking peoples discussed above suffered severe cultural shake-ups that more or less obliterated their distinctive native mythologies (in our sense of fantastic traditions of legendary heroic adventure). The Vikings were converted to Christ; the era of raiding and conquest had already given way to settled kingdoms and constituted law. Though saga literature continued to flourish, the old heathen magic waned and the legends of the gods were ephemerized or forgotten. The Anglo-Saxons were conquered, and their society and literature eclipsed by the language, feudal order and literary heritage of the continental invaders; and before long the Celtic nations were subjected to Norman England. In place of the purely national mythologies of the Dark Ages, there evolved an international and cross-cultural repertory of traditional stories, freely transplanted from one language to another and often back again. Similarly, secular ideals of chivalry and love, as well as popular traditions of monsters and the Supernatural, become diffused over all of western Christendom in broadly identical forms, and we don't sacrifice much to convenience if we treat the age's mythology as a product of a single cosmopolitan culture.

Outside the Christian mythological traditions of apocryphal Biblical narrative and hagiography, there were three main legendary traditions in the High Middle Ages. All followed the pattern of an accretion of fabulous magical and heroic adventures around a historical figure, incongruously got up in contemporary dress, arms and literary language; and all followed the general style of heroic adventure favored by the age, which is customarily termed *romance* and contrasted with *epic*. Broadly speaking, epic is characterized by unity, seriousness, tragedy, and a certain restraint or spareness in the use of fantastic elements, and is best instanced by *Beowulf* and the French *chansons de geste;* while romance is more diffuse and episodic, lighter in tone, often comic, and much freer with unlikely and supernatural events.

The three traditions are the legends of Alexander, Arthur and Charlemagne. The romances of Alexander the Great deal with his apocryphal fantastic adventures in the East; both their locale and their quasi-historical date oblige their reluctant exclusion from this book. The Carolingian legends are too varied in their conceptions to be readily simulated in a game: the two best-known works in this tradition, the 11th-century epic *Chanson de Roland* and the 16th-century romance *Orlando Furioso,* are set in quite different worlds.

The "Matter of Britain" is another matter. The world of the Welsh, French, German and English Arthurian romances is coherent enough to be gameable, and the tradition benefits from a definitive, culminating expression in Sir Thomas Malory's *Morte D'Arthur*. The historical Arthur died early in the 6th century, Malory in 1471; and as these more or less correspond to the limits of the period simulated in *Fantasy Wargaming,* we offer here a few brief guidelines for putting an Arthurian adventure together. Arthurian fantasy comes in at least three different flavors, and we set them out in turn.

The *historical Arthur* was a Romanized Celtic war leader who, as commander in chief of the previously disorganized and shambolic Briton armies, scored a spectacular series of victories against the invading Saxons around the year 500, culminating in the decisive battle of Mount Badon, before falling 20 years later at Camlann, a victim of internecine political rivalries. A historical Arthurian adventure will be a largely military affair, between Christian Celts and pagan (Teutonic) Anglo-Saxons; magical color at GM's discretion. The Britons are farmers (arable and livestock) organized for tribute and military service under warrior kings, who are themselves subject to King Arthur as supreme

commander of allied forces. They operated in armies from about
50 to several hundred in number, with swords, spears, shields and
chain mail; though they tended not to build fortifications themselves, they relied frequently on abandoned Roman hill and ring
forts, many of which were still intact and defensible. They fought
in the heroic style, as massed individuals rather than an organized
force, and sometimes fought from horseback. Their English enemies fought primarily with spears, both throwing and thrusting,
and swords and axes were of lesser popularity. Though the
leaders would wear chain armor, on the whole they are restricted
to shields and leather jerkins. Neither side wore helmets except
very occasional individuals. The English did not use horses in
warfare, nor do they seem to have gone in much for fortification.

The *Welsh Arthur* of early legend falls into the category of
Celtic myth described in the previous section. Marvellous tales
about the heroic king began to be told within a couple of generations of his death, and five splendid specimens survive in the *Mabinogion*. There is as yet no definitive Arthurian legend, but rather
a wide range of unconnected tales about the King and his knights.
Sometimes Arthur takes the lead himself, accompanied by his select band of warriors, on a magical quest on earth or into the
Otherworld of Annwn (see below on *Faery*). At other times the
protagonists are individual knights like Peredur (Percival) or
Owein, and Arthur appears only as a magnanimous but sedentary
center of action at his magnificient palace at Caerleon, though
occasionally venturing abroad to hunt or to intervene in adventures. The Welsh romances of Arthur tend to be marked by
quests, individual feats of arms, and a lot of magical embellish-
ment; the knights are highly self-conscious about their honor and
prowess, without being terribly courtly about it. Women are
treated with esteem and are nearly always beautiful; and the Celtic
knight shows none of the studied erotic continence of the hero of
later chivalry. Of the familiar characters of Arthurian myth, some
are already established and characterized in the tradition: Gwen-
hwyfar his queen (not yet adulterous), Cei the fiery No 2,
Gwalchmei and Bedwyr (but if Welsh names boggle you, stick to
Guinevere, Kay, Gawain and Bedevere). Others, like Lancelot,
Galahad and Merlin, don't come in till later; the historical
Medraut or Mordred doesn't figure in the Welsh romances. In

general, this is a lovely adventure scenario allowing GMs a wide latitude for invention.

The *Arthur of chivalry* is the product of an international tradition of court poetry, and is the Arthur of legend familiar from stage, screen, Tennyson, Burne-Jones, T. H. White, Monty Python . . . The Welsh legends were conveyed to the continent mainly by itinerant Breton bards, and thence entered French, German and English romance, culminating in Sir Thomas Malory's *Morte D'Arthur,* the first printed classic of English literature. By this time the historical Arthur had been blessed with a substantial legendary career at the hands of Geoffrey of Monmouth, whose imaginative *History of the Kings of Britain* contributed the figure of Merlin and the sword Excalibur, and the adventure of the Holy Grail was added by Chretien de Troyes from hints in Welsh sources.

Arthur and his court became the embodiment of contemporary ideals of chivalry, courtly love and Christian knighthood; knighthood is the highest calling there is, demanding in its requirements, which include the renunciation of personal goals, and dedicated to the upholding of order and justice against disruptive elements natural and Supernatural. In spite of the tendency to regard adventures as spiritual exercises, this tradition still follows much the same adventure patterns as the Celtic: quests (now generally religiously motivated, rather than for magic items), monster bashing, individual wanderings and combat. Arthur is rarely a main actor in such adventures—his part of the story takes place largely at home. If you're gaming this type of Arthurian adventure, piety has to be hoarded jealously or your knight may forfeit his honor, and God won't support him in battle and general appeals like he does his true Christian servants. Remember that the courtly idea of love tends to sublimate and spiritualize sexual impulses, and non-consummation is the best way to go about it; so watch that lust, fellas!

The adventures will generally be conducted in High Middle Ages dress—the nominal historical date doesn't really figure, and feel free to incorporate wild anachronisms. The landscape of the adventures will be typically naturalistic English, with a lot of woodland and castles, but substantially running over into Faery. In the romances, a knight may cultivate such outstanding piety as to attain mystical experience (visions, celestial visitations, even assumption); but in practice if his piety ever gets that high he'll more normally throw knighthood over for a monastery, and most knights remain rather practical and unmystical in spite of their high ideals.

Faery

Celtic Britain was converted to Christianity with the Romans, and the old Celtic gods went underground in a variety of different ways. Many of the old gods persisted in legend as mortal heroes and heroines, and one even crossed the floor of the House to find a new career as the Irish St. Brigid. But most retained some of their Supernatural identity while fading and diminishing in status over the whole of the Middle Ages, and survived as a race of rather low Higher Powers on the periphery of worship despite the steady ebbing of belief in them (and hence, in *FW* terms, their mana). One particularly strong tradition that survived with them was that of a realm contiguous with this earth but not of it, in which these Supernatural beings dwelt and to which men too could be drawn. In Welsh legend, it is called Annwn, and is sometimes thought of as the land of the dead; its lord, who bears its name, seems to be a lapsed Celtic god, and sometimes personifies death, but often this connection is missing. Arthur once led a daring and costly raid on Annwn in quest of a magic cauldron, and the *Mabinogion* relates how Pwyll, Prince of Dyved, formed a close friendship with Annwn and even ruled the realm in his place for a year. In Irish legend the magical realm is particularly associated with, and called after, the *sid* or hollow hills, and sometimes is also thought to lie across the sea (where it is called Tir na nOg, "the land of youth").

With the diffusion of Celtic mythology all over Europe in the High Middle Ages came a more generalized conception of this unhuman land, which in *Fantasy Wargaming* we call *Faery*. Faery is neither divine nor diabolic, and certainly not human; it is a place that exists neither wholly on Earth nor wholly in the Otherworld. Its live inhabitants step between the two worlds freely—a whole series of spirits who have no obvious place in the divine or diabolic hosts, who (in Christian tradition) laughed at exorcisms and were morally neutral. Foremost among these beings were the great immortal spirits of the Celtic underworld: fairies, brownies, kelpies, etc. Here too are monsters which have become much rarer on Earth proper: goblins, trolls, banshees, water horses and so forth.

The Ethereal plane, the Otherworld, has no proper geography. Faery, by contrast, is a world with visible topography, which can be entered and walked in by men of Earth. Faery is, in medieval myth, overwhelmingly rural—a place of woods and copses, of open heaths, of waterfalls, springs and deep pools; of hollow hills, where the elves hold revel; of open barrows, and fairy rings. It is at these places that Earth and Faery meet, as gates. Here pass the elves and other spirits into Earth. They may be benevolent towards men, and graciously perform small feats of magic in return for offerings of food and worship. They may tempt handsome young men and women back into Faery, for the pleasure of their company; or even steal human babies, leaving a changeling in their place. Mischievous rather than evil, their power for good and ill declines in Western tradition from the conquest onwards. In Anglo-Saxon times, "elf-shot" was deadly, bringing sure death of men and cattle alike. The elves themselves were substantial creatures, the size of a slender youth. By 1500, they had shrunk to tiny, winged fairies and curdlers of milk.

To someone who has read this chapter, it is not hard to make sense of Faery and its decline within the *FW* system. Faery is an *Enchanted place*, "Enchantment" being the magical process whereby an object and its Ethereal spirit are indissolubly united. Enchanted creatures live and move simultaneously in both worlds, and exorcism is useless because of the unity between spirit and body. But not only the denizens of Faery are enchanted: the entire landscape and all its individual elements are likewise bonded to their Ethereal spirits, so that not only the living inhabitants but the realm itself exist in this strange borderland between Earth and the Otherworld proper. We can imagine that the magic used to set up the enchantment originally was of titanic scale, and carried out by the old Celtic gods in their heyday before the Roman conquest. As belief in Faery and its natives ebbed, so did the realm itself, because the mana needed to support it was not continually injected in sufficient supply. So the decline in the worship of and belief of Faery would have affected its survival considerably. Its creatures more rarely visited earth, and adopted smaller forms that required less mana to maintain. Like the Scandinavian gods after the conversion, the vestiges of Faery

faded away after the Reformation. From the three main elements
of medieval mythology—Christianity, Diabolism and Faery—had
emerged only two. Yet in the period covered by this book, adventures involving or entirely located in Faery are just as feasible as
the Gothic conflicts of God and Devil.

Saints and miracles

We should not forget that the Christian Church had a kind of mythology of its own besides all these traditions of fantastic adventure in secular literature. In bulk, of course, hagiographic writing
ponderously outweighed the whole of Arthurian literature several
times over; but it only calls for a brief mention here because it
has only the smallest part to play in fantasy adventures. Most of
the Saints to whom miracles were attributed lived before our period or outside our geographical radius; in Britain in the Dark
Ages, miracle-working Saints were primarily a feature of the missionary era, and though some of the Celtic Saints had some rather
exciting adventures their day was done by the time our period
opens. But holy men continue to work occasional miracles thereafter, and they will certainly arise occasionally in gaming, so a
short word on varieties of miracle will be perhaps helpful.

The great pastime of the Irish Saints was subduing giants and
monsters (St. Columba's was the first recorded encounter with
the Loch Ness monster), generally in unarmed confrontation
(daunting the beasts, no doubt, with divinely-enhanced missionary charisma), although the late St. George is a distinguished
martial counter-instance. Otherwise, miracles fall under the two
general headings of community benefits and displays of the Deity's power to the blasphemous or sceptical. The former category
includes miraculous influences over natural foodstuffs (multi-
plying crops, filling garners, herding herrings into nets) and general miracles of curing and resurrection, ending droughts and so
forth.

The second sort of miracle was more spectacular but rarely encountered as the number of complete unbelievers fell away; God
doesn't mind showing off if there's a large catch of potential mana
to be culled from the operation, but generally the mana expended
on a miracle of walking on water or raising mountains will not
justify itself in a cost-effective way.

One further tradition deserves special mention; there is a strong hagiographic tradition of holy men communing with wild things, either conversing with birds and animals or subduing and pacifying ferocious creatures like boars and tigers, even taming them to hand. Strictly speaking, these are two different sorts of miracle, communication and imposition of will or personality.

Chapter III

The Book of Physiologus

(*or "Oh God! It's a Thesaurus!"*)

Fabulous beasts and races make up the terrestrial department of the marvellous. In an age when the Supernatural was viewed as a part of the real world, not a thing apart but simply an extension of the natural order into realms unseen, it is not surprising that there should be wonders on the face of the Earth as well as beyond it. Our own era is regrettably intolerant of marvels, and insists when looking back on the Middle Ages upon a firm distinction between the real and the imaginary. But role-playing historical fantasy games go beyond history and try to view the medieval worlds from the inside. In *Fantasy Wargaming,* reality is not what was, but what was believed. In the last chapter we explained how this principle applies to the Supernatural, to myth, magic, and religion; in the present, much briefer, survey we guide the player round the marvellous menagerie of monsters and mythical beings that were, to the medieval imagination, at least as real as the elephant and the tiger, and in many cases more believable than the fantastic attributes then ascribed to many *bona fide* forms of exotic wildlife.

The encounter with monsters is the oldest form of heroic adventure there is. It features in *Gilgamesh,* the earliest fantasy fiction we know; and in the Middle Ages it is the only type of fantastic exploit as freely undertaken by Saints as by pagan heroes. Modern fantasy games teem with monsters to be overcome, but they have tended, as we remarked in the last chapter, to pay only the most haphazard attention to actual beliefs, even when trying to be historically authentic. It seems a pity, in view of the broad and splendid medieval teratological tradition, to throw it all over for feeble coinages in the Clark Ashton Smith vein, or to attach real names to shoddy travesties of the creatures they originally designated. Naturally, we don't want to inhabit GMs' invention in this field, and we would urge them to be as free as they want in their resort to anachronism or other departures from strict authenticity. After all, when you're dealing with creatures who never trod this earth, it doesn't much matter whether you locate them in Madagascar or Shropshire. We have taken a few such liberties ourselves, in including in our lists creatures not normally expected to be encountered in Western Europe, on the perhaps rather tenuous pretext that heroic literature did freely populate its adventures with unlikely wildlife, such as lions in Wales. Still, we hope to illustrate something of the range of delicious monsters found in medieval literature and art, and in this as elsewhere to show the charm and fertility of the medieval imagination, and the particular pleasures to be had from gaming it.

Accordingly, we offer in the Rules section a list of some 60 monsters and magical beings, with playing characteristics and a brief description of each. In this chapter, we hope to explain the different varieties of fabulous creatures, with suggestions on how to evolve new ones of your own in the same mold; and to introduce the various non-human races encountered in *Fantasy Wargaming,* whose characteristics will be found in the same section of the Rules (pages 267–91).

The different traditions

Medieval monster lore consists of two largely distinct traditions, the literary and the scholarly. We have said a little about the literary mythology in the last chapter: the monsters of the Dark Ages tend to have the shape (if not the scale or attributes) of men and well-known domestic and wild animals, while the inventions of the High Middle Ages become more extravagant and diverse. Scholarship follows a rather different course. The interest in zoological descriptions of fabulous beasts goes back to the natural historians of classical antiquity, people like Aristotle, Pliny and Aelian, who were often driven to unreliable hearsay and travellers' tales for their accounts of non-Mediterranean wildlife. From these beginnings, the science of zoology got liberally and charmingly saturated with folklore, and in the Middle Ages their branch of monster lore divided further into two sub-traditions that could loosely be called scholarly: the *bestiaries,* which flourished right through the period, and *heraldry,* which established itself as a curious new learning in the High Middle Ages only. Our own monster catalogues have drawn from all of these sources, and we offer here a quick view of the style distinctive to each.

Anglo-Saxon monsters have already been touched on. The *Beowulf* monsters are not circumstantially described, which gives a mysterious and sinister effect of something only half-glimpsed. This is very much in keeping with the shadowy, teasingly hinting quality of the Anglo-Saxon poetic imagination and the misty feel of the heroic landscape; the innumerable water monsters Beowulf battles in the sea and glimpses around Grendel's mere are swift, fierce, secretive and deadly, either half-perceived from a dim shape, splash or movement or else suddenly embroiled in lethal combat with the hero too close and quick to be fully seen. Grendel and his mother are loosely anthropomorphic, but similarly furtive and elusive to view. Grendel slays men in secret, silently and rapidly; there's no razzamatazz about Old English monstrous combat, no showy challenges, set-piece drawn-out tussles and victorious exultation. Death is swift and somber, and monsters powerful agents of deep terror and menace.

Much of Old English monster lore is that of the continental Germanic tradition; so with dragons and the undead, and GMs should feel free to import other Teutonic monsters like trolls and giants if they want to expand the range. The *Beowulf* dragon is a flying fire breather, bound to a hoard, which goes on a destructive rampage when the hoard is disturbed after three centuries of quiescence. A point of departure from some continental tradition is that the dragon is non-sentient, and instead of being a man in origin who was transformed into a dragon by his miserly association with his hoard, it took over a pagan burial hoard left undefended by the death of the last guardian of those relics of ancient heroes. The dragon is envenomed, presumably on his fangs and perhaps on his talons and tail spike as well, and is slain with the thrust of a shortsword in the belly. He leaves his hoard only at night.

Barrow-wights are substantial ghosts (animated corpses, the deceased's remains inhabited by its necromantically conjured spirit, or alternatively by a demon) dwelling in and operating from their place of burial. The Anglo-Saxon burial mound or barrow is a more or less rudimentary chamber varying from a simple pile of stones over the dead and his possessions to a pillared structure of wood and stone, all heaped over with earth and soon grassed over. The door to the mound is physical but concealed; it has been added to the original design by the Barrow-Wight itself. Some barrows are haunted by insubstantial ghosts, in which case they need no physical egress.

Norse monsters and magical beings range from the routine to the apocalyptic. The divine sagas include some colossally powerful creatures that not even the gods can overcome, such as the world-encircling Midgard Serpent and the titanic Fenris Wolf (bound until the doom of the gods thanks to Tyr, who lost his hand in the process). These are essentially denizens of the Ethereal plane, and feature only in adventures of the gods. The same is largely true of Norse *Giants,* who are much the largest of the races of that name; many are literally mountainous in stature, and mercifully their wanderings are largely confined to the Ethereal realms, particularly their own Ethereal land of Jotunheim. Such giants as dwell outside Jotunheim are of three strains according to habitat: the Frost Giants and Fire Giants, who live respectively in the Ethereal realms of frost and fire and will remain there until Ragnarok, and the Hill Giants, who very occasionally haunt terrestrial rocks, forests and especially mountains. Though basically humanoid in form, Norse giants often have multiple heads or hands, and strangely enough can sometimes breed perfectly normal and rather attractive females. Their attitude to the Asgardian deities ranges from grudging tolerance through mild indifference to open hostility. They never trust them, perhaps because the gods are a lot more intelligent.

As in Anglo-Saxon belief, the main category of Undead is *Barrow-Wights;* like their English counterparts, they guard the treasure buried in their mound against theft, and the more adventurous of them can wander among men for ill or good (sometimes they offer prophecy or advice to their kin). Like their Christian counterparts, they have to have had their spirits conjured back into their remains at some time in the past (by themselves, of course, if they've the magical resources), and this can only be done for spirits in Niflheim (Hel).

Norse *Werewolves* are voluntary shape shifters, unlike in some other traditions, and usually effect their change by donning an animal skin, upon which they take on the likeness of the beast while retaining their human mental faculties. They don't always specialize in wolf form, either; sometimes they take on a bear shape, and very occasionally other animal guises. Treat involuntary lycanthropes as ordinary, non-sentient wolves, whose characteristics are in the *Animals* table on page 291.

Dragons follow the general Teutonic, as against Celtic, model, with their associations with hoards and fire-breathing abilities. Norse dragons differ from Anglo-Saxon in being occasionally sentient, having metamorphosed out of human form by the adoption of draconic characteristics of sedentary, surly miserhood; but they don't think much, and their intelligence drops with age. The winged ones are still in the minority, but in the High Middle Ages the flying strain comes to predominate.

The most numerous of the species of Norse monsters are the three non-human races of elves, trolls and dwarfs, on all of whom see below. On the whole, Norse monsters are much more bogeyish, and often comical, than their English relations, and there are other ways of dealing with them than simply fighting to the death; often they're vulnerable to trickery, and dwarfs and trolls have a powerful (in the latter case fatal) aversion to sunlight.

Celtic monsters, as remarked in the last chapter, tend to be relatively simple variations on real terrestrial creatures, even quite ordinary domestic beasts with no reputation for ferocity. They can be enlarged to superhuman size and in Irish legend invested with venomous properties of tooth, claw and hide, but they don't become sentient or command magical powers. These are reserved for the *Giants,* who don't constitute a separate race in the way that the Fairies or the Norse giants do, but nevertheless have a lot of recurrent features: usually between eight and 20 feet in height, they are belligerent and perverse without being necessarily evil, and some of them show considerable courtesy in combat with heroes. They are not always wild, either; Ysbaddaden, Chief Giant in the *Mabinogion,* has a castle and a beautiful daughter, even if he has a rather treacherous way with his poisoned stone-headed spears. But many, particularly in Arthurian romance, are simply wicked, often attaching themselves to a particular spot and slaying all who try to pass. Some have a passion for mortal women, but they seem to prefer bondage and flagellation to

straight consummation, thereby affording the hero a chance to
rescue the dishevelled captive with her clothing tantalizingly awry
but her virtue blessedly intact.

Celtic *Dragons* are a different species from Teutonic, though
there seems to have been a good deal of interbreeding. The typical Celtic dragon is flightless, variable in color, and missing the
flaming breath of the Scandinavian strain, though its breath can
often be poisonous or caustic. It tends to inhabit fresh water
places, particularly small lakes, and to be more interested in
nubile human females than boring old treasure. But this pure Celtic
type gets early mingled with the continental breed, and wings
and fiery breath and stinging tails are widely encountered, particularly when you get into the era of cosmopolitan Romance. You
need armor to be able to engage with them properly. The Irish
version is called a *Péist* (same as "beast") and inhabits loughs,
either in the waters or in a lair on an island or on shore. Sometimes they guard magical spots or treasure, coiling round trees of
magical fruit or lurking in a pool by a treasure site. Heroes kill
them by chopping off the head, as the vitals are hard to locate in
the long, undifferentiated body; Celtic Saints tend to bind them
within their waters, as St. Columba did the Loch Ness monster, or
to scare them away from the haunts of men. It is from the cross-
bred continental-Celtic strain of dragon, incidentally, that the familiar bat-winged, spiny dragon of heraldry derives.

Bestiaries owe their origin from a (now lost, except in adul-
terated translations) Greek treatise of the early Christian era
called *Physiologus,* which was translated and expanded throughout the Middle Ages to become the period's chiefest fount of
beastly lore. In addition to a wide range of monsters and semi-
fabulous creatures, the bestiarists (whose purpose was generally
religious and allegorical rather than scientific) ascribed all sorts
of bizarre characteristics to perfectly genuine terrestrial creatures.
Elephants copulated backwards, pelicans fed their young by dig-
ging chunks out of their own breast, beavers eluded pursuit by
biting off their testicles; all such snippets were imputed to the
inarguable authority of Physiologus, and duly allegorized into ingenious sacred significance. Many bestiaries were copiously illus-
trated, and these images were a major inspiration to early heraldry. The bestiary monsters come from a diverse range of
sources; some are wholly imaginary creatures that originate in

classical zoological treatises, while others are evidently garbled versions of real animals. Under the first heading fall such as the Amphisbaena, Griffin and Yale; under the second, the intriguing Bonnacon (a highly mythologized version of the bison) and the Parandrus (in spite of its alleged Ethiopic habitat, a fanciful derivation from the reindeer). Any creature not readily observable by the naturalist was likely to sprout strange legendary attributes, especially Asian and African wild animals, serpents, and uncommon birds. On the whole, though, these are physical properties rather than magical, and the main interest of bestiary monsters will tend to be in combat. It is worth remarking that such beasts are never any more than beasts; they are not sentient, have no souls, and behave like animals rather than fiends.

Heraldic monsters are easy to build your own, full of variety, and immensely stylish, so it is surprising they have been relatively neglected in fantasy gaming. Heraldic design was largely a Norman invention, and as the number and range of armorial bearings widened in the 13th and 15th centuries, so the repertory of mundane animals available became rapidly exhausted, and more fantastic creatures started coming in. Some derived from the classical zoologists of antiquity, more came from the bestiaries, a great many were simply made up to look good, and the origins of the great majority remain entirely opaque. Although the heraldic tradition spawned an astonishing range of fantastic creatures, their method of construction is not all that hard to outline. The bestiarists used to try and convey a picture of an exotic or obscure creature by likening various parts of its body to the nearest familiar equivalents: so, for instance, the Cambridge Bestiary describes the Parandrus as having the body of an Ibex, the head of a stag, and the color of a bear. This kind of piecemeal verbal construction of monsters was carried over into the pictorial invention of monsters in heraldic art, with the result that most such creatures are what's called *chimerical,* made up of bits of real animals stuck together in odd, effective new combinations. The range of such elements is rather limited, in fact, by the range of terrestrial animals thought suitably dignified for use on arms; they tend to be beasts that are powerful or obviously distinguished, with some that have obvious allegorical significance. The most common are birds of prey, large wild animals, and occasional smaller creatures like reptiles, particularly serpents and oddly enough newts (admired for the stars imagined on their backs).

The result is that a great many chimerical creatures of heraldry have common features like eagle's talons, antlers, forked tongues, and the like. Bodies tend to be supplied from lions, antelopes, panthers, stags and horses; heads are human, reptilian, feline, or like boars or eagles; the feet may be cloven, taloned, pawed, or sometimes (in the case of quadrupeds) two of one and two of the other, front and rear. Tails and horns come in a wide variety of styles, and there are optional extras like wings, spines, stings, or extra heads. The exigencies of heraldic posture mean that many can go bipedal as readily as on all fours, and the fact that many such beasts are known only in appearance means that GMs can devise further attributes and characteristics with complete freedom.

Magical races

Medieval myth, later folk belief and modern literary fantasy have all peopled the world with species of non-human (but sentient) creatures who exist in considerable numbers with a race and society of their own. In the last chapter we explained the origins of these secret peoples who reside outside the Christian world yet mingle with it, and whose own kingdoms lie both in this world and in the other, while belonging to neither. Here we identify the individual races of magical being more closely, and follow the decline of the Faery races over the period covered by the book. Certain species familiar from other systems, such as goblins, gnomes, hobbits and orcs, don't feature because they're not encountered in the Middle Ages; others, like giants and dragons, come in more than one flavor and are separately discussed above.

Elves and *Fairies* are the Faery races proper: survivors of a pre-Christian paganism who maintain a slowly dwindling existence in an enchanted realm apart from but contiguous with this world. Originally distinct, the two peoples mingled throughout the Middle Ages so as to become ultimately one; but they originated in quite separate heathen heavens. *Elves* are the Teutonic strain, originally equal to and worshipped with the Asgardian gods; they lived and feasted in Asgard, and dwelt in the region of the Ethereal plane called Alfheim under the rule of Frey. They were related to the gods and giants rather than trolls and dwarfs, and were benign and not much individualized. The Norsemen called them *alfar,* the Anglo-Saxons *ylfe,* and Snorri Sturlusson tells us that there were two species, the Light Elves of Asgard and the Dark Elves who dwelt on Earth or in what was to become Faery. Both strains were of human form and stature, but the Light Elves were fair and extraordinarily beautiful, while the Dark Elves were black, and preferred to dwell underground. With the waning of Germanic paganism, we may imagine that the Light Elves opted out of waning Asgard to join their terrestrial kin, for we hear of elves of forests, water and mountains as well as underground. Eventually the two strains blended and the Elves became a people very much like the courtly Fairies of Celtic romance, with whom they came to be merged, before their size began to diminish and their societies to become much more secretive.

Fairies are the Celtic equivalents to elves. Originally the pagan gods of Britain and Ireland known in Irish legend as the Tuatha de Danaan, they passed with the coming of Christianity into a Faery realm called the *síd,* which was entered through ancient pagan mounds and through loughs. (Don't confuse them with Teutonic Barrow-Wights, who are conjured Undead who dwell in the barrows themselves.) There they established a vast, mainly subterranean realm rather like that of the Teutonic dwarfs (see below), itself partitioned into several extensive kingdoms, and continued to adventure in the world of men as powerful, handsome heroic magicians, intermarrying freely with humans both openly (like Morgan le Fay, greatest of the later fairies) or by theft (as in *Sir Orfeo*). The heyday of Arthurian romance was also their fullest bloom; the Celtic fairies absorbed the Teutonic elves to form a single race, but thereafter their mana declined badly and with it their stature and powers.

The later, diminutive elves and fairies ("elves" being the usual name in Germanic countries, "fairies" in Britain and France) vary considerably in size even within a single period, but tend to get smaller with time, from the stature of 12-year-old children to the familiar flower-sized tinies of Victorian art. In the 13th century they are already beginning to develop into the secretive, mischievous, rather weakly magical fairies of later folktale, and by the end of the Middle Ages their typical size is about half that of humans. Intermarriage has stopped, though they still steal human children away and replace them with changelings if they can get at them before Christening.

Dwarfs (the plural "Dwarves" applies, strictly speaking, only in Tolkien) are a Teutonic race of little people, again originating in pagan Asgard and diminishing in size and majesty throughout the Middle Ages. Created separately from the Teutonic gods, they have always lived underground, in an Enchanted realm of considerable splendor, whose entrances are through hills and rocks. In their pagan heyday they were about two-thirds human size, and employed their considerable skills in magic, engineering, architecture, metallurgy and runic lore to manufacture a wide range of Enchanted items to those who could either afford their steep rates or cheat their suspicious, wary intellects out of payment. They specialized in Enchanted weapons (their finest creation was Thor's hammer Miollnir), but all their produce was jealously coveted by the gods, with whom they coexisted in an uneasy relationship of mutual mistrust. They were, and have always been, extremely miserly, amassing huge hoards for the mere pleasure of ownership; not surprisingly, several have ended up as Teutonic dragons. With the passing of Asgard, they carried on business as usual in their Enchanted subterranean kingdom, but as their mana ebbed they grew uglier (not that they were ever pretty), and unable to venture comfortably into daylight, a property which is already appearing in pagan times. Their size and skills diminish, too, until by the end of the High Middle Ages they are only a few inches in height, and are reduced to doing petty tasks for human gold: a piece of metal to be forged or a piece of wool to be spun may be left, with an appropriate fee, outside their holes overnight and will be found done in the morning. They continue to carry off mortal women to interbreed with well into the High Middle Ages; it's never really been ascertained whether they have females of their own, and if so whether they're as plug-ugly as their menfolk.

Trolls are a purely Scandinavian race, though they have migrated as far as Shetland (where they are called Trows) thanks to Viking seamanship. Strictly speaking, they are not a Faery race at all, having no actual Enchanted habitat. Unlike the other magical races, trolls are of superhuman stature (though they too diminish over time) and definitely evil. Huge and ugly, they're strong in combat and magic alike, and can possess pagans of low piety in just the same way as Judeo-Christian devils; conversion is the only safeguard. With the advent of Christianity, many went over to the Satanic hosts, but some remained independent, solitary agents of mischief. All trolls turn to stone in daylight. The females are called Troll Wives, but in point of fact trolls rarely go about in company and don't form couples.

Undead

In *Fantasy Wargaming* the souls of the departed can only wander around on Earth, whether discorporate or in their mortal remains, if they're Conjured by a necromancer (or, of course, by themselves); see the section on Conjuration, page 193. Certain kinds of soul cannot be Conjured under any circumstances, while all will have a resistance to Conjuration according to their method of interment and their post-mortal status. If the necromancer fails to secure the spirit's full obedience, or if the Command to obey wears off, the spirit may continue to lead an autonomous Conjured existence in or out of its mortal remains, exercising magical powers in its own interests. Any soul may animate its own mortal body (or what's left of it) as though it were alive, even if the muscles, brain, central nervous system, and other physical agents of motion are decomposed or removed, without expenditure of mana. This applies even when all that's left is a bone or two, or when the remains are separated into more than one part (in which case the different bits are all animated and moved independently). If a spirit is inhabiting its mortal relics, it will normally want to keep them safe from interference; leaving them in the tomb is the normal way, so that many Undead (particularly Barrow-Wights) tend to use their tombs as a base. Medieval *Vampyres* are not undead, but a species of east European magical monster that can take a variety of human or animal shapes, *not* including bats—they hadn't discovered vampire bats yet, and the association with bats belongs to a much later stage of the legend. See the rules for further description.

Chapter IV

Mortal Combat

(or "A poignard in your codpiece")

Weapons

This section deals with the history of various families of weapons from about 600 AD to 1500 AD in the Christian calendar, and in most fantasy universes will parallel the period from the decline and fall of the "old empire" to the rise of the new. The weapon that most men have felt easiest with throughout much of history is the sword, a weapon which gradually evolved from a heavy, clumsy, sharpened club to a precision instrument of death when wielded by a master of the art.

The first swords of this period were used mainly for sweeping or hacking blows designed to cut, the balance of the weapon being well forward of the hilt with most of the weight in the third of the blade nearest the well-rounded "point." The main reasons for this were the method of fighting and the inability of early armorers to forge a weapon which could both hold a point and remain light enough to make an accurate thrust possible. Blades were usually 60–80 cm in length with a simple cross hilt and a heavy pommel. They were nearly always double-edged and single-handed. A smaller group of swords used in this period had a heavier but shorter blade and were predominantly single-edged. They could be likened to a long machete and must have been very effective at close quarters; the name given to them was the *seax*.

As methods of manufacture improved the length of sword blades increased to 70–90 cm and they became dual-purpose weapons used for stabbing as well as cutting. Blades became noticeably thinner, although the cruciform hilt and large pommel remained; these improvements date from around 1000 AD. The next phase was designed to counteract improvements in the

Weapons of war

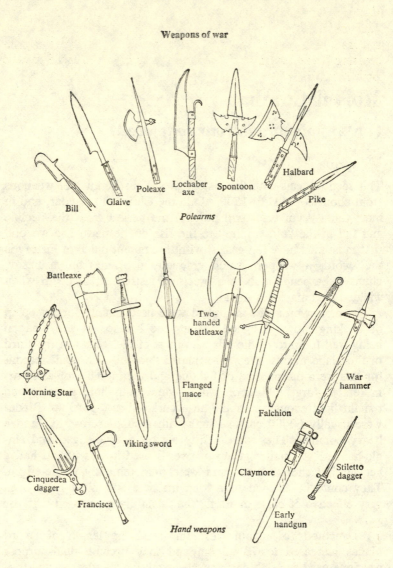

Bill
Glaive
Poleaxe
Lochaber axe
Spontoon
Halbard
Pike

Polearms

Battleaxe
Morning Star
Cinquedea dagger
Francisca
Viking sword
Flanged mace
Two-handed battleaxe
Falchion
War hammer
Claymore
Early handgun
Stiletto dagger

Hand weapons

strength of plate armor, and involved two developments: the *falchion,* which increased the power of the blow by being heavier; and the one-and-a-half handed ("bastard") or double-handed swords which created more power at the point of impact by increasing blade length and allowing the user to put more muscle power into the blow.

As more and more plate was added, the *estoc,* or thrusting sword, was introduced. This concentrated the power of the blow in the point, which was supposed to penetrate between the joints of plate armor and gaps in the links of mail. These developments, which take us to about 1390 AD, then remained virtually unaltered until the end of our period (when the earliest forms of rapier appear), although sword hilts began to acquire finger guards and curved quillions.

The next family of weapons to consider is the axe, both single- and double-handed, which remained essentially unchanged throughout the whole of our period. (The one exception is the *fransisca,* which was used early in the period; this was a short, well-balanced throwing axe which would normally be hurled underhand prior to close combat.)

Pole weapons can basically be split into two groups; those based on the spear, and the rest. The earliest spears would have been about 2–2½ metres in length, increasing to around 3–4 metres in the case of the lance carried by a mounted soldier or knight and to some 5½ metres in the case of the pike. These thrusting weapons, among which should also be included the heavy boar spear and the spontoon, were designed for use by troops in close formation and were essentially equally effective against both infantry and cavalry. Length and weight gradually increased throughout our period, the cavalry lance ending up as a hollow wooden weapon some four metres long which widened to the grip, itself protected by a circular guard, and the infantry pike as the formidable weapon most people are familiar with through the battle re-enactments of the English Civil War Society and the Sealed Knot. Because these weapons were designed for use by troops *en masse* and in close order, when they were extremely effective, they became less deadly when formations were broken up by rough ground or missile fire. This was where other pole weapons came into their own. Being designed for slashing (in addition to thrusting in some cases), such weapons as the bill, battle axe, halberd and Lochaber axe were much more flexible and effective in the hands of troops operating in looser formation. Pitchforks, scythes and other agricultural implements can also be counted as pole weapons but would have been relatively ineffectual in the hands of their untrained peasant levies.

The most basic form of missile weapon was the sling, either the simple sort comprising a leather thong which was whirled around the head then one end released to send a lead ball or, *in extremis,* a pebble, hurtling towards the enemy; or the staff sling which imparted greater velocity and thus either additional range or armor-piercing power.

Bows fall into three groups: the short self or composite bow, the Welsh longbow, and the crossbow; the latter is usually thought of as being a medieval weapon but had, in fact, been in use since Macedonian times. The longbow, used exclusively by English and Welsh archers as a military weapon from the early part of the 13th century, is generally recognized as being more powerful than the short bow, having longer range and greater armor-piercing ability, but its effective use demanded longer training than either the short or crossbow. Until the introduction of effective firearms, the crossbow was the infantryman's weapon *par excellence* throughout most of Europe, possessing greater range than the bow and impressive armor-piercing ability. Needless to say, despite a succession of Papal edicts against its use, the crossbow was an extremely popular weapon, despite taking longer to reload than the bow.

The earliest handguns began to appear in the later part of our period. They were very crude and extremely unreliable, the chance of a misfire being high and even that of the barrel exploding in the user's face not uncommon. However, they required very little training to use and would have had an effect on the morale of any enemy troops unaccustomed to such weapons.

Other weapons available throughout this period include such things as mauls (heavy hammers), maces, morning stars and clubs, all of which could inflict heavy blows but obviously needed a fair bit of strength and agility to use. Daggers of various sorts and sword breakers used as a left-handed weapon were also available. A successful parry with a sword breaker in the combat rules shifts the breakage table two columns to the right.

Armor

From the beginning of our period armor was being constantly improved until it reached the heavy and often elaborate full plate armor at the end of the period. Two factors influenced changes in armor design: improved weapons, necessitating better defense; and improved workmanship, which made it possible.

From 600 to 1100 AD, basic armor remained virtually unchanged, although it became more common as the years rolled by. From being something that only nobles could afford to purchase, it increasingly became worn by ordinary soldiery of all types. The basic armor was a *hauberk* of mail, scale or ring mail, initially covering only the torso and upper arms but eventually being extended to cover the thighs and lower arms. A simple helmet, usually of conical shape, with or without a nasal guard and possibly ear flaps and an *aventail* of leather or mail, was worn with the hauberk. Viking and Byzantine troops may well have had lower leg and forearm protection consisting of splints of horn or iron linked with leather to form greaves.

Worn under the hauberk was a heavy cloth or leather garment which eventually became known as an *aqueton*. This not only protected the wearer from chafing but also helped absorb the energy of a blow and reduce the chances of heavy bruising or fractures. This type of garment would have been the only "armor" worn by light troops.

Almost all troop types would carry a shield. Originally this was circular, made of wood with a metal boss (which in turn was sometimes spiked so that the shield itself could be used as an effective weapon). Later, shields became increasingly kite-shaped as horsemen discovered the need to protect the left leg; the kite shield was, however, also used by foot soldiers.

Following the early Crusades (1096–1195 AD) the conical helmet gained a flattened top and a *surcoat* was worn over the mail. The original intention of the surcoat was to help keep the armor, and its wearer, cool, but it is equally likely that it was often worn for appearance only, and by the end of our period had become flamboyantly decorated in heraldic symbology.

The later Crusades (1201–1254 AD) saw the introduction of the barrel-shaped great helm and plate armor, initially over the knees with, perhaps, a plate under the mail covering the chest. For lighter troops padded armor, made of cloth tightly stuffed with cotton, was introduced. This was remarkably effective and could, perhaps, be equated with inferior ring mail. The mail itself was extended to include protection of the legs and hands, and a mail *coif* could be worn over the head.

By the turn of the 14th century plate began to be used to protect the lower legs and forearms and the shield decreased in size. The *brigantine* and *jack* began to be worn by richer infantrymen, while the flat-topped great helm became pointed to provide a glancing surface. During the century a plate *cuirass,* either splint armor or single piece, appeared and, by 1400 AD, the majority of knights would have some plate equipment.

The introduction and widespread use of the longbow and heavy crossbow necessitated an increase in armor protection and extra pieces of plate armor were added until, by 1475, complete suits of plate were common. A fine example of this can be seen in Dürer's engraving of "The Knight, Death and the Devil," printed in 1513, a good portrayal of the Gothic knight. The introduction of full plate led to the disuse of the shield, except in jousts.

Organization of a medieval army

The army would have consisted of the king or his appointed commander, knights called to the army by their liege lords, men at arms, mercenaries and often militia units from the surrounding countryside. It would be organized in a number of "battles" (three being the usual quantity), each comprising a mixture of all arms. Knights, nobles and men at arms would be in the center, screened to front and flanks by more mobile missile-armed troops. The ill-trained levies would normally be left to guard the camp and could not usually be trusted in battle.

The main problem with a feudal army was its short-lived nature since troops could normally only be called upon to give service for a comparatively brief period. This eventually brought about an extension of *scutage* (literally, shield money), whereby one could elect to pay cash rather than fight. The funds raised could then be used to employ mercenaries instead.

On the field, the battles could be aligned in line, column or echelon, or with one flank refused (i.e., drawn back to cover a

weaker flank). The English usually fought dismounted with perhaps a small mounted reserve. This was due mainly to the
efficiency of longbowmen drawn up *en herse* as shown in the accompanying diagram. Where possible, English armies would
adopt a defensive position, with woods or other natural obstacles
to protect their flanks. Continental armies usually assumed an
offensive posture, attacking with their battles in column. When
they did try to fight on foot to prevent their knights' horses being
decimated by arrows, it simply meant they had to suffer the
archers' fire for longer.

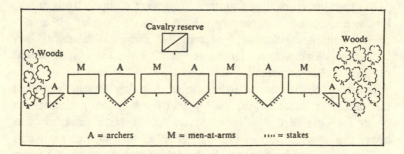

Tradition imparts to the knight an impetuosity in attack which
is probably exaggerated. With good officers, knights could be held
back until the right time for a crucial charge. Under bad officers,
however, the charge would be made the moment the enemy was
sighted, no thought being given to fighting a tactical battle.

Castle development

The development of the castle was a continuous process throughout the period, alterations occurring according to changes in fashion, improvements in siege warfare, and foreign influence. The
earliest castles, defined as a defended base for one lord and his
family, were of the motte and bailey type. These consisted of a
steep hill, which could be natural, artificially augmented or entirely artificial, surmounted by a wooden stockade and the lord's
hall. At one side, forming a figure of eight with the motte, was the
bailey, or outer pallisade, which formed the peacetime living
space required for stables, storehouses and accommodation for
servants and men at arms. All this was surrounded by a ditch and

bank topped by a wooden pallisade. At this stage, all the buildings would normally have also been of wood. Even in later years, this form of castle would be used in the Marches as it could be constructed quickly and used to cover the building of more permanent fortifications.

By the beginning of the 12th century stone had increasingly begun to replace wood. The first alteration would usually be to the motte, where the wooden stockade would be replaced by a rectangular keep or a circular shell keep. The bailey walls would follow and occasionally a stone gatehouse would also be built.

Because the corners of a square keep were comparatively weak, by the end of the 12th century the keep was becoming either circular or multi-angular. If a rectangular keep had already been built it would not normally be replaced, but new castles would reflect the changing trend.

During the 13th century the use of flanking towers increased the defensive value of the bailey walls by enabling archers to cover the base of the walls in safety. At the same time, wooden hoardings over the top of the wall enabled arrows, hot sand and boiling oil to be dropped on the besiegers working at the bottom of the wall. These hoardings were later replaced by stone structures which gave even greater protection.

The final development of the medieval castle was the concentric type, whereby the main castle was encircled by a lower wall which had to be breached before the castle proper could be attacked.

A variety of siege weapons had been developed throughout history to deal with castles and other fortifications, and their use continued throughout this period. The main types were the pick or ram, used to bring down castle walls by attacking their bases; the trebuchet and the mangonel, which were mainly used to attack the tops of walls and towers by throwing heavy stones on a high trajectory (or plague-ridden bodies into the castle—an early form of germ warfare); siege catapults and crossbows which threw lighter anti-personnel weapons from a greater distance than the castle defenders' hand-held weapons; belfrey towers for close assault of the castle walls; and primitive siege guns which fired large stone balls.

Conduct of sieges

The besieged

As the enemy approached the inhabitants would gather into the castle all the cattle, sheep and other mobile food supplies partly for their own use and partly to deny them to the enemy. Supplies of forage would also be gathered into the castle. Trees growing near the castle walls would be cut down to give a clear field of fire for the archers. Small parties would harry the scouts of the approaching enemy so that the castle's strength would not be known until the last possible moment.

Once the besiegers arrive before the castle, raids of varying size should be made to destroy the siege works and engines and to demoralize the attackers. If relief is unlikely it is usual to agree a date when the castle will be surrendered, the garrison marching out with the honors of war and allowed to return to their own forces. If relief is coming then the castle would be held to the last possible moment even if this means forcing non-combatants outside the castle walls. If this course of action is taken then the results of any assault are on the conscience of the garrison commander.

The besiegers

On the approach to the castle every effort should be made to stop the garrison gathering in the supplies from the surrounding countryside and a cordon should be thrown around the castle to stop reinforcements reaching the garrison. When the main army arrives siege works should be built around the castle to guard the army's camp. If the garrison appears weak an attempt should be made to storm the walls using scaling ladders and, if gunpowder is available, a petard on the gateway. If this fails await the siege train with its engines. When the engines arrive concentrate on the enemy's engines on the walls and try to breach part of the curtain wall. If this succeeds and the moat is a dry one attempt to storm the castle. If the moat is wet it must be filled with fascines (bundles of brushwood) and then a storm attempted. If the walls should prove too strong the only option is to starve the defenders out which regretfully takes the longest.

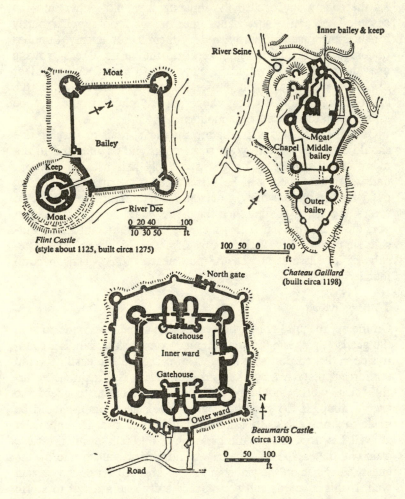

Three types of castle

Moat

Bailey

Keep

Moat

River Dee

0 20 40   100
10 30 50   ft

Flint Castle
(style about 1125, built circa 1275)

River Seine

Inner bailey & keep

Chapel   Moat   Middle bailey

Outer bailey

100 50 0   100
ft

Chateau Gaillard
(built circa 1198)

North gate

Gatehouse

Inner ward

Gatehouse

Outer ward

N

Beaumaris Castle
(circa 1300)

0 50 100
ft

Road

Glossary of arms and armor

Aqueton. Padded garment worn under all types of armor.

Arbalest. Heavy crossbow.

Armet. Closed helmet with bevor and movable visor.

Aventail. Leather or mail neck armor attached to helmet.

Banded mail. Ring mail linked by passing leather straps through links.

Barding. Horse armor.

Bardische Axe. A pole axe where one point of the axe is extended down the shaft.

Bascinet. Helmet shaped like a sugarloaf, with or without visor.

Bastard sword. Two-handed or one-and-a-half-handed sword.

Bevor. Armor fixed to the plate armor covering the chest, protecting the neck and chin, and connected so that it could turn.

Bill. Late English infantry pole arm.

Bracer. Leather wrist guard used by archers.

Brassard. Plate armor covering the arm.

Brigantine. Light armor constructed of small steel plates riveted to cloth.

Chamfron. Armor covering to front of the horse's head.

Chapel-de-fer. Kettle-hat, a broad-brimmed helmet used by infantry—a little like a British World War I helmet. So much for progress!

Chausses. Mail coverings for the lower legs and feet.

Cinquedea. Short broad-bladed Italian dagger.

Claymore. Scottish two-handed sword.

Coif. Mail hood, rather like a Balaclava helmet.

Coute. Plate armor for the elbow.

Crinet. Armor for the horse's neck.

Cuirass. Plate or leather armor for the trunk.

Cuir-boulli. Leather armor molded by boiling, for man and horse.

Cuisse. Thigh armor, usually plate.

Destrier. A warhorse.

Estoc. A thrusting sword.

Falchion. Single-edged infantry sword.

Fauchard. A form of glaive.

Flamberge. Two-handed sword with wavy blade.

Gambeson. Quilted tunic, similar to an aqueton.

Gisarme. A form of glaive.

Glaive. Pole arm, similar to a bill.

Gorget. Throat and neck protection, usually plate.

Greaves. Shin defense.

Gusset. Small pieces of mail filling gaps in plate armor, e.g., under arms, behind knees, etc.

Halberd. Pole arm consisting usually of axe, spear and hammer.

Hauberk. Mail shirt.

Jack. Leather tunic reinforced with plates of metal or horn.

Jupon. Short surcoat.

Kettle helm. Open helmet—see Chapel-de-fer.

Lames. Riveted steel strips similar to Roman armor.

Lochaber axe. Scottish pole arm.

Main gauche. Left-handed dagger.

Maul. Heavy hammer or mace.

Morning Star. Flail with one heavy spiked ball on end of a chain.

Partisan. Short pole arm usually carried by officers.

Pauldron. Shoulder armor, usually plate.

Pavise. Large free-standing shield used by bowmen.

Pike. Very long infantry spear.

Plastron. Upper part of cuirass when made in two pieces.

Poignard. Narrow-bladed thrusting dagger.

Pole-axe. Horseman's axe with spear point and often a hammer or beak.

Poleynes. Knee armor.

Quarrel. Crossbow bolt.

Quillions. Cross hilt of sword.

Ranseur. A type of partisan.

Ring mail. Rings sewn individually on to leather.

Rondelle. Plate protecting armpit.

Salet. Helm with wide brim at back, with or without visor.

Scale armor. Armor made of small pieces of overlapping horn or metal.

Seax. Long slashing knife.

Solleret. Plate protection for the feet, jointed.

Splint armor. Overlapping narrow plates.

Surcoat. Light garment worn over armor.

Sword breaker. Heavy dagger used to catch and break an opponent's sword.

Taces. Plates at bottom of cuirass.
Tassets. Plates to protect thighs.
Vambrace. Plate armor covering forearm.
Visor. Movable part of helmet, protecting eyes and nose.

Chapter V

Moorcock and More . . .

(or "Whatever takes your fantasy")

Since the theme of this book, as explained in the Revelation, has been to firmly root fantasy gaming in our cultural past, the following remarks are necessarily brief. Nevertheless, a chapter on the modern fantasy novel is necessary, not only because many games designers base their scenarios on worlds extracted from these books (see also Chapter Six), but also because an awareness of what has been written can give a new player a heightened awareness of what might be going on in an adventure, and even allow him to recognize or anticipate particular devices or ploys which the game designer may have built in to his filthy plot.

I would be willing to lay heavy odds that virtually a hundred per cent of the readers of this book have read Tolkien and would think of *The Lord of the Rings* first if asked for the title of a modern fantasy novel. So, I shan't say anything about the contents of the book itself except that it is probably the closest thing in modern literature to a concept of another world which is really rooted in the above-mentioned cultural past, and the closest in terms of depth of treatment to the type of fantasy scenario which I hope this book will inspire you to create for yourself.

In terms of making a setting for a fantasy adventure game, however, it has to be admitted that *Lord of the Rings* is BORING because Tolkien has done all the work for us and the only way to produce surprises in a game is by going outside his framework and introducing alien influences. It would not have been so bad if his posthumously published *Silmarilion* had not filled virtually every gap, but as things are, Middle Earth is almost as well documented as the historical Dark Ages and does not allow your imagination rein to roam. Besides, who the hell wants to play the role of a hobbit?

Please don't imagine that I am decrying Tolkien. I first read *Lord of the Rings* in 1960, long before the book had become a fashionable cult, and I still have my school library's volumes at home (they may even have forgiven me by now!). I have re-read it so many times that I can mentally read it almost word for word without having the printed text in front of me. It is, without doubt, a *tour de force* and among the outstanding novels of the 20th century. But it isn't fertile ground for a fantasy gaming adventure.

Of course, the preceding comments are subjective, and if I encountered a Balrog in a game I'd try to do a fast bunk. But I do feel that there is much more to be garnered from other fantasy novels which have not, and may never, acquire such status; at least in terms of designing fantasy adventures.

Talking of garnering, another early acquaintance was Alan Garner. Like *The Hobbit,* his early books were written for children, although they have a depth and roundness which should make them equally compelling for the fantasy gamer. Of particular interest to us here are two titles which involve the same characters and setting, the *Weirdstone of Brisingamen* and the *Moon of Gomrath.* Despite the fact that the two central characters are children, the plot and the standard of writing are both worthy of adult attention. Set in Cheshire, they revolve around one of the sites which has been postulated as the resting place for Arthur and his knights, from whence they will emerge again when England is in danger. After various struggles, good inevitably triumphs over evil, but one of the best characteristics of these books is that neither white nor black are wholly either, the characters are fairly well rounded, and the old, wild or pagan magic is never far from the surface. Garner's other novels, such as *Elidor,* the *Owl Service* or *Red Shift* in particular, are also well worth reading, pitched at a progressively more adult audience (although still billed as "juveniles"), and providing much food for thought.

As with Tolkien, it was inevitable that Arthur would enter any discussion of the modern fantasy novel at an early stage, because of all our cultural myths, his must surely be the most prevalent, most reworked and assuredly most fascinating. The modern

novels which treat of Arthur and Merlin are legion, from *Raven**
at the bottom end of the literary scale (being based on a TV children's series) to T. H. White and Mary Stewart at the top.
White's books, *The Sword in the Stone* and *The Once and Future
King,* are rather "Alice in Wonderland"-ish, particularly the former which, again, was mainly written for children. It is rather like
reading *The Hobbit* before *Lord of the Rings;* if you can perse-
vere through the former, the latter repays careful reading—so
don't be put off.

Mary Stewart is entirely a different kettle of fish. Her superb
trilogy, comprising *The Crystal Cave, The Hollow Hills* and *Last
Enchantment,* follow the life of Merlin from young boy to old
man. They are firmly based in what one might call the "historical" Arthurian world rather than that of Geoffrey, Wace, Laya-
mon, Malory *et al,* and one of the most attractive points about
them from a fantasy gaming point of view is the very subtle treatment of magic, which is right in line with how it ought to happen
if you follow the guidelines in this book. There is a carefully and
sympathetically constructed interplay and low-key conflict between
the forces of Mithras, the mystery cult god of Roman soldiery to
whom Merlin gets introduced at an early age, and the old Norse
gods of the invaders plus, of course, the burgeoning figure of
Christ. This trilogy is not only absorbing reading but provides a
ready-made backdrop for virtually any adventure you care to
design, being sufficiently "elastic" to give you the freedom which
Tolkien denies.

Even more than Arthur himself, Merlin (who is not always
given the same name) seems to exercise a fascination on modern
fantasy writers, and many other books, such as H. Warner
Munn's *Merlin's Godson* and *Merlin's Ring,* are well worth reading.

With the exception of *Raven,* all the books so far mentioned
are ones which I first read or own in hardback, but it is to the paperback that most people will turn, and here the scope is so vast
that all I can do is give some pointers towards personal favorites. Top of the list must come Fritz Leiber's "Swords and Sor-

---

* Not to be confused with Richard Kirk's excellent series of novels about
the beautiful warrior woman of the same name, the "swordsmistress of
chaos" and *FW*'s answer to Modesty Blaise!

cery" series concerning the adventures of the brawling northerner
Fahfrd and his inseparable companion, the wizard's apprentice,
the Grey Mouser. With this pair we enter the realms of pure fantasy, the alternate world of Newhon, with its grotesque city of
Lankhmar, its Thieves' Guild and its sorcerers. Leiber's books are
entertainment, not "literature," as I am sure he would be the first
to admit. Try *Swords and Deviltry* to get the feel of the series,
and if you like it, go on to *Swords Against Death,* a collection of
short stories which introduces some diabolical ideas for your adventures, such as the living skull of a long-dead sorcerer, a tower
which is "alive," its brain being made of diamonds (which our
heroes try to steal!), or the golem in the "bizarre bazaar." Another favortie is *Swords of Lankhmar,* in which intelligent rats try
to take over the world, the Grey Mouser dons an unusual disguise
and the Old Gods suffer a nasty setback! Leiber's other books in
this series were, for a long time, only available in hardback and,
although I understand they are now appearing in paperback, they
are—to my mind—rather disappointing, particularly *Swords and
Ice Magic* which, unusually, I never even managed to finish.

Still in the realms of "pure" fantasy, but on a much more serious and more carefully constructed level, are Andre Norton's
"Witch World" titles. These concern a man of our own Earth
who escapes from this world into an alternate universe where
magic, as used by the witches of Escarp and others, does work.
Unlike Leiber's sorcerers, however, Norton's have to work at
their magic, and its use not only involves careful preparation but
also physical and psychical energy loss which can, *in extremis,*
put the magic user in dire peril. The basis of the "Witch World"
series is an Earth which is essentially feudal and on which a
diminished population is struggling back to a civilized level after
a devastating war long ago which has left "pools" of evil littered
around the landscape as traps for the unwary or weak. There are
many strange races, such as the Were "Riders," each of whom
can assume a different animal shape, the peoples of the woods
and of the waters, plus Mages of different persuasions and even
some unpleasant characters who belong more in science fiction
than fantasy who have created a "gate" from their own universe
into "Witch World." The individual books in this series include
*Witch World, Web of the Witch World, Spell of the Witch World,
Sorceress of the Witch World, Warlock of the Witch World* and,

among others, *Year of the Unicorn* which, although outside the main sequence of the others, is perhaps my favorite. Several short stories have also appeared in various publications.

For some reason I cannot explain, I always mentally link the "Witch World" books with Anne McCaffrey's "Dragonflight" series about the planet Pern. Although these involve dragons, they are not really so much fantasy as SciFi. Admittedly, the dragons are real firebreathing creatures with enormous appetites, but they would never hurt a human being since they are an artificially evolved race designed to work with man. They also have other qualities, including the ability to fly "between" in space and time, an almost instantaneous transition to wherever they wish to be, and telepathic communication with their riders. But Pern is a delightfully "real" world in which to set an adventure, with its various Craft Guilds, rival barons and unexplored tracts in which anything could—and often does!—happen. The main sequence of books is *Dragonflight, Dragonquest* and *White Dragon*, with subsidiary plot and characters complementing these through *Dragonsong, Dragonsinger* and *Dragondrums*.

Another favorite series of mine which lines in the grey area between science fiction and fantasy is Marion Zimmer Bradley's "Darkover" novels. As with Pern, Darkover is a planet settled some time in the misty past by the survivors of a crashed starship who evolve their own culture and legends and who, at the time most of the stories are set in, have achieved a culture which appears feudal, being run by the heirs of the Seven Domains, but which in fact is far more sophisticated. Psionic ability ("laran") rests with the red-headed men and women of the Domains and closely resembles magic. It is also "magic" in the same way that Andre Norton's is, in that it exerts terrible demands on the user and requires long preparation. However, one "failing" of the Darkover books which must be pointed out is that, although each possesses internal similarities, there is no real consistency of historical or even geographical detail, so they cannot be read truly as a sequence. This creates many anomalies and can be frustrating for anyone trying to design an adventure set on Darkover, as only very basic elements such as the Trade Town, the Hellers (a mountain range), the red sun and the bitter cold remain consistent from book to book. Titles in this series begin with *Darkover Landfall* but the others do not fit any particular sequence: *Bloody Sun, Door Through Space, Forbidden Tower, Heritage of Hastur, Planet Savers, Shattered Chain, Spell Sword, Star of Danger, Sword of Aldones, Wind of Darkover* and *World Wreckers*. In at least one instance, the planet, although identical to Darkover, is not even called Darkover but Wolf! Nevertheless, they make most enjoyable reading. Also set on another planet, and involving both space travel, magic and derring-do, are Arthur Landis' pseudo-Arthurian fantasies, *A World Called Camelot* and *Camelot in Orbit*. Pug-Boos do *not* feature in *FW!*

If one contemporary writer of fantasy fiction can be said to have influenced fantasy wargaming or "dungeons and dragons" more than any other, however, the "Oscar" must assuredly go to Michael Moorcock, former editor of *New Worlds* and author of over 50 novels, both science fiction and fantasy. Probably the best, although certainly among least-known of these is *Gloriana,* a modern *Faerie Queene* set in an Albion which rules not just most of America but most of Asia too. The rich, flowery language, endless intrigue and the background of spies, assassins and seducers are truly Elizabethan in flavor.

Better known to most Moorcock addicts, however, are the series concerning Corum, last scion of an ancient race able to move at will on the Ethereal plane, and his battles both on Earth and in the astral with the three ruling gods of Chaos; the superb Elric of Melnibone series, and the tales of Hawkmoon.

Moorcock's imagination is fertile and far-reaching, although morbid and often—usually—pessimistic, giving little credence to free will. It comes as no surprise when you eventually read *The Eternal Champion* to find that Elric, Corum, Hawkmoon and other central characters from his novels are all in fact one and the same, a hero fated never to die but to reappear in endless incarnations fighting what appears to be the evil of the time, and often destroying those whom he best loves through ignorance of the true state of affairs in any given incarnation.

Nevertheless, for the fantasy wargamer seeking new ideas outside those already outlined in this book, the rigid caste system of GranBretan, in which everybody wears an intricately wrought animal mask which is never taken off in public; or the beloved Camargue of Count Brass with its horses and flamingoes; make really worthwhile reading. Although, as discussed earlier, Moorcock's universe, with its constant battle between "law" and "chaos," does not truly fit in with the ideas we have tried to put forward in this book, it is undeniable that most existing fantasy rules and commercial games lean on them heavily; and since you are presumably going to venture into other people's adventures and "dungeons," a knowledge of Moorcock can serve you well in giving you an inkling of what might be going on.

Progressing in no particular sequence, a gem of a one-off fantasy novel is Clifford D. Simak's *Goblin Reservation,* set in a not too far distant future in which scientific research into the occult has resulted in physical contact actually being made with the "elder" beings—goblins, trolls, banshees and the like. The story also involves a mysterious artifact; a timid ghost, a Neanderthal Man and a saber-toothed tiger. It is basically a jolly romp, although with serious undertones, but if your tastes run to creating a fantasy adventure set in a more or less "modern" world it will certainly give you some ideas.

In this context another modern writer worthy of mention is Dennis Wheatley, whose stories of Satanism and Voodoo in the 20th century provide many ideas for contemporary fantasy scenarios. Wheatley writes in a rather ponderous, slightly old-fashioned style which can prove irksome, and most of his books are fairly long when compared with the average fantasy novel. However, psychic battles on the astral plane, reincarnation, witches' covens and Black Sabbats, "elementals" and other nasties from The Pit all make interesting reading. When I first came across *The Devil Rides Out* at the age of about 13 my mother wouldn't let me read it, so I had to sneak a flashlight under the bedclothes—then had nightmares for a week so I suppose she was right! Other Wheatley titles in this vein include *Strange Conflict, To the Devil a Daughter, The Satanist, The Haunting of Toby Jugg* and *The Ka of Gifford Hilary,* but *The Devil Rides Out* is undoubtedly my own favorite.

Most modern fantasy novels, however, root their stories either in the dim and legendary past, in a far future after a nuclear holocaust, or on an alternate Earth running on a parallel time track. An example of the first of these is Lin Carter's Thongor of Lemuria series, Lemuria being the name for a lost continent (like Atlantis) somewhere in what is now the Indian Ocean. These books are traditional fantasy of the Edgar Rice Burroughs genre with the usual bejewelled semi-naked princesses, brawling warriors, airships supported by a mysterious gravity-defying metal, jungles full of hostile tribesmen, good and evil sorcerers and the dying remnants of the inimical lizard men (intelligent dinosaurs). The central character is the swashbuckling barbarian warrior Thongor and the books trace his inevitable career from wandering mercenary to powerful warlord and ultimate ruler after a final confrontation with the lizard men.

In much the same vein are Robert E. Howard's 14* books about Conan the Cimmerian and John Jakes' Brak the Barbarian tales. The three heroes, Brak, Conan and Thongor, are almost interchangeable, being typical semi-naked, brawny northern swordsmen who run foul of the various powers that be in their respective universes. Of the three series, the Conan books are, in my opinion, the best-written and most interesting, although all should really be classed as "pulp" fiction.

A more recent author is John Norman, whose fantasy adventures are set on Gor, the mythical counter-earth which is in the same orbit as this planet but on the other side of the sun, so it is never visible. His central hero is in some respects a rather pathetic character, Tarl Cabot, who gets mysteriously transported to Gor by the Priest Kings where he becomes a tarnsman—a warrior trained to fight from the back of the giant birds which give him his name. From simple "thud and blunder" writing in the first two or three books of the series, they become more deeply psychological, and the central character eventually evolves into a most unsympathetic "hero." My favorite in the whole series is *Nomads of Gor,* one of the early titles, which sees Cabot living on the steppes with a wild nomadic race obviously based on the ancient Mongol warriors of Genghis Khan. Unfortunately, John Norman suffers from a deeply rooted bondage fetish which he obviously expects his readers to share, for all of these books are full of nubile slave girls who are forced to call all men "master," who are kept permanently chained and whose erotic instincts are usually aroused by a touch of a whip. I'm no great advocate of women's lib but these books are sufficiently strong in places to be more than mildly offensive, and you'll have to form your own

---

* In addition to which, Lin Carter, L. Sprague de Camp and Fletcher Pratt have compiled several others from Howard's unfinished writings.

judgement of them. For heaven's sake don't let a "liberated" wife or girlfriend read them, though, or you'll never hear the last of it!

Another strange author whose central character, although totally unsympathetic because so totally selfish, has begun to acquire "cult" status, is Stephen Donaldson. His first trilogy (*Illearth War, Lord Foul's Bane* and *Power That Preserves*) concerns the adventures of a modern-day leper (yes, leprosy still survives) who periodically manages to knock himself on the head and, while unconscious, becomes transported to a land of "faerie" where, despite his thoroughly unpleasant character, the locals hold him in high respect and expect great things from him. Despite the fact that Thomas Covenant "The Unbeliever" thoroughly screws things up most of the time and only muddles through as a result, presumably, of the same sort of divine intervention which sends him into "faerieland" in the first place, hurting people who befriend him right, left and center, he must have some redeeming characteristic since I could not put these books down. I'm blowed if I can find it, though! I don't *like* Donaldson's books, but have to admit they are compulsive. Maybe Covenant will improve in the second series, which I have not yet read. Other books which fit into this category of ones I have read but don't particularly like so can't recommend include Patricia McKillip's *Riddlemaster of Hed* trilogy, which concerns a world in which the old magic is falling apart because it lacks the one man who can talk to the winds, the waves and the earth; and Tanith Lee's *Storm Lord, Birthgrave* and *Shadow Fire* trilogy.

Perhaps I am old-fashioned, but I dislike dithering heroes or heroines who don't understand what is going on around them and who muddle selfishly through with no respect for the feelings of others. If this is a new trend in fantasy fiction, give me Conan any day!

Much more to my liking is yet another triology, written this time by one of my favorite science-fiction authors, Ursula Leguin. Although apparently written (and certainly sold) as juvenile fiction, her "Earthsea" books treat magic in the right way for anyone who is intending to use *this* book as a basis for fantasy adventuring, the plots are good and the relationship between the higher powers, or gods, and man, is excellently depicted in all its uncertainties.

One could go on almost endlessly drawing names out of the hat

containing titles of books one has read but—and please feel free
to disagree—I don't really think it worthwhile in the context of
fantasy wargaming discussing the works of Bram Stoker, Conan
Doyle, Edgar Rice Burroughs or even such classics as E. R.
Edison's *Worm Ouroborous,* which I found *very* heavy going. But
I suppose, if we have included Simak we ought to mention L.
Sprague de Camp's hilarious *Incompleat Enchanter* trilogy which
concerns the midadventures of a mad professor who has found a
way to travel into alternate worlds, the best of which is that of
Spenser's *Faerie Queene.* This is also a favorite device of several
straightforward science-fiction authors—the idea that the characters of fiction, through repeated re-reading by countless millions
of devotees, can achieve genuine substance in some alternate universe. But no one has yet surpassed Robert Heinlein who, in *The
Number of the Beast,* transports his heroes through a succession
of fictional worlds, including the land of Oz, Carroll's Wonderland, "Doc" Smith's Lensman universe and, the ultimate in
self-congratulation, finally into that of *Time Enough For Love*
where Heinlein addicts like myself can revel in getting re-
acquainted with Lazarus Long & Co.

Which is perhaps a good time to end because the purpose of
this chapter really has been to point the way not only to some
good, or at least enjoyable, reading, but also to suggest that the
worlds of fiction created by modern writers can be as rewarding
in their own way as scenarios for your own adventures as can the
"real" mythological worlds of our historical past.

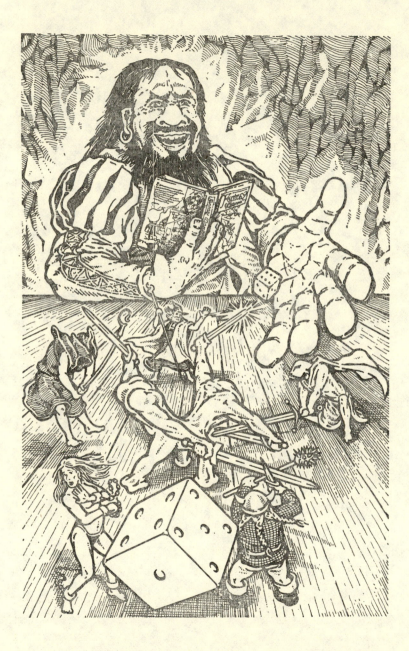

Chapter VI

The Compleat Enchanter

(*or "What in Hell do I do now?"*)

Let me start off by saying that, of course, all Gaming Masters are "compleat," in that they are presumably doing the job to their own satisfaction. If this was not the case, they would not be enjoying the game and so would not be playing. However, a job reference stating that you had performed your duties in your previous job, entirely to your own satisfaction, would be likely to see you signing on at your local Labor Exchange for a long campaign. The judge of a Gaming Master must be the players. If he does not provide them with an enjoyable, efficient, fair game, then as a GM, he is very "incompleat."

The purpose of this section is to set out advice for new GMs who need guidance in the art; for GMs of slightly more experience who wish to improve themselves; and for GMs of considerable experience to examine, by way of interest, if only to prove to themselves that they are already perfect. (At this point there will be slight pause while the author adjusts his halo, amid cries of "conceited twit.") Picking up his pen once again, and wiping off the worst of the rotten eggs, he continues.

I realize that the above sounds highly pretentious and, of course, the lowly advice I offer can be completely ignored, taken as gospel or any stage in between. However, no one is beyond finding the odd little piece of useful advice, and I offer my own humble ramblings as a suggested procedure whereby a GM can give his players a fast-flowing, interesting game, free of the arguments, shufflings through loose pieces of paper, incessant rattlings of large numbers of dice of all shapes and sizes, searching through books of rules, counting squares on the map and other common distractions that follow a simple statement of action from a player.

So, jumping in with both feet, let us look at what I consider to be the major problem with all role playing games: the ambivalent position of the GM.

Suggest to any football or cricket team captain that a crucial match should be refereed by the captain of the opposing team and there would be screams of protest and riots from the supporters. Yet participants in role playing games happily submit to a situation where, not only is the referee the opposition captain, but play on a field sown with proximity mines and with a ball given to exploding on a random basis. In other words the GM has it all rigged in his favor.

"Great," I can hear you yelling, "I'll be Gaming Master." And you can play it like that. A massive kill session in which you liquidate 95 per cent of the party on the first level and leave the players with a distinct feeling that they need not have bothered. After a few games you will find it harder and harder to get players to venture into your adventures. Alternatively, players will appear with wonderfully high level characters they "just happen to have." Either way, the game suffers and both GM and players rapidly lose interest, to the great detriment of the hobby.

There is, therefore, a need for a very fine balance on the part of the Gaming Master, and he must make considerable effort to achieve this balance if the game is to be enjoyable for both parties. To see how this balance is to be obtained I would first like to consider the major areas in which the problem manifests itself.

Firstly, there is the construction of the adventure itself. The temptation of the designer is always to come up with newer, more vicious traps and greater, more powerful monsters, in a setting that becomes more and more inimical to the survival of the adventurers. It is very easy to overstep the bounds of what the party can fairly be expected to have a chance of coping with.

Secondly, as the Gaming Master is describing the rooms, passages or other encounter areas, he has the opportunity to unfairly disguise or hinder the party in discovering traps, treasure clues or other hidden aspects. He is, in effect, the players' eyes and to a certain extent their intelligence as well, insofar as he has to tell them what they notice. Too often in playing a character have I heard the phrase "Unfortunately, you didn't notice . . ." In some games it has seemed as if the party were blind, stumbling about with the aid of white sticks, while the GM made gleeful sounds as they set off yet another trap.

The next area of ambivalence is that non-player characters are played by the GM, giving yet another situation where reality would indicate that this character would follow a certain course of action, impart certain information, or give the party the benefit of his special knowledge; but where, because the party has not asked, the Gaming Master has not passed on the information. It is far too easy for such an encountered person to be merely an extension of the Gaming Master, rather than a personality in his own right, who thinks and acts for himself. To see some of these non-player characters picked up during an adventure, one would think they had had a prefrontal lobotomy, neither speaking nor acting unless directly addressed. In fact, anyone joining a party would be prone to talk to his new companions, finding out about the quest, discovering what they knew, giving out what he considered to be relevant information. In other words, being generally helpful to the communal effort. A very difficult situation for the Gaming Master to play fairly.

The final area of conflict is the matter of saving throws and percentage chances of events occurring. On many occasions during a game a character will instigate an action, or claim a chance of some event happening, which had not been planned or forseen by the Gaming Master. He has to set a percentage chance of this action being successful. A saving throw is claimed by a player and again the GM has to decide at what level the throw shall be made and what modifiers, if any, to apply to the throw. This is possibly the most crucial area where a GM can find himself in conflict with his duty to the players. Saving throws are, almost by definition, matters of life and death to a character, or at least a matter of major damage. A poorly calculated saving throw may cause the death of an important member of the party, who may be vital to the overcoming of some problem later on. Or, it may so weaken the party that they are no longer up to the level of difficulty of the adventure. Again, some unforseen action may be equally vital to the party and the Gaming Master has to set a percentage chance for the success of the action. Situations like these give the Gaming Master the dangerous opportunity to unfairly affect the balance of the game.

I know many of you will say that this is the name of the game. The party has to take its chances and suffer the effects of its actions. If they aren't prepared to die, they shouldn't be down there. I agree that this is perfectly correct, where the chances are clearly set out in the rule book and the player should know what his likely chances of success are for a given action. What I am concerned with is the situation that is not covered, that has to be decided by the Gaming Master on the spot. There is far too often the temptation for him to rig the odds in his favor (I hesitate to say cheat; that implies a breaking of existing rules, while this is constructing the rules to benefit himself).

In all these areas the GM is trying desperately to ride two horses in two different directions at once. To continue the metaphor, if he can grasp both sets of reins and with a foot firmly in each saddle, steer them both on the same course, then he is close to becoming the "compleat" Gaming Master.

To strike this perfect balance is not easy and many will feel it is not worth the effort, especially if you feel that your own style of play is satisfactory. However, regular players will soon get the idea that they have little chance with this kind of Gaming Master and will become reluctant to play. You will find it increasingly difficult to get players to agree to your mastering an adventure. While seeming enthusiastic for the hobby, they will always have something on when you offer an adventure. You may even suspect that there is something that even your best friend won't tell you! Also, you are in effect cheating yourself if you don't try to obtain this balance. It is nice to win, but what is the point, where is the achievement if it is all rigged in your favor? It is much greater fun and far more stimulating if you can nail an experienced player through your skill, without any unfair manipulation.

Having set out this problem of ambivalence in the role of Gaming Master, I should like to wave my magic wand and dispel all these problems "at a stroke." Unfortunately, as we do not live in the world of magicians, or in the minds of politicians, this is much harder to do. There are no perfect solutions. What I would like to do is give you some ideas which will help, but cannot solve every problem. In the long run it is going to depend on yourselves. A real attempt by a Gaming Master to combat the temptations of his ambivalent position is "best cure for all our ills." You have got to recognize a situation which is becoming unbalanced; a point where piling more and more on to a party is getting beyond the normal level of fair competition, passes through the range of overkill into the nasty realm of megadeath. Regrettably, this depends to a certain extent on experience. The few suggestions I can make will, at least, take the edge off the major problems.

In the following sections I intend to set out, first of all, detailed instructions on how to go about designing an adventure; and secondly, suggestions on how to master a game. Within these sections will also be contained a procedure which I hope goes some way to maintaining balanced games.

Designing a "dungeon" or adventure

This will take the form of a set of ideas and steps to help on the practical side of designing an adventure, and in passing go some of the way to meeting the problems of balance.

The basic idea. Surprisingly for games that are claimed to have infinite possibilities, the design of "dungeons" seems to take on a strange sameness: a deserted or ruined building, a secret entrance, a number of levels inhabited by monsters and containing traps, treasures and magic in various forms. Some of these complexes are so large that it must have taken a gang of navvies with JCBs a couple of centuries to excavate them. The traps and monsters become boringly repetitive after a while; the fantastic becomes commonplace. Once that happens the Gaming Master can easily be tempted down the path of overkill and megadeath again. A Gaming Master should be looking for more original scenarios to hold his players and maintain their interest, rather than always increasing the level of difficulty.

Obviously the next question is, "where can I find such ideas?" Springing first to mind is fantasy fiction, as outlined in the previous chapter. The number of fantasy novels now available is staggering and reading a few is an excellent way to get new ideas for scenarios, either one-off or campaigns. I have, since reading Fritz Leiber's *Swords Against Wizardry,* harbored a desire to make a scenario based on Quarmall, the fantastic underground city, with its weird customs and weirder magic-using inhabitants, its mushroom beds, mushroom wine inducing fantastic visions and the pervading sound of slaves' feet, forever turning vast fans to

ventilate the lower levels. Another idea I have been considering
for a long time is a version of the city in the Conan story *Red
Nails* by R. E. Howard. In this story two warring tribes inhabit
different parts of an ancient, deserted city. An ideal game for two
opposing groups of players, but requiring considerable preparation on the part of the Gaming Master.

Other sources of ideas can be surprising. The real, mundane
world has many ideas, if looked at in the correct way. An ornate
stone hut in the grounds of a local Grammar School gave me the
idea of the tomb of a Saint in a monastery, which is being used as
the meeting place of a witches' coven. One of my cities is based
on the street plan of my own town. The Salvation Army hall is
the chapter house of a sect of fighting monks and the Labor Exchange is the house of a local slave trader.

Legends and myths, either local or general, can be useful
sources, either for full scenarios or for embellishing your campaign. Another very successful scenario came to me from hearing
a radio program on archeology; a study of an Egyptian tomb.
This became a truly tortuous testing ground for thieves and
clerics. Looked at the right way, most things can give you an idea
for a scenario.

Next, I feel it is most important to have your scenario set firmly
in a world and society. Role playing games cannot take place in a
vacuum if you wish to enjoy their full potential, as this whole
book has taken pains to explain. Your adventurers must live
somewhere, they must have somewhere to spend the money and
treasure they accumulate. Their characters must have been
formed by the mores and dictates of a society, the gods of the
clerics must have worshippers.

I can hear the groans and protests already. No, I don't want
you to design a new world for each adventure. What I feel is far
better is to set all your adventures in one world, which develops
and fleshes out as you expand your situations. Some of you will
feel that even this is an imposition and for you I offer a suggestion for a quick and simple method of setting your adventure in a
ready made world. *Fantasy Wargaming* does just this—offering
you the world of the Dark and Middle Ages. Alternatively, take
one of the worlds of the fantasy novels and use that as a setting
for your dungeon or adventure. This has the major advantage that
you can ask your players to read the book first, so they all have

the same detailed background in which to base their characters. Of course, you will have to take care not to include too many aspects of the plot of the novel in your scenario, or you will find that your players have too much information. There is also the possibility of an actual character from a book appearing occasionally, as a non-player character. I strongly advise against allowing players to take a character from a book, as they are invariably very high level and would destroy all balance.

Now you have an idea and a world to set it in, you must decide various things about the adventure you start planning. Firstly, do you intend it to be for a particular level of character? Your approach has got to be very different for low level characters, compared to that for higher level ones. Decide now what level it is designed for. Secondly, is it for a particular type of character, a testing ground for their particular abilities; a general adventure for a wide range of characters; or a limited range where certain types are going to be under some kind of hardship? Next consider the length of your scenario. Is it going to be something to last for an afternoon or an evening, in which case two or three small levels are required; or a larger game over a number of sessions, in which case you are more or less unrestricted. In assessing the length of time an adventure will last, two factors must be remembered. The less experienced the players, the longer, in general, they will take to make decisions and solve puzzles. Also, generally speaking, the more players in a party, the longer they will take over a scenario. The number of characters does have some bearing, but not as much as the number of players, most of whom will want to get his or her oar in when decisions are taken. Of course, if you are designing an adventure for a group with whom you play regularly, you will be able to assess quite accurately how much you will get through in a session of play.

The next stage is to rough out in note form the general scenario of your adventure, including its legends and history. Once you have "compleated" your adventure you will be able to decide how much you are going to allow your players to know of its history in advance. Keeping in mind the scenario and level of characters you are designing for, prepare a list of various monsters, of all levels. Similarly, prepare lists of treasure, magic items (if any), inhabiting characters and traps.

Once you have prepared these lists, you can start roughing out the map of your dungeon, city or landscape. Decide where you are going to put which monsters, treasures, magical items, etc., and make a few notes for each location. Remember, when placing monsters that, however fantastic they are, most of them are living creatures, with such creatures' needs for food, air and water. A living monster, shut in a room on its own, fairly quickly becomes a dead monster, through starvation, thirst and lack of air. There must either be fairly easy access to the surface from all levels, or a steady supply of food underground. You would only get a self-sustaining ecology in a fairly large complex. Such sources of food underground are rivers and lakes with fish, large-scale fungal growths and much smaller vermin like rats, mice and insects. (Adventurers are not going to be frequent enough to provide a steady food supply.) In many respects, it is far easier to allow easy access to the surface. Adventures in the culture of *Fantasy Wargaming* are, indeed, more likely to take place *on* the surface, in towns and wildernesses.

Similarly, the structure of your scenario must have a purpose. If you are designing a "traditional" dungeon, did it develop as living quarters for a large tribe of monsters? What is the purpose of all the chambers in a tomb? Secret doors and passages are there for some reason, not just for the hell of it. How did the treasure and magic items get where they are? Who normally leaves valuable items lying about in various rooms? They are usually locked safely away together in some strongroom, guarded by locks, puzzle combinations and back-up traps. Anything lying around, and there won't usually be much, has probably been dropped by previous parties from their own personal possessions.

Mechanical traps have a greater likelihood of malfunctioning the older they are. In the damp atmosphere underground (and it almost certainly will be) wood and cloth will rot in about a hundred years. Unprotected metal will begin to corrode fairly quickly and serious damage can be expected after 15 to 20 years, unless protected by oil or grease. Even oil or grease will dry up, given a few hundred years. Also, clean pieces of metal, pressed together, tend, over a long period, to fuse together. All these are reasons why traps may malfunction. Complex, mechanical traps must be given a moderately high chance of misfiring, or be replaced in some way quite frequently. Traps depending on disturbed balance are the longest lasting. Partially balanced floors or ceilings, collapsing door lintels, roof falls due to rotting timber supports and rotten floors and stairs are all long-lasting traps with good chances of success. Shooting traps with crossbows or spears will probably be rotted away after two hundred years. Spring needles and spikes will probably have seized up after a century. All this should be borne in mind when deciding what traps to use and where to place them.

Also, when placing traps, it is a good idea to have a clear concept of, and to describe, the mechanism by which it works. Thus, when a player describes his action to you and then complains when he sets off a trap, possibly despite precautions on his part, you will be able to explain to him why he is dead. Also, the more detail you put into your scenario, the more it comes to life.

Once everything is positioned and decided, make a fair, detailed copy of the map and description. I strongly recommend that colored felt pens or markers be used to mark out areas in rooms and positions of items. Highlighting pens are also useful to mark out areas of effect of traps and magic. Secret doors should be clearly marked in a different color as I find otherwise they are very easily overlooked. Remember, walls have thickness, more than just a pencil line width. Again, broad black felt lines help in achieving this and in making the plan more visible. I also find it a great help to note down by each wall and passage its length. This saves the frantic counting of squares, which sends me cross-eyed! This is really the burden of this section—do all you possibly can to make your plan easily readable, you'll be spending a good deal of time looking at it. Choose a scale of squared paper that is not going to make your life hell. For most dungeons 5 mm squared A4, each square representing five feet, should be adequate.

When it comes to writing the description of each room and passage, if anyhow possible, type it out. It really does make life so much easier when playing the game, and if your handwriting is anything like mine, it's probably going to save you one or two serious mistakes and a lot of eye strain.

Now we come on to one of the solutions I mentioned earlier to the question of ambivalence. If you give a very detailed description of each room, you can quite fairly give all the necessary clues and information a party requires, while disguising them in a your adventure and giving it a feeling of realism. I also strongly superfluity of room detail. This also has the effect of fleshing out advise that you adhere to the following sequence of writing your description and reading it to your players.

Room dimensions should be given to the party, as far as they can see from the position they are in and with the light they have available.

The general appearance of the room should then be described, followed by the fine detail.

The furniture or other contents of the room should then be outlined, in as much detail as can be seen from the party's position.

As the party moves into the room, any areas which come into sight should be described, e.g., the area behind the door, alcoves or irregular sections of the room or portions previously masked by objects in the room. At this stage, any finer detail, omitted earlier, should be added.

If the room is occupied, the occupant should be described in the second of the above stages. I say described, because I feel it is unrealistic that all adventurers be assumed to recognize a rare creature, which is semi-mythical. The more common type of non-human creature can be named, but players will have to rely on their skill and knowledge in recognizing the rest. If the party wish to converse, or do not immediately attack, proceed with the rest of the description sequence. If they or the occupants attack, then the combat should be resolved before the finer detail is given. The rationale is that, while you would see a general impression of a room, you would not notice the finer detail while concentrating on fighting.

While writing the description of the occupants of a room, I find it saves much thumbing through the rule books to put down a brief description of the monster, along with its statistics and any other information likely to be needed to play the beast. This may seem tedious while writing your scenario, but it keeps play flowing much faster and I feel is therefore worth the effort.

Next, go through the adventure and decide which of the occupants is likely to leave its location. These are going to form the basis of the "wandering" creatures in your dungeon. You may, of course, add others, of no fixed abode, to your list. You must also decide which, if any, will be capable of wandering between levels and so can appear on more than one encounter table. It is worth writing out the creatures' statistics again on the "wanders" list, so you don't have to search for the room from which they come. Likewise, for non-player characters that the party are likely to encounter, prepare character sheets, which, if necessary, can be handed over to the players.

All this is to avoid the situation where a Gaming Master tells you that you have met someone interesting, and then spends the next ten minutes rolling dice to obtain his interesting character!

Penultimately, prepare any lists of rumors or legends which players may know or discover before they enter the scenario. These may be the common tales found in the folk lore of the area or locality, specific rumors or scraps of information which individuals may be able to pass on to the party; physical clues or documents. Of course, there will always be a fair chance of false information, or information so vague or wrongly stressed so as to be misleading.

Also at this stage, if there are any maps to be found in your scenario, or documents, draw them out. Use plain paper rather than lined and try as much as possible to reproduce the document in the condition in which it would be found by the party. The use of a quill pen would be perfect, but a felt tip can give a reasonable facsimile. Adopt a style of syntax and writing suitable to the person supposed to have written it. A merchant will write differently to a monk, who will have a different style to a nobleman. If possible, age your document (cold tea works wonders). It's not necessary, but it looks good. My personal favorite was half a map which was found in a fireplace, well and truly charred. This was found to be all wrong—which presumably is why it was burned.

Finally, assemble your sheets in order in a presentation folder or similar binder. Again, this is not vital, but keeps things tidy and orderly and looks much more impressive when you meet your players. I like to put a title page, with a suitable style of lettering and, if possible, embellish it with a sketch of something found in the adventure.

How to master a game

Before play commences, there are a number of things you must do, especially if you are using one of the commercially prepared scenarios. The most obvious is to read it through first, so you know everything that's in it and are thoroughly familiar with all the levels. It seems amazing, but I have seen someone try to master a game he has just bought, without looking beyond the introductory section. To say the least, it was a slow, disjointed game. If you are not fully conversant with the rooms, contents, traps, secret doors, etc., there is a very strong likelihood of missing out some vital aspect, or completely unbalancing the game in some way or another. If the scenario uses an aspect of the rules you are not familiar with or are unsure of, read it up and make sure you know how to play it. It is most disheartening for players to watch while a Gaming Master dithers about in uncertainty over the rules. If nothing else, it destroys your credibility as a Master and reinforces the players' tendency to argue.

When actually setting up the game, try to have everything set out before the players arrive. If you are using the printed floor pieces, try to have them cut ready to the size of the rooms and passages you expect to be using; have something on hand to fasten them down. You may reasonably gibe at the expense of these playing aids, and I offer you two alternatives.

What I have found to be much more flexible is a sheet of posterboard, an off-cut is usually available quite cheaply, covered with inch-squared paper. Over this stick a layer of clear plastic. (A useful tip here, is to make a pin prick to let out the air from the bubbles that invariably form.) This can now be drawn on with grease pencils, or the felt markers for use with overhead projectors. You, or the players, can mark out each room as they come to it and then wipe it off when you've finished. I have four of these boards which, when placed together, correspond exactly to the number of 5 mm squares on an A4 sheet, which I use for all my plans. The result is that a whole level can be drawn out as the party explores.

An alternative a friend of mine uses requires less preparation. He has a 24-inch-square sheet of expanded polystyrene, marked with one-inch squares. By using pins and black thread, any shaped room can be delineated. The only disadvantage of this system is that you have to take it apart for the next room.

If you are using figures, rather than simple markers, as I assume most of you are, use ones that are at least of a reasonably accurate size. We all at some stage have to use a figure of a different type of monster, to represent one which we don't have. If this is not the correct size, inaccuracies can easily creep in. Likewise, insist that your players move their figures exactly as they wish their characters to move. Too frequently I have seen a clump of figures left in the middle of the table, unmoved, while the party has gone through various actions. When it has become necessary to know where the characters are, at the commencement of a fight, players miraculously find that their characters are in the most advantageous of positions. Figures must be moved each time an action dictates, even if it is only changing the direction it is facing. Similarly, all movement must be carefully monitored and a close eye kept on encumbrance. You should check the load of each character at the beginning of the game, take a note and add to it any time he picks up treasure, weapons, armor or other weighty matter.

At the beginning of the game you should state to your players clearly any conventions you play with, or amendments or alterations to the rules you wish to operate during the game. This makes it clear for the players and will help to reduce any arguments or disagreements that might possibly arise if you spring what they regard as an unfair interpretation of the rules.

Now we come on to the first area of ambivalence discussed earlier. If you follow the sequence in which you noted down the room contents, putting plenty of detail into your description, you will find it easy to camouflage any item you wish to. A ploy by players which you should not allow, is to say as a general order, that they are feeling for secret entrances, checking for traps, tapping for hollow walls or similar actions and assume they are doing it all the time. Unless a player states specifically, at a particular time, that he is carrying out that sort of action, you have every right to assume he is proceeding with only normal vigilance. He will notice anything glaringly obvious, but subtler things will escape him. You will find that, just as in even the most dangerous situation a person's attention will wander and concentration relax, so players will frequently fail to make this detailed search specifically, and so you legitimately and fairly fail to tell them of the crack that betrays the secret entrance, or the hollowness of a trap beneath their feet. This also conveys the advantage of benefitting the careful, thoughtful player, while penalizing the "thud and blunder" merchants.

Next, we come on to the problem of non-player characters. There are two choices here, either to play the character yourself for the rest of the game, or to allow one of the players to take it over. As far as realism is concerned, it would be best if you played the character yourself and so gave him a separate personality. However, you are up to your ears in running the game and giving your players a fair, balanced adventure. Running an extra character is going to be too much. Also, you would find it difficult to play him fairly. The danger in giving him to the party is that you are likely to be giving them too much information, if your character is one who has a good knowledge of the area.

On average, though, I feel it is best to allow one of the party to play the character, and for this reason I include in the design steps the preparation of sheets for such characters. What you can do is omit any information you don't want the players to have from the sheet. Thus a high level magic user can pose as a simple first or second level magician, until such time as he chooses to reveal himself. If he is benign to the party, then he can help them and the player can continue to run him. If he is inimical, then you will have to take over and run him as a normal "wandering monster." However, if you do adopt this technique, you must keep an eye on the player, to see that he does not have the character do anything that is grossly against his personality. If he does, you will quietly have to override him, or find some reason to tell the player why he shouldn't do it.

A similar technique can be used when players encounter something which takes over or substitutes for one of their characters. As an example, in one dungeon I ran, a character released the trapped spirit of a high level female magic user, who took over his body and mind and changed his sex. I told the player that he had suffered a sex change and had picked up a few memories from the body he had disturbed because there was a fragmentary telepathic ability preserved with the body. The player continued to run the character, while I occasionally dropped hints as to "vague recollections" of this or that. The effect was of the magic user surreptitiously steering the party in the direction she desired, till at last they reached their goal and she revealed herself in her true colors, at which point I took over playing her. I escaped with all the loot, but I did leave the party with another treasure map with which to console themselves.

Now we come to the vexed question of saving throws. Many Gaming Masters are very sparing in allowing characters a chance to save, especially from traps. I feel that in most cases, where a player requests it, a saving throw should be allowed. Very few things happen so instantaneously that there is absolutely no chance of any reaction of any kind. The mechanical contrivances of the societies which we represent in our scenarios, for the most part, are not the slick mechanisms to which we are accustomed today. Fine measurements and tolerances were extremely difficult prior to instruments like the micrometer, assuming that tools existed to work to such a fine level. Moving joints were crude and bearings virtually non-existent. Spring steel was very unreliable and imperfect. (For example, in the 16th and 17th centuries, wheel lock pistols could not be left wound up for any length of time, overnight even, or they would not function.) Lubrication was also very difficult. All these are reasons why traps or mechanisms will not work instantaneously, and thus there is an opportunity for a character to make a desperate lunge for safety.

How, then, do you assess such a chance? A simple roll under your agility is one method, but rather crude. I prefer to set a percentage chance, and have the player roll under it with percentage dice. This leaves us with the problem of setting the percentage. Here you have got to be really honest with yourself and your players. Assess whether there is a substantial or a negligible chance of saving, or somewhere in between. If substantial, allow a chance of 35–40 per cent, if negligible, a chance of 10–15 per cent and 25–30 if in between. Modify this by 5 per cent for above or below average agility, with an additional 2 per cent for exceptional scores. Also modify by 5 per cent if the character's level is higher or lower than the level of difficulty of the dungeon. The final result is the percentage saving throw.

This may sound a tedious process, but once you are familiar with the process, it is fairly quick. It can also be adapted for saving throws for other situations by substituting other characteristics as the modifier, though you must be careful not to allow a modifier for experience where this would not be applicable. One further comment; this is intended only for situations where saving throws are not covered in the rules; where the situation *is* covered the rules should be used. My system is really only a rule of thumb for guidance.

Finally, if you do feel that there is no chance whatsoever of a saving throw, then obviously don't give one. However, you should, in fairness, have your reasons ready to give the players, either there and then or, if your reason would involve the disclosure of too much information, at the end of the game.

When it comes to dice rolling, I know some Gaming Masters like to do it all themselves, even the combat rolls of players; some go so far as to keep these rolls secret, merely informing players they have scored some damage. This is going too far. Players are going to feel they have lost control of their own destiny. Possibly they have, but they should not feel so. Wherever possible, players should be allowed to roll their own dice, as this keeps them closely involved in the process of the game. The only exceptions are where searches or detections are concerned, where, if a player is not successful, he should not be able to tell whether he is unsuccessful or there really is nothing there. For that reason I make such rolls in secret and merely say something like "you find nothing."

A vital aspect of mastering an adventure is keeping your players under control. Keep a close eye on all their actions and make sure they tell you each action in advance. Take nothing as understood, and insist that there are none but the most simple and basic standing orders. An example is hand-carried objects. As a player I have been guilty of carrying a lantern and a drawn sword and when combat ensues, I have gaily claimed benefit of shield without having a hand free to hold it. What is more, the Gaming Master has allowed it and not taken into account the hazards of a lighted lantern in combat. I presume he assumed I put it down, unslung my shield, and commenced fighting; but I was not penalized the seven or eight seconds it would have taken me to do it. I must admit, I have been equally guilty, as a Gaming Master, of such errors. It is something we all do but should try hard not to.

Another thing you should be fairly tight over is cooperation between characters run by the same player. Where they can be claimed to be friends or associates a reasonable amount of cooperation can be allowed. However, such things as large-scale loans, to help equip characters at the beginning of the adventure, should be eyed with suspicion and a realistic rate of interest enforced. Likewise, characters of radically different alignment who act hand in glove with each other, should be penalized with a possible change in alignment. No one is perfectly altruistic and while the good of the party can be used to justify a fair amount, there are times when characters in trouble should be abandoned to their fate.

As Gaming Master, you should also add as much color to your adventure as possible. Do all you can to make your game come to life and be out of the ordinary. I have one adventure which starts off with the characters hearing a minstrel in a tavern, singing of a legendary ancient emperor. This sends them in search of his tomb. I have a recording of the musical setting of a poem by Rudyard Kipling, which was the original inspiration for the scenario, and I play this to the players as a starting point. You could even try writing and singing your own song for such a situation.

Tape recorders can also provide sound effects, for specific situations or for general background. In one game the party were discussing their next action and I was waiting and idly blowing down an empty beer bottle (well, I get a very dry throat, you know), making a moaning sound. The players heard it and got quite worried over it, thinking it a new monster about to burst on the scene. After that, at irregular intervals I produced the noise again, justifying it as draught through small holes. It did not really affect the players' actions or the outcome of the game, but it did add further color and interest as they scrambled into a protective circle. Of course, if you don't occasionally have the noise linked to something nasty, your players will get blasé.

When introducing encountered persons, don't give what they say in the third person, always do it in the first. You are the person speaking to the characters, so try to put what you are saying in the form in which they would say it. Remember that their perception of events and the adventure are going to be entirely their own. They may not know what a monster is, but just describe it as something big and hairy. They could quite easily underestimate or overestimate the strength of something they have encountered and misrepresent it to the party. Also, they will have their own pattern of speech and tone of voice and accent. While not vital, it contributes considerably to the dungeon color to act these as closely as possible. On one occasion, my players met a wandering old man who was very wandery and doddery. He spoke in a high, quavery voice and his dialogue consisted for the large part of the phrase "many years, many years, oh so many years," sprinkled with a few other connecting phrases. The party spent quite a while in growing frustration, which became hysterical laughter as a Norse warrior, one Bang Olafson, went berserk and, spurred on by frustration, tried to kill him. The old man proved remarkably agile.

While stressing as I have the necessity for planning and realism, I do not wish to proscribe the *ad hoc* occurrence which presents itself and is too good to miss. A good laugh occasionally, or frequently even, is very definitely an important aspect of role-play games. If a situation arises, which you can use for a bit of fun, without too much spoiling the direction of the game, go ahead, "make 'em laugh, make 'em laugh." I had a party once who managed to talk their way past a guardian Djinn. I knew a player was going to have to break off soon and leave the game, and so when he said "shalom" to the Djinn, as he passed, my thoughts went like this. "Djinns are Arabic; Shalom is a Jewish greeting." The rest of the party stood obsequiously back, waving PLO flags, while I smeared him all over the dungeon wall. I am also very fond of bad puns (I have restrained myself with great difficulty while writing this) and some of the names of my characters and occupants of my dungeons are quite excruciating.

There will always be a time when a player will disagree with you and accuse you of unfairness. That is why you should strive for balance and fairness in your adventures, have your reasons ready and be prepared to give them to back your decision. Again, stating your conventions to the players at the beginning of the game gives that much more strength to your arguments. A dungeon where as much as possible is done as realistically as possible is always easier to justify, and gives rise to fewer arguments anyway. When it comes down to it, the Gaming Master has always to be right, just as the referee in a sports match has to be right, even if he is proved wrong later; but you will find it easier to make your players accept this if it is always clear to them that you always attempt to be as scrupulously fair as possible. A player should always be able to say to you, to paraphrase the poet Gerard Manley Hopkins: "Thou art indeed just, Gaming Master, when I contend with Thee."

Chapter VII

Playing Rules

Constructing a fantasy character

Characters in *Fantasy Wargaming* are defined by a series of characteristics. Some of these are physical attributes, some mental, while others briefly define the personality—virtues and vices—of the individual. In most cases, these characteristics are produced by throwing three six-sided dice. These are the characteristics outlined in the chart on the following page. Those wishing to give their characters authentic medieval attributes may then wish to modify these variable characteristics to take account of astrological influences. They should do this before turning to the rest of the chart. The meaning of the different attributes, and the means of calculating non-diced characteristics are set out thereafter. Finally, all characters should throw against the "Bogey Table"—a list of special factors giving individual quirks to the adventurer, and in some cases arbitrarily altering a characteristic (ignore "follow-on" effects).

Astrological alterations to characteristics (optional)

ASTROLOGICAL ALTERATIONS

Dice	Star sign	Physique	Agility	Endurance	Charisma	Greed	Selfishness	Lust	Bravery	Intelligence	Faith	Social class
1	Aquarius	-1			+1	+1					+2	
2	Pisces	-2		-2			+1	-2	-1		+3	-1
3	Aries	+1	-1			+1			+2			+1
4	Taurus	+2		+1	-1		-1			-2	-1	
5	Gemini		-2	-1	-1			+2		+1		
6	Cancer			-2		+1	+2			+3		+1
7	Leo	+1		+1	+2		+1		+1		-2	+1
8	Virgo		+1		-1	+1		+2		+1		
9	Libra	-1	+1	+1				-1	-2	+2		+1
10	Scorpio				-2		+1		+1	-2	+1	
11	Sagittarius	+1	+2		+1			+1				+1
12	Capricorn	+1		-1	-1	-1		-1	+1	-1		

Compare your character's star sign against the table and alter his characteristics accordingly. No characteristic may, however, increase beyond 18 or be lowered beyond 3.

SAMPLE CHARACTER SHEET

Name: Sex: Nationality:

Physical attributes

Height: Weight:

Physique: Agility:

Endurance:

Mental attributes/magical and religious factors

Intelligence: Faith: Star Sign:*

Literacy: Languages:

Mana: Piety:

Personality factors

Charisma: Social Class: Bravery:

Greed: Selfishness: Lust:

Leadership: Special attributes:

Social background

Father's social position: Age:

Family rank: Occupation:

Social position:

Material possessions

Equipment: Money:

Skills

Riding: Tracking:

Swimming: Stealing:

Climbing: Singing:

Experience

Combat/adventuring level: Religious level: Magic level:

* Throw one 12-sided dice against the Astrological Table on previous page.

Aspecting

Astrological lore includes the influence on character of good and poor aspecting in the stars. To simulate this with your character, throw two six-sided dice and subtract seven. The resultant plus /minus number is the total of points by which you may alter the set of characteristics. No characteristic may be altered by more than two points, or one point for factors of 14 and above, and the same upper and lower limits (3 and 18) apply. Greed, selfishness and lust, being vices, must be raised rather than lowered by a minus factor.

Example: a Pisces character looks at his raw characteristics, and amends them by the star chart. This leaves him as an impossible warrior, but a fair Mage or Cleric. His selfishness, however, is high, dangerously so for a Christian priest. He throws two six-dice, and gets 10—a plus factor of 3. He decides to add 2 to his faith, bringing that to 15, and to better his character by reducing selfishness 1 point, to 13.

Explanation of characteristics

Name, sex, nationality. These are entirely open to the player's choice. The player should, however, choose a name suitable to the character's nationality, and a nationality covered by the geographical scope of *Fantasy Wargaming*. Players wishing to play a female character must unfortunately take the penalties of a patriarchal society. Make the following adjustments to diced characteristics: physique and endurance —3, charisma —2, social class —3, bravery —2, greed/selfishness/lust —3. They will be excluded from combat, from all parts of the Church save the nunnery, and expected in most cases to adopt a domestic position as wife, housekeeper and servant. These factors are invariable.

Physical attributes

Height. 4'7" + 1" per physique point. Invariable.

Weight. 50 lb + 10 lb per endurance point. Invariable.

Physique. This defines your ability to carry weights, lift objects, administer blows, etc. It is a prime characteristic for warriors. Variable by level.

Agility. This defines how easily and gracefully you move, wield objects or weapons, dodge, etc. It is a prime characteristic for warriors and a secondary characteristic for Mages. Variable by level.

Endurance. This defines your ability to survive hardship, disease, or other physical damage (e.g., through combat). It is a prime characteristic for warriors, a secondary characteristic for clerics and Mages. Endurance points are lost during adventures, but return during rest towards this maximum. Variable by level.

Mental attributes/magical and religious factors

Intelligence. This is your capacity to comprehend situations, analyze a problem, learn new facts or otherwise exercise the force of reason. It is of general importance in all aspects of adventuring. It is a prime characteristic of Mages, a secondary characteristic of clerics and warriors. Variable.

Faith. This is your intuitive understanding of the Ethereal plane, and the hidden workings of the universe. It is a prime characteristic for clerics and Mages. Variable by level.

Star sign. This is the astrological influence under which your character was born. It has considerable effect on characteristics (see above), and on the exercise of magic. Invariable.

Literacy. This defines how well your character can read or write. Add intelligence and social class points over 12 (subtract points below 8) and multiply by 10. Add 10 per cent if the character is a Mage or cleric, subtract 10 per cent if a warrior. Throw percentage dice. If they are below the percentage figure, your character is literate, can read and write any language he knows. Variable; once intelligence and social class have both altered upwards, test again.

Languages. Halve the percentage required for literacy. This is your chance of knowing any of the human languages you will encounter in an adventure. Invariable.

Mana. The emanation of the Ethereal plane, and the source of magical power on Earth. Mana has to be accumulated, and is limited by magic level.

Piety. This defines your relationship with the Higher powers you serve—God, the Devil, the Norse deities, etc. It is of particular importance to clerics, but can also affect drastically the lives (and afterlives) of other characters. Piety varies from hour to hour, being gained and lost by certain actions approved of by your powers.

Personality factors

Charisma. This characteristic defines your popularity, plausibility, persuasiveness, charm, physical attractiveness and, above all, self-confidence. It is of considerable importance in determining the ease of your relations with others. It is a secondary characteristic for Mages, clerics and warriors. Variable with level.

Social class. The most important characteristic of all, in hierarchical medieval society. Social class affects your wealth, standing, leadership, etc. In the short term, it defines what kind of social position and occupation your character will hold at the start of his adventuring career. Social class increases at certain set points in that career (see "Experience"), and can be purchased—at great cost!

Bravery, greed, selfishness and lust. These four factors define the personality of your character. The higher the factor, the more pronounced the tendency. *Bravery* (includes anger) is a prime characteristic for warriors, a secondary characteristic for clerics and Mages. *Greed, selfishness* and *lust* are prime characteristics for clerics—the lower the factor the better! Variable (up or down!) with level.

Leadership. This defines your capacity to command men and obtain obedience and respect from others, especially to the adventuring party. Apply the calculation:

$$\frac{(3 \times \text{charisma}) + \text{physique} + \text{intelligence} + \text{bravery} + (4 \times \text{social class})}{10}$$

Then add half (rounded up) your character's highest experience level.

Special attributes. These reflect the "bogey table." (See following pages.)

Social background

The normal age of a new character is 16—unless he is a character artificially promoted to a higher experience level than 0 (see below). The social background of the character—his father's social position, his own rank within the family, his present social position and occupation—must be constructed and chosen by the player, after comparing his social class with the options available. Work of this kind is invaluable in "fleshing out" a new character.

Social class is increased by one point at the following level breaks: combat experience levels: 2, 5, 8, 11; religious experience levels: 3, 5, 7, 9, 11; magic experience levels: 4, 8, 11. Social class is subject to a maximum of 22 and minimum of 0.

"Bogey table"

Despite its name, the "Bogey table" has as many good as bad factors within it. The factor uniting them is their unpredictability, inability to quantify and effect on the behavior of the character. Throw a six-sided dice. 1-2: throw once with percentage dice against the table. 3-4: throw twice. 5-6: throw three times. Note the results (if any) down in the "special attributes" section of your personality factors. Note: 01-34 indicates no result.

BOGEY TABLE

%	Roll Factor	Notes	%	Roll Factor	Notes
35	Homosexuality	Attraction only to own sex.	36	Bisexuality	Attraction to both sexes.
			38	Beauty	+ 1 charisma.
37	Homophobia	Violent fear of homosexuals.	40	Sexual charm	You are sexually irresistible.
39	Sexual fetish	Leather, transvestitism, etc: your choice.	42	Amiability	Never takes offense. +1 charisma.
41	Ugliness	–1 charisma: repellent to others.	44	Extroversion	+ 1 charisma.
			46	Presence of mind	Does not fail morale or control tests. + 1 leadership.
43	Impotence	Cannot consummate in sex.	48	Oratory	+˙1 leadership. Could talk hind legs off a centaur.
45	Poor sight	–1 agility: cannot read.
47	Deafness	Can hear only the loudest noises.	50	Born organizer	+ 1 leadership. Will carry out jobs efficiently within limits of intelligence.
49	Stammer	–1 charisma: cannot speak in emergency.	52	Gift of sleep	Can sleep anywhere, anytime. + 1 endurance.
51	Limp	–1 agility: movement at slow rate.	54	Resistance to alcohol	Never gets drunk.
53	Asthma	Allergy to *either* dust & pollen *or* animals: sneezing constantly.	56	Resistance to fatigue	Takes twice as long to get exhausted.
			58	Resistance to pain	Halve factors in calculations for EP loss (round down).
55	Poor health	–1 endurance: susceptible to colds, etc.
57	Shyness	Difficulty in relationships: –1 charisma.	60	Keen eyesight	50% chance of spotting concealed objects, etc., within 30 ft. Ignore illusions.
59	Belligerence	Will take offense at any criticism.	62	Keen hearing	50% chance of hearing concealed enemies, etc., in same range.
61	Snoring *or* body odor	–1 charisma. People avoid you.	64	Keen smell	10% chance of smelling concealed animals, etc., in same range.
63	Insomnia	–1 endurance. Fitful sleep.
65	Hypochondria	Imaginations of illness.	66	Good health	+ 1 endurance. Resists illnesses.
67	Alcoholism	Perpetual craving for alcohol. –1 lust.	68	Good with animals	Can calm any animal (non-sentient). Good horseman.
69	Obsessional gambling	Will not refuse to bet or game.	70	Green fingers	Can make any plant grow.
71	Spendthrift *or* hoarding	Obsessional spending *or* accumulation of money.	72	Mechanical genius	Can understand any machine's workings.

%	Roll Factor	Notes	%	Roll factor	Notes
73	Depression	−1 charisma. Deep melancholy.	74	Born swimmer	+1 agility: +1 over water obstacles.
75	Paranoia	Suspicious of persecution.	76	Born climber	+1 agility: +1 over climbing obstacles.
77	Psychopathy	Sadistic enjoyment of killing.	78	Sense of location	Knows exactly where he is (relative to previous places).
79	Misanthropy	Distrust of all men.	80	Sense of direction	Knows which way is north.
81	Kleptomania	Always stealing small objects.	82	Healing hands	Can restore 1-6 EP loss once a day.
83	Claustrophobia	Fear of confined spaces.	84	Empathy	Can sense what sentients are feeling.
85	Agoraphobia	Fear of open spaces.	86	Intuition	One question to GM a day: 01-75% brings accurate answer.
87	Fear of water	Cannot swim.	88	Prophecy	Likewise: applies only to what is likely to happen in future.
89	Fear of heights	Cannot climb (up or down).	90	Clairvoyance	40 ft. range. Can see through walls, etc., once every 12 hours.
91	Fear of spiders *or* snakes	Will "freeze" in terror.	92	Clairaudience	Likewise.
			94	Gift of tongues	Will learn or decipher any language/inscription within a day.
93	Fear of mice and rats	Will run away in opposite direction.	96	Good luck	+1 on all luck dice.
95	Jewish	You will be persecuted and shunned by all right-minded Christians.	98	Lycanthropy	Voluntary change to wolf, bear or dog once a month for 12 hours.
97	Heretic		100	Trance	Can suspend body functions for a day. 10% chance of a vision.
99	Atheist				

Material possessions

Equipment. Initial adventuring gear must be purchased from the available money, according to the cost charts which follow.

Money. This varies with your success in adventuring. Initial money depends on your social class, and is calculated later.

Skills

There are certain skills which may be needed in *Fantasy Wargaming* adventures and which are not covered elsewhere in the rules. These are: riding, swimming, climbing, tracking, stealing and singing. GMs should take these skills into account when considering probabilities (e.g., of negotiating a physical obstacle).

Riding. Any member of the nobility (including clergy) can ride. Warriors with agility of 10+ will ride well. Clergy with agility of 14+ will ride well. For freemen, add agility plus social class, double, then throw a percentage dice under to ride. Freemen with agility of 14+ and able to ride will automatically ride well. The unfree, poor free and slaves have a chance to ride equal to half their agility (rounded down). They cannot ride well unless possessed of maximum agility (18).

Swimming and climbing. The chance of swimming equals agility, unless the character lives beside a sea, lake or river, when the chance is multiplied by five. Agility of 14+ equals swim well. Chance of climbing equals agility, unless the character lives in the mountains, when the chance is multiplied by five. Agility of 14+ equals climb well.

Tracking. Only nobility and rural dwellers can track. Add agility and intelligence, double, then throw a percentage dice under to track. Rural dwellers (including nobility) with intelligence of 12+ will track well.

Stealing (including lock picking, stealthy movement, pickpocketing, etc.). All poor free and slaves with agility of over six can steal; agility of 10+ qualifies as thief. Unfree peasantry have a 50 per cent chance of being able to steal; agility of 14+ qualifies as thief.

Singing. All clergy can sing; those with charisma of 10+ sing well. Lay nobility have a 66 per cent chance of singing; those with charisma of 14+ sing well. Slaves have a 50 per cent chance of singing; those with charisma of 14+ sing well. All others have a 33 per cent chance of singing.

Experience

At the start of your character's adventuring career, he will have no experience—levels of 0 in each category. (Exception: players may artificially create experienced characters, at GM's discretion, using the rules below for the increase of factors.) As he progresses, he will acquire three different types of experience—combat and general adventuring, religious and magical. Obviously, a warrior will accumulate more of the first than the other types of experience, but he may also acquire some religious or magical knowledge. These experience levels very largely determine how well, over a period, the character is likely to do in combat, and in the exercise of religion and magic. Characters accumulate experience points in each category. At each 1,000 points, they go up a level in that category. Each type of experience is added to only by activities that are appropriate to the category—and higher level characters will receive less experience from the same activity than lesser mortals. The calculation of experience is handled in the combat, religion and magic rules. Certain characteristics will also vary as the character increases his level. At each "level break" (1,000 points), the player receives two points with which to alter (up or down) his character's characteristics. One must be assigned to a prime characteristic in the experience category for which the points were awarded; the other must be used to alter a secondary characteristic in the same category. No characteristic may be altered in successive level breaks, whether within a single category or across categories.

No characteristic may be increased beyond 20, or lowered beyond 0.

CHARACTERISTICS: PRIME AND SECONDARY

	Prime characteristics	Secondary characteristics
Combat and adventuring	Physique	Charisma
	Agility	Intelligence
	Endurance	Greed
	Bravery	Selfishness
Religious		Lust
	Faith	Intelligence
	Greed	Endurance
	Selfishness	Bravery
	Lust	Charisma
	Piety*	
Magical	Faith	Endurance
	Intelligence	Agility
	Mana**	Bravery
		Charisma

* Piety may be increased by the width of one piety band, and **Mana may be increased by 16 points, instead of altering a characteristic.

Social class and background: character generation

Social class	Landowning and warrior classes	Clergy ('noble', lesser)	Townsfolk	Rural dwellers	Cost in Gold Sovereigns (GS) to purchase increase into rank
22	Emperor	Pope			500,000
21	King	(Anti-Pope)			150,000
20	Duke	Cardinal			40,000
19	Marquis	Primate			13,000
18	Count, Earl	Archbishop			4,000
17	Rich Baron	Bishop, Abbot of a Mother House	Lord Mayor (of a city)		1,500
16	Poor Baron, Rich Knight	Archdeacon, Abbot (1)	Alderman (city), Mayor (town)		600
15	Poor Knight	Dean, Prior (1), Abbot (2)	Guild Master (1)		250
14	Landless Knight	Rich priest, Monk (1), Prior (2)	Guild Member (1), Guild Master (2)		150
13	Mercenary captain	Middling priest, Monk (2)	Guild Journeyman (1) Guild Member (2) Guild Master (3)	(Lord's agent) Reeve	90
12	Sergeant/mercenary NCO	Poor priest, Friar	Guild Journeyman (2) Guild Member (3) Self-employed tradesman	Rich freeman	56
11	Man-at-Arms, basic soldier	Lay brother (free)	Guild Journeyman (3) Employed skilled laborer	Poor freeman	40
10	Mercenaries, bowmen	Lay brother (free)	Employed laborer	Sokeman	30
9	Conscript peasant, militia/POW	Lay brother (serf)	Servant	Rich villein	22
8	Conscript peasant militia/POW	Lay brother (serf)	Unemployed	Poor villein	16
7	Outlawed soldier	Common serf	Pimp, thief	Cottar	12
6			Beggar, whore	Bordar	9
5			Recently escaped serf	Waste/forest dweller/outlaw	6
4			Recently escaped slave	Slave	5
3				Slave	4
2				Slave	3
1				Slave	2
0				Slave	1

(Vertical labels: NOBILITY and FREEMEN for upper ranks; UNFREE, POOR, FREE, and SLAVE for lower ranks)

Explanations

The social position of these groups is described in the text. The following are, therefore, only notes.

Rural dwellers. Waste/forest dweller/outlaw: this class belongs to a community completely isolated from mainstream agricultural society, by birth or choice. It is the right (and duty) of all men to kill outlaws on sight. Reeve: this is a freeman installed by an absent Knight or lord to run his estate. He must pay 20 per cent of the annual income to the lord, as profit, every year.

Town dwellers. Guilds are divided into three classes: the rich (merchants, bankers and, sometimes, clothiers); the poor (bakers, candlemakers, grocers, cobblers, butchers, tinkers, etc.); and the middling (anything else). The exact composition varies from town to town, depending on the nature of local industries. There is no Thieves' Guild (sorry Fritz!). Alderman: usually a Guild Master as well; has policing rights over his part of the town.

Clergy. Monasteries are divided into rich and poor houses. A rich monastery will have estates equal to that of a rich Baron. A poor monastery will have estates equal to a rich Knight or poor Baron. A Mother House has estates equal to those of an Earl.

Landowning and warrior classes. Basic soldier: any military man (e.g., engineer) employed as part of the regular complement of an army or castle, etc. Landless Knight: will normally make his living either as an itinerant mercenary or as a waged vassal of a Baron, Earl, etc. Will always be on the search for an estate, either by conquest or by marriage.

Choosing a father/family rank

The table above is not directly usable by new, zero-level characters. Since most characters in the game will start at age 16 (unless artificially aged and experienced), they cannot immediately "jump" into positions like Guild Member, man-at-arms, or (with rare exceptions) King. The table instead gives the *average* (not absolute) social class of established, adult figures in different positions. From this table, the player must choose a father consonant with his character's own social class (see below). The player will also develop his character over time, and may find himself falling into these general categories.

In choosing a father, the player may elect to be the heir of a man with a similar social class to that of his character, or a more distant child of someone with a higher social position. The differences between the social class of the father and character depend on the latter's family rank, and are:

Nobility

+1 Eldest legitimate son (Heir), wife; eldest daughter if no legitimate sons (Heiress).

+2 Other legitimate sons, eldest daughter (if not Heiress); bastard son if no legitimate children at all (Heir).

+3 Bastard son (if not Heir), bastard daughter if no other offspring at all (Heiress).

Freemen

+1 Eldest legitimate son (Heir), wife; eldest daughter if no legitimate sons (Heiress).

+2 Eldest daughter (if not Heiress), other legitimate sons, other legitimate daughters; bastard Heir.

+3 Other bastards.

Clergy

None; all children automatically bastard.

Eldest son (Heir), mistress; eldest daughter if no sons (Heiress).

Other sons, eldest daughter (if not Heiress, other daughters).

Unfree and poor free

All legitimate sons (joint Heirs), wife; all bastard sons if no legitimate ones (joint Heirs). All daughters, all bastards (not Heirs).

Slaves

All Sons of slaves have the same rank as their father. All daughters are one rank down.

Add the factor you want to your class, and start looking for a father!

Costs

Normal annual income is ⅓ × cost needed to purchase increase into the rank, rounded *up*. Normal inheritance is equal to the cost needed to purchase increase into the next rank. Available income at the start of an adventuring career is *proportionately* greater for those in lower social classes, who have less tied up in investments. All the following calculations should be rounded up: classes 0-5, ½ × rank purchase cost; classes 6-9, ⅓ × rank purchase cost; classes 10-13, ¼ × rank purchase cost; classes 14-16, ⅕ × rank purchase cost; classes 17-18, ⅙ × rank purchase cost; classes 19-20, ⅛ × rank purchase cost; classes 21-22, ⅒ × rank purchase cost.

Cost charts

The following coinage is used: 1 Gold Sovereign (GS) = 5 Silver Marks; 1 Silver Mark (SM) = 2 Ducats; 1 Ducat (DT) = 2 Florins; 1 Florin (Fn) = 2 Shillings; 1 Shilling (Sg) = 5 Groats; 1 Groat (Gt) = 5 Pennies; 1 Penny (Py) = 5 Copper Farthings (CF).

Gems and precious goods. At GM's discretion.

Weapons. Broadsword 60 Fn; falchion 30 Fn; heavy mace 30 Fn; lance 40 Fn; calvalry spear 20 Fn; two-handed axe 35 Fn; single-handed axe 25 Fn; estoc 36 Fn; pike 20 Fn; infantry spear 17 Fn; halberd 28 Fn; arbalest 60 Fn; light crossbow 27 Fn; two-handed sword 67 Fn; bill 15 Fn; claymore 36 Fn; cinqueda 32 Fn; dagger 18 Fn; sling 3 Fn; glaive 27 Fn; main gauche 30 Fn; morning star 32 Fn; poignard 26 Fn; poleaxe 33 Fn; longbow 18 Fn; short bow 14 Fn; arrows (20) 12 Fn; quarrels (20) 13 Fn; seax 35 Fn; sword breaker 36 Fn; javelin 4 Fn; boar spear 18 Fn; farm tools (average) 8 Fn.

Armor. Open helmet 17 Fn; helm 20 Fn; helm with visor 25 Fn; leather body armor 80 Fn; mail 135 Fn; ring mail 90 Fn; plate 240 Fn; half-plate (upper body) 160 Fn; brigantine 40 Fn; gambeson 25 Fn; hauberk 60 Fn; jupon 15 Fn; cloth horse barding 65 Fn; leather 70 Fn; metal 190 Fn; bracer 3 Fn; buckler 17 Fn; large shield (wood) 8 Fn; (metal faced) 12 Fn; small shield (wood) 7 Fn; (metal faced) 9 Fn.

Miscellaneous equipment. Scabbard 5 Fn; sword belt 7 Fn; dagger scabbard 2 Fn; iron nails/spikes (15) 1 Fn; cloth sack 1 Fn; leather sack 2 Fn; candles (10) 2 Fn; lantern 15 Fn; flint (12) 1 Fn; tinder (5) 1 Fn; paper (per sheet) 1 Fn; parchment (per sheet) 1 Fn; gunpowder and lead balls (per shot) 1 Fn; 50 ft rope 5 Fn; water skin 3 Fn; tarred torch (8) 1 Fn; tinder box 5 Fn; horse harness 67 Fn; mule/donkey pack harness 15 Fn; riding harness 48 Fn; warhorse harness 120 Fn; two-wheeled cart 300 Fn; 4-wheeled cart 400 Fn.

Animals. (Each type is followed by three prices—purchase cost /feeding cost per day/stabling cost per day.) Slave 4 GS to 10 GS/4 Py to 10 Py/4 Py to 10 Py; donkey 3 GS/1 Gt/1 Gt; mule 84 Fn/1 Gt/1 Gt; riding horse 12 GS/6 Py/6 Py; warhorse 40 GS/2 Gt/7 Py; guard god 50 Fn/1 Gt/-; hawk 4 GS/2 Py/-; carthorse 20 GS/ 7 Py/1 Gt; ox 8 GS/2 Gt/-.

Living expenses. Minimum food (including salt, herbs and spices) 6 Py per day (four days' supply allowed, then "goes off"); iron rations 9 Py per day (ten days' supply allowed in addition to above food allowance); lodging per night (including food)—country inn 10 Py, town inn 1 Sg, good town inn is 1 Fn, monastery 1 Sg.

Other costs can be arrived at by finding something similar and charging a like amount. All prices quoted are for new, unused items. Secondhand items may be purchased for D6 × 5 per cent less but may well have a defect (00-10 per cent, defect at GM's discretion). If selling equipment, the price is calculated at 2D6 × 5 per cent less than the new price (we've all got to make a profit!). These costs, in fact, represent fairly late medieval prices, but are from authentic accounts. Dark Age prices would be perhaps a third or half as high. Income in the Dark Ages would, however, be proportionately reduced by at least the same amount. For simplicity's sake, we have nevertheless assumed costs to be the same throughout our period.

Role-playing rules

Luck

The influence of "Lady Luck" affects most calculations at some point or other. It is simply calculated by throwing one six-sided dice (1D6) and scoring as follows: $1 = -2; 2 = -1; 3, 4 = 0; 5 = +1; 6 = +2$.

Leadership factor

A character's leadership is decided by the following equation:

$$\frac{(3 \times \text{charisma}) + (1 \times \text{physique}) + (1 \times \text{intelligence}) + (4 \times \text{class}) + (1 \times \text{bravery})}{10}$$

Then add ½ character's highest experience level to achieve a final figure (rounded up).

The character in a party with the highest leadership (ignore any difference in fractions) will be the party leader and the ultimate source of decisions and orders. Note also who has the highest leadership in the other factions (i.e., magicians and clerics if leader is a warrior). These are sub-leaders. If two characters in the party have the same leadership, the party is split. Unless one of the two characters is willing to stand down (reduce his leadership by 10 per cent and his charisma by 1 point), there must be a challenge. Leaders receive +50 per cent experience. Sub-leaders receive +10 per cent experience. Deputy leader (second highest leadership in party) gets +10 per cent (cumulative if also sub-leader).

Challenging the leader

Parties in most fantasy games have a habit of being monolithic; they stick together in an unnatural fashion, without disagreements or jealousies. While it makes sense that a party should have a great deal of natural cohesion, when faced with common dangers, provision should also be included for jealousy, competition and rebellion.

The best way of resolving a challenge to the leader of the party is by calling him out in physical combat (if a warrior) or magical duel (if a cleric or Mage). Mages may decide on a magical contest (i.e., to try their magical strength without combat) if so desired. The victor of this struggle, if unchallenged by either a sub-leader or the deputy leader (the character in the party with the second highest leadership under the new order), is the new party leader. Other party members, whatever their personal feelings, will not interfere before or during combat: "calling out" was an ingrained and unchallengeable right in the cultures covered by this book. However, a defeated challenger who has earned the unpopularity of the party may face retribution, if the victorious leader does not expressly forbid it.

Only the deputy leader may challenge the leader directly. However, third or lower leaders (i.e., characters with the third highest leadership, and so on) may secure a chance to challenge the leader by defeating those who stand between them and the party leader.

Where the challenger is of a different type from the leader (i.e., cleric or magician in a party led by a warrior), or where the challenger wishes to elevate himself above the leader without combat, he may appeal to the party as a whole for support. Challenger and leader each have one minute real time to put their case, the challenger going first. The other party members must then individually decide, in turn, between them. Add the leadership factors of members on either side and compare; only if there is 10 per cent clear difference in favor of the challenger does he prevail.

Challengers with a bravery of under 8 must always choose the second method.

The defeated character (challenger or old leader) will lose 2 points charisma for the rest of the adventure, and 10 per cent leadership. These will revert to him either upon a successful counter-challenge at some later stage, or at the end of the adventure. Sub-leaders may be challenged or questioned on the same terms.

Questioning the leader

This occurs when a character calls into question any decision or order given by the party leader. The procedure is again by appeal to the party, with questioner and leader each having 40 seconds' real time to put their case. Total leadership factors of supporting party members: there is no requirement here for a 10 per cent difference.

No party member with a leadership more than 8 points lower than that of the leader may question him, except as the result of a temptation or morale test. Members not wishing to resort to an open appeal may of course put their case privately to the leader and attempt to persuade him to reverse his decision.

The effect of the question is to confirm or overrule the decision, and to lower the leadership and charisma of the defeated party by 10 per cent for the remainder of that day. If this takes the leader below any other party member, an automatic challenge by council of war will take place unless the deputy leader gives way (minus 10 per cent on leadership and charisma for the remainder of the day; then revert to ordinary leadership and increase original charisma by 1 point for the remainder of the adventure).

A challenge will take 1 turn (20 minutes). A question will take ½ turn.

Temptation

The aim of these rules is to bring the personality characteristics into adventure play, and to encourage players to act in character when faced with situations, e.g., in a dungeon. The rules also allow GMs to consider subtler traps for characters; instead of merely killing or capturing them, he may seek to win them over. Personality clashes and interaction between members of the party are thereby made easier.

The rules below apply equally to attempts by the party to tempt a monster or non-player character. The "degree of temptation" must here be decided between party leader and GM, the latter having the final word.

When trying to tempt a party or a member thereof, the GM may appeal to his greed, selfishness, lust or bravery (as anger). The calculation is very much the same in each case.

Stage one. When drawing up his adventure, or at the time of temptation, the GM must assign to the temptation three factors:

Degree of temptation. This is normally a factor between 0 and 20. It is directly comparable to the greed, selfishness, lust or bravery of the character tempted, and defines how greedy, selfish, lustful or angry the character has to be before he begins to be tempted. Characters with factors under this figure need not take at all. Thus the *lower* this figure is, the *greater* the temptation: "It would have tempted a saint."

Degree of visible danger. This indicates the degree of danger which the tempted person can see in accepting the temptation (not including retaliation by the party). It is normally a factor between 5 and 20, and is directly comparable to bravery. Note: there may be very little visible danger in what is in fact a very dangerous temptation; the factor is not necessarily a true measure of the peril in accepting the temptation. The greater the figure, the greater the visible danger.

Intelligence. This indicates how intelligent the tempted person has to be before he begins to have a chance of realizing (or inventing) disadvantages and "catches" in the temptation.

Stage two. Apply the following calculation: character's greed /selfishness/lust, minus the degree of temptation; add his bravery, minus the degree of visible danger; add his intelligence, minus the degree of required intelligence; luck, as described earlier; plus special factors as follows.

Character is leader of the party, —2; leader orders him not to accept, —2; members of the party threaten retaliation, —1 to —4

(GM's choice); endurance below half, —2; endurance 3 or below, —2 (accumulative); exhausted, —2; members of the party encourage him, +1 to +4 (GM's choice).

Subtract ½ highest experience level or *all* religious experience level.

Results	−5 or below	−4	−3	−2	−1	0	1	2	3	4	5	6	7	8	9 or over
Accept with alacrity	—	—	—	100	100	99–100	97–100	95–100	90–100	85–100	80–100	75–100	70–100	65–100	60–100
Accept	—	—	100	96–99	91–99	86–98	81–96	75–94	68–89	51–84	41–79	24–74	10–69	06–64	0–59
Accept if offered more	—	100	93–99	83–95	76–90	66–85	56–80	50–74	41–67	33–50	23–40	11–23	02–09	0–05	—
Reject	41–100	36–99	31–92	26–82	21–75	17–65	14–55	11–49	08–40	06–32	04–22	02–10	01	—	—
Reject with indignation	01–40	01–35	01–30	01–25	01–20	01–16	01–13	01–10	01–07	01–05	01–03	01	—	—	—

TEMPTATION

Effects

Accept with alacrity. Character is in GM's control.

Accept. Character in player's control.

Accept if offered more. Offer must be increased 10 per cent or more.

Reject. No other action.

Reject with indignation. Character will seek to prevent anybody else accepting the temptation, and may also (if bravery exceeds visible danger) seek to destroy the tempter.

The player whose character has accepted with alacrity may not recover control of his character until he has taken a second test and achieved a different result. He may demand a second test under the following circumstances (each of which carries a —3 factor in the calculation): he has suffered physical, financial or other loss from the temptation (down to ½ EPs or ½ money or other); the tempter has disappeared, or himself suffered ½ EP damage; or the player succeeds in identifying precisely the danger or catch in the temptation.

Players whose characters have accepted but remained under their own control will normally revoke their decision automatically under these circumstances unless the party is seen to be losing the struggle. GMs may, however, demand a retest.

Notes

The temptation test should only be used if a character's player refuses a temptation which in the GM's view it would be out of character for him to reject; or having initially accepted the temptation, the player wishes to withdraw his character in circumstances which the GM believes inadequate. It is thus a court of appeal and should not normally interfere with the direct personal play between GM and player.

If there are several characters eligible for a test, take the one with the highest greed/selfishness/lust/bravery first. If the GM wishes to test the whole party, take the leader first, then the character with the highest greed/selfishness/lust/bravery.

A party leader may demand a temptation test on a monster or non-party character.

GMs may reduce the charisma and leadership of successfully tempted or persuaded characters by up to 15 per cent, at their own discretion. Successfully tempted characters automatically lose piety (see religion rules). The test may be extended to cover tempting situations as well as actual tempters.

Persuasion

These rules are again designed to provide a court of appeal in cases where the refusal of a player or a non-player character confronted with a reasoned and persuasive argument is out of character. It should be used sparingly, and mainly in cases where one character is trying to persuade a party member or a non-player character to change his natural allegiance. Note: persuasion is by words only.

The calculation is broadly similar to that for temptation, and the same table is used. Add: charisma of persuader minus charisma of subject; leadership of persuader minus leadership of subject; luck (in the ordinary manner); intelligence of the persuader is 2 or more greater than subject, +1; same as (within two of), 0; 2 or more lower than subject, —1; subject is leader of the party, —2; party leader has forbidden persuasion, —2; members of the party threaten retaliation, —1 to —4 (GM's choice); party members encourage him to accept, +1 to +4 (GM's choice);

subject's endurance is below half, —2; is 3 or below, —2 (accumulative); subject is exhausted, —2; brave (over 13), —1; cowardly (below 9), +1; appeal is backed by bribes or promises of favor, etc., +1—3 (GM's discretion).

Temporary handicaps

Characters do not always feel on top of their job, however heroic they may be! For added realism, the GM should throw at the start of the game day for each character, with two six-dice. A score of 12 will bring any one of the following minor irritants, as seems most appropriate to the GM: head cold, violent diarrhea, splitting headache, abject melancholy, appalling hangover, post-coital tristesse, stabbing pains (in the arms, legs, trunk or groin), inexplicable tiredness, feelings of rejection or inadequacy, etc. Each will last 2-12 hours (two six-dice), and reduce all luck throws by 1.

GMs should also be aware of the possibilities of more serious infection, when designing their adventures. Certain places or people—a malarial swamp, a carrier of typhoid, etc.—can be designated dangerous, with a set percentage chance (normally below 10 per cent) of infecting anyone who comes into close proximity.

Fatigue

Characters become exhausted in the following circumstances: after ten combats in one day (3 hours' rest/6 hours' moderate effort); after three turns (one hour) of continuous combat (1 turn rest/1 hours moderate effort); after three turns (one hour) of continuous pursuit or rout (as combat); after 9 turns (3 hours) of continually carrying beyond your own weight (5 hours' rest/12 hours' moderate effort); after 24 hours (8 hours) of carrying 75-100 per cent body weight (8 hours' rest/24 hours' moderate effort); after 24 hours without sleep (8 hours' sleep only); after 24 hours without food (8 hours' rest or food); after 16 hours without water (water); when endurance points fall to 3 (increase in endurance); moving when seriously ill or wounded, below half endurance (1 turn rest each hour).

The bracketed figures explain how a character may return to his normal state from exhaustion. "Rest" means sleep or complete lack of effort while in a comfortable stationary position.

"Moderate effort" means movement at walking speed unencumbered by armor or shield or other weight; only minor physical obstacles may be undertaken without exhaustion continuing.

Fasting/Starvation

A character without food at all will lose 1 point endurance, physique and agility per day; double that if active (anything but "Rest"). A character fasting (light food and water) will lose points at ¼ × the applicable rate. A character without water will die in 3 days, losing ⅓ EPs per day.

Recovery of endurance points

Characters lose endurance points (EPs) by combat, accident and disease. In the first two cases, the loss is immediate, and has no carry-on effect. Disease, and spells of wasting, ebb endurance points from the body until either death occurs or the patient is cured. Once loss of EPs has ceased, the character (if still alive) will begin his recovery. This will occur at the following rates: 1½ EPs per day if totally rested and nursed at all times; 1 EP per day if character undertakes light effort, looks after himself, moving not more than ½m per hour and eight hours during a day; ½ EP per day if character undertakes moderate effort, keeps pace with adventuring party, etc.; 0 if character remains a fully operational member of the party, undertaking all duties.

Combat and general adventuring experience

For convenience, we have assumed a connection between combat experience and experience at general adventuring. The latter covers activities like the negotiation of traps and physical obstacles, the carrying out of thefts and other difficult missions, the organization of the party—and others, at the GM's discretion. The calculations below are intended only as rough guidelines, and should be used by GMs only with consideration of all the individual circumstances. We recommend the giving of experience only at the end of an adventure, or at the end of each adventuring day —each character making a list of the circumstances for which he would wish to claim, and the amount to which he would be entitled under the experience calculations.

Combat.

Experience gained = (Opponent's combat level × 100)

or

$$\frac{(monster\ value)}{own\ combat\ level}$$

General adventuring.

$$Experience\ gained = \frac{100 - likelihood\ of\ success^*}{2}$$

* This is normally the percentage likelihood of success given in the tables in the section on physical obstacles, thefts, etc. For activities not covered in this section, GMs must use their discretion. *Fantasy Wargaming* awards no experience merely for gathering money or other valuables—picking up 100 "gold pieces" and carrying them for a day and a half is not physically different to picking up and transporting two medium-sized bricks; it is what you have to do to get the money that counts! No experience is awarded for gallant failures, in either combat or general adventuring: sorry!

Physical obstacles

This section discusses and quantifies the means of deciding whether members of the party have successfully negotiated physical obstacles to be found down a dungeon or in another adventure: locked doors, traps, chasms, cliff faces, etc.

How to identify a secret (non-magical) door or compartment

GMs who have followed the admirable procedure noted in "The Compleat Enchanter" of copying down the factors of party members into their own "crib" can use this calculation to discover whether secret doors not protected by magic have been discovered during the exploration of a room or passageway. This section may also be used to discover if a character recognizes a trap before stepping on it. Identification of secret doors is dependent upon intelligence, profession and time. The latter factor is taken into account by allowing one calculation to be taken for every five minutes spent exploring the room.

In designing an adventure, the GM should assign to each secret door or compartment an "intelligence": this defines how intelligent a character must be before he stands a reasonable chance of identifying it. Then follow the calculation. Add: character's intelligence minus "intelligence" required (double); luck (in the ordinary manner); special factors—subject is a professional thief, +2; a warrior, 0; a magician/cleric, −1; combat and adventuring level, +1 for each; exhausted, −2; half endurance, −2; endurance 3 or below, −2; using artificial aids (magnifying glass, tapping the wall), +1 to +3 (GM's choice).

Refer to the following table. Note: doors disguised by magic may only be identified by magic.

SECRET DOOR IDENTIFICATION

Results	−5 or below	−4	−3	−2	−1	0	1	2	3	4	5	6	7	8	9	10 or over
Success	01	01–05	01–10	01–20	01–33	01–45	01–54	01–65	01–74	01–79	01–84	01–89	01–95	01–98	01–99	Success
Partial success	02–50	06–55	11–59	21–64	34–71	46–77	55–82	66–86	75–89	80–92	85–95	90–98	96–99	99–100	100	—
Failure	51–100	56–100	60–100	65–100	72–100	78–100	83–100	87–100	90–100	93–100	96–100	99–100	100	—	—	—

How to open a locked (non-magical) door or compartment

In designing an adventure, the GM should assign to each lock in the adventure the following factors:

Degree of required agility. This defines what agility a character must have if he is to have a chance of opening it.

Degree of required intelligence. This defines what intelligence a character must have if he is to have a chance of opening it.

Apply the following calculations. Add: character's agility minus required agility; character's intelligence minus required intelligence; luck (in the ordinary manner); special factors—subject is a professional thief, +2; a warrior/other, 0; a magician /cleric, −1; combat and adventuring level, +1 for each; exhausted, −2; half endurance, −2; endurance 3 or below, −3; using thieves' tools, +1; using makeshift tools, −1; without tools, −3; subject has tried to open lock before, −2 per failure.

Refer to the preceding table. Note: doors locked by magic and locks enforced by magic may not be opened until the magic is removed.

How to recognize and escape a trap as it is sprung

There are two ways in which a character may recognize a trap *before* reaching it: by the procedure outlined in "how to identify a secret door or compartment"; or by the normal intelligence of the player confronted with the visible evidence of the trap. Note: GMs feeling that this realization is out of character for the player's character may require a recognition test: if the character fails it, he walks into the trap!

This section is somewhat different: it defines what chance the character has of realizing and escaping the trap at the very moment that it springs. It is thus in the nature of a "saving throw."

In designing the adventure, a GM should give each trap the following factors:

Degree of intelligence required for immediate recognition. This should be used for trap recognition before it is reached.

Degree of intelligence required for immediate recognition. This should be used for the "saving throw" calculation.

Degree of agility required for immediate escape. This defines how agile a character must be to have a reasonable chance of escape.

Degree of physique required for escape. This defines how strong a character must be to have a reasonable chance of escape as the trap springs.

Apply the following calculation. Add: character's intelligence minus degree of required intelligence; character's agility minus degree of required agility; character's physique minus degree of required physique; luck (as per normal); special factors—subject is a thief, +2; a warrior/other, 0; a magician or cleric, —1; combat/adventuring level, +1 for each; exhausted, —2; below half endurance, —2; endurance of 3 or below, —3; wearing chain mail, —1; wearing plate mail, —2; otherwise encumbered, —1 to —4 (GM's choice).

Refer to the preceding table. Note: in creating a trap GMs should also note its physical dimensions, the damage it will do if successful, and the degree of required agility and physique to escape from the trap if caught in it: see "how to negotiate an obstacle." These will normally be higher than the degree of required physique and agility for escape as the trap is sprung.

How to negotiate an obstacle

This section is designed to cover every type of obstacle: from a chasm or a sheer cliff face to a loose paving stone. It will also cover escape from a sprung trap (as above). The method of calculation is almost identical with the other calculations in this section.

In designing an adventure, the GM should assign to each obstacle the following features:

What it is.

Its physical dimensions.

Any special difficulties involved in it.

Damage done if not negotiated successfully.

Degree of required physique. This defines what physique a character requires to have a reasonable chance of negotiating the obstacle.

Degree of required agility. Likewise.

Apply the following calculation. Add: character's physique minus required physique; character's agility minus required agility; luck (in the ordinary manner); special factors—subject is a thief, +2; a warrior/other, 0; a magician or cleric, —1; combat and adventuring level, +1 for each; intelligent (14 or above), +1; unintelligent (8 or below), —1; brave (14 or above), +1; cowardly (8 or below), —1; exhausted, —2; below half endurance, —2; endurance of 3 or below, —3; using artificial aids: the GM may assign any + figure he feels appropriate depending upon the nature of the aid; +1 to +5 would be the normal range.

How to pick a pocket

This section tells you how to calculate an attempt to steal money or other valuables from the person of a monster, character or non-player character. It covers stealing from pockets, pouches, handbags and other appurtenances actually in the possession of the object of theft. It does not cover more elaborate thefts like breaking and entering: see above for locks, doors, compartments and negotiating a physical obstacle.

Once the person attempting the theft has got within reach of the target, apply the following calculation. Add: the difference between the agilities of the thief and his victim; the difference between the intelligences of the thief and his victim; luck (in the ordinary manner); special factors—person attempting the theft is a professional thief, +2; a warrior/other, 0; a magician or cleric, —1; combat/adventuring level difference, ± difference; exhausted, —2; below half endurance, —2; endurance 3 or below, —3; brave (14 or above), +1; cowardly (8 or below), —1; charismatic (14 or above), +2; uncharismatic (8 or below), —2; target of theft is particularly difficult, —1 to —4 (GM's choice); target of theft is particularly easy, +1 to +4 (GM's choice); previous attempts have failed, —2 per attempt.

Effects (refer to table)

Success. Character has succeeded in picking the lock/identifying the secret door or compartment or trap/recognized and escaped the trap as it sprung/negotiated the obstacle without damage /picked the pocket.

Partial success. The lock is partially picked: try again with an extra +2 (ignore the —2 factors for previous failures). The secret door, compartment or trap is suspected but not recognized: try again at an extra +1. You are half-caught by the trap; try again with no extra factor. You have half fallen from the obstacle: try again at an extra —1 factor. You have failed to pick the pocket but are not detected.

Failure. Self-explanatory. The lock is intact. The trap, secret door or compartment is unrecognized. The trap is sprung. The obstacle has claimed a victim. You are caught trying to pick the pocket.

Group combat rules

Who can fight?

Anyone bearing arms can engage in combat unless the notes in their character descriptions prevent them.

Selecting a warrior and weapons

Once the culture in which the adventure is to take place has been chosen, the player should consult the relevant table detailing the normal types for that culture together with the usual weapons and armor and any special points which it may be necessary to bear in mind. Taking special note of the social standing of his character, the player should then choose a suitable warrior type. Besides the usual weapons and armor, one further item of armor or one additional weapon may be chosen. If a weapon is selected, this cannot be treated as a "favored weapon" until the player has gained sufficient experience in its use. The cost of additional items of equipment is tabulated elsewhere. Also included in the warrior tables is the "heroic" character, which can only be used if the Gaming Master agrees. The weapon tables detail the performance of the various weapons and the minimum character abilities needed to use them. Players should note that the speed of fighting with a weapon is taken into account when working out overall effectiveness: thus a dagger is reasonably effective in close combat due to the ease with which perhaps two or three blows could be struck in the same time as it would take to deliver one with a double-handed axe. The armor tables detail the protection conferred and the abilities required to use different items effectively.

Combat

Combat is based on a simultaneous flurry of blows; however, missile weapons and those with a significantly longer reach are allowed a first strike. Missile weapons can obviously be used repeatedly until the enemy's proximity forces a character into hand-to-hand combat.

Combat sequence

The combat should always be conducted in the following sequence.

Pre-combat phase. 1 All characters who have to take a check on their morale calculate their enforced reactions, if any, in accordance with the procedure below. 2 Control check for all characters who are likely to go berserk (see page 148). 3 Characters with free choice make a note of their choice of action, either in writing or mentally, for the next phase (ten seconds in game time). They should make this decision in less than 45 seconds. 4 Long-range (missile) weapons engage the enemy. 5 Magical spells made ready beforehand, and instantaneous magic, may now be cast. (The preceding sequence may be omitted in the case of a surprise attack *on* the party.)

Combat phase. 1 Characters with a weapon effectively two feet longer than their opponent's, or whose surplus agility is greater than 4, have a first blow. 2 Opponents then strike back against the first blow unless killed or severely wounded (i.e., endurance halved). 3 Simultaneous combat then takes place. This can be a simultaneous flurry of blows or an attempt by one party to dodge, disengage or parry the blow. If a lunge is attempted, it should be declared at the beginning of this section. *Post-combat phase.* 1 Check if any morale tests are required. If so, take them and apply their effects. 2 Return to combat phase. (Note: magical or missile weapons should not be used into an existing mêlée unless you are willing to have the effects fall on friend and foe alike.)

Morale

Morale should be tested in the following circumstances by the Gaming Master, and its effect should be hinted at to the player concerned. If the player consistently ignores such remarks as "Gregor's not too happy about going in there," the Gaming Master should take over the character for that phase.

Before engaging in physical or magical combat

When endurance falls to half its original level; again when it falls to 3 or below

When 5 points of damage are received in a phase

By any character whose bravery is under 7 or who failed his last morale test when faced with apparent danger

On entering a level higher than that of the party leader

When up to three characters are isolated from the rest of the party and do not know how to rejoin them

When deserted (i.e., at least half the party killed, severely wounded or in flight)

When first losing endurance points in an adventure

When the party falls below half strength or when three characters are killed in one turn (20 minutes)

At the Gaming Master's discretion

When morale is tested, the party leader is taken first, then the character with the lowest bravery, then any who have failed a previous test.

Testing procedure

Add together the character's combat level and bravery, then make the following (accumulative) adjustments: +1 Each victory in this day; in a level lower than that of your party leader (+1 per level); selfless (8 or below). +2 Unharmed; in a secure position (GM's decision); character is party leader; least brave member of party passes a test; greedy or lusty (14 or over) faced with the object of your desire; party intact. —1 Magic user faced with higher level magic; below original endurance; unintelligent (8 or below); party member fleeing this phase; shieldless (physical combat only); unarmored (physical combat only); under missile fire this phase; each defeat in this day; in a level higher than that of your party leader (—1 per level); selfish (14 or over). —2 Isolated (GM's decision); deserted; at or below half original endurance; below an endurance of 4; demoralized by last test; unarmed (physical combat only); leader fails a morale test; party has suffered half casualties; warrior faced with magic/miracle *or* mage/cleric faced with combat. —4 Fleeing. ±1 If the player's astrological sign is exercising an influence on the situation (+1) of if the opposite (diminishing) sign is exercising influence (—1). Finally, throw an ordinary six-sided dice, for luck, in the usual manner. Correlate the results in the following table and make the character act accordingly:

Test score	Below 8	9	10	11	12	13	14	15	16	17	18	19	20	21	22	23+	
Obey orders	1	1-5	1-12	1-21	1-33	1-44	1-54	1-65	1-73	1-80	1-86	1-90	1-93	1-96	1-98	1-100	
Dither	2-12	6-31	13-42	22-53	34-64	45-70	55-77	66-83	74-88	81-90	87-94	91-97	93-99	97-100	99-100		Throw 2 percentage dice
Act selfishly	13-26	32-45	43-60	54-69	65-75	71-82	78-89	84-94	89-97	91-98	95-100	98-100	100	—	—	—	
Panic or surrender	27-50	46-66	61-76	70-82	76-85	83-90	90-94	95-97	98-99	99-100	—	—	—	—	—	—	
Flee	51-100	67-100	77-100	83-100	86-100	91-100	95-100	98-100	100	—	—	—	—	—	—	—	

Effects

Obey orders. Do as the player requires in accordance with the wishes of the party leader.

Dither. Continue if in combat or other dangerous enterprise but deduct (−1) from all subsequent dice throws and do not initiate a new action until passing a further test.

Act selfishly. You will pull out of personal danger and refuse orders to get involved in any new enterprise. If involved in combat, −1 on throws to hit but +1 on disengage.

Panic or surrender. Character is "taken over" by GM and will flee if forced to engage in combat.

Flee. Character is "taken over" by GM and will flee at top speed by the route he imagines will best avoid danger.

Subsequent tests

Anything less than "obey orders" counts as failure. "Dither" ceases once the situation that caused it has ended (GM's decision), as does "act selfishly." "Panic or surrender" and "flee" will continue until the character is in a safe place (GM's decision) or outruns the cause of his problems, when he will take a further test.

Control, or "berserk," test

All Viking characters and others with a bravery factor of 12 or over coupled with an intelligence of 9 or less may go berserk in the following circumstances if they pass (fail?) the following test, which should be taken at the start of physical combat, or during physical combat when endurance falls below half, or when the GM decides by an Act of Dog that the situation is such that a character *ought* to go berserk.

Procedure

Halve the character's combat level (rounding fractions up), treating the result as negative for a "normal" character, positive for a Viking, then make the following (accumulative) adjustments: +1 Bravery of 14; intelligence 6-7; Viking; shieldless; unarmored. +2 Bravery of 15-16; intelligence 5; berserk in last two days. +3 Bravery of 17 or over; intelligence of 3 or below; cornered (GM's decision). −1 Alone; party member dies, flees or surrenders this phase (−1 per member). −2 Exhausted; failed last morale test; leader of party. −3 Unarmed; endurance 3 or below. Finally, throw a six-sided dice, scoring and allowing for astrological influence as under morale, then check the resultant total against a throw of two percentage dice on the following table:

	4 or less	5	6	7	8	9	10	11	12	13 plus
Stay in control	1–98	1–94	1–89	1–81	1–69	1–53	1–35	1–19	1–7	—
Go berserk	99–100	95–100	90–100	82–100	70–100	54–100	36–100	20–100	8–100	1–100

Effects

A berserk character is ferocious, immune to pain and incapable of reason, he is —1 on all attempts to hit, may not disengage and scores +3 on damage. He will not take a morale test until his endurance falls to 3 or below. Ignore effects of exhaustion or damage in working out strike probabilities. A berserker *must* engage in combat if it is offered and will not stop until his visible enemies are killed.

Combat procedure

During an adventure two elements usually remain constant, agility and physique. If these are more than those required to wield the weapon used in the combat they count as "surplus" agility and physique. This surplus will, however, be reduced by the encumbrance factor of any weapon or other accoutrement not actually being used in the combat.

To calculate surplus agility, compare the character's basic factor (as amended by any encumbrance) with that needed to wield his weapon effectively. The difference counts as surplus—but may be negative. If it *is* negative, apply it absolutely. If it is positive, halve it (rounding fractions up) and apply.

Distance weapons (i.e., missile weapons and firearms). Take the character's combat level and to this add the surplus agility and physique, if any. Then apply the following (accumulative) factors: +1 Large target; slow-moving target. +2 Very large target; very slow-moving target. (0 Medium size or medium-moving target.) —1 Small target; fast-moving target; over half range; opponent sees you fire. —2 Tiny target; very fast-moving target; at extreme range (last 10 per cent).

Now add ±1 as applicable for astrological influence and ±

from a six-sided dice throw for luck, then run through the following mêlée factors (except those marked *) and apply the results to the combat table.

All other weapons. Add combat level, surplus agility, factor for astrological influence and dice throw as above, and apply the results to the combat table.

Mêlée factors

—1 Intelligence of 4-8; bravery of 4-8*; endurance of 4-8*; character is berserk; character is outnumbered (—1 for each outnumbering opponent). —2 Intelligence of 0-3; bravery of 0-3*; endurance of 0-3*; character damaged in last phase ("flurry"); character using a non-favored weapon; blow is carrying over from a parry in which the opponent's weapon broke*; blow is partially parried or dodged; character is exhausted. —3 Blow is substantially parried. —4 Blow is substantially dodged. +1 Intelligence of 14+; bravery of 14+*; endurance of 14+*; opponent damaged in last phase ("flurry"); opponent is exhausted; first strike used; opponent is outnumbered (+1 for each outnumbering ally, to a maximum of +3). +2 Not applicable. +3 Blow is a free hack (i.e., on an unaware, fleeing or stunned opponent).

The result of the foregoing additions and subtractions will be a final factor of, usually, between —6 and +14 (below and above being rounded back to the minimum/maximum on the striking table). Cross reference this with a percentage dice throw to determine which part of the target has been hit. In the case of any multi-limbed or -headed beasts, the organ affected will be at the GM's discretion.

Now roll to see the damage caused to the part of the target hit by your character's weapon according to the weapon table, *adding* to your score any surplus physique (calculate as for agility above) and *deducting* your opponent's armor value. The resultant total is deducted from your opponent's endurance.

Special effects. Some blows have a special effect. On heart or throat, double the endurance loss. If this makes the endurance level fall to zero or below, your opponent is dead. On the head, 4 points damage will stun, providing you with a free hack in the next D4 "flurry." On the face, 3 points damage will temporarily blind (blood from cuts) for further D4 "flurries." In the guts, 4

STRIKING TABLE

Parry/dodge/ disengage effect	Part of body hit	-6 or less	-5	-4	-3	-2	-1	0	1	2	3	4	5	6	7	8	9	10	11	12	13	13+
Failure	Miss	1-41	1-40	1-38	1-37	1-35	1-34	1-32	1-31	1-29	1-28	1-26	1-25	1-23	1-22	1-20	1-19	1-17	1-16	1-14	1-12	1-10
	Shield or trunk if unshielded	42-52	41-49	39-47	38-45	36-43	35-42	33-41	32-39	30-37	29-36	27-35	26-33	24-30	23-28	21-25	20-23	18-20	17-18	15	13	11
Partial Success	Trunk	53-63	50-60	48-58	46-56	44-55	43-54	42-53	40-51	38-49	37-48	36-46	34-45	31-42	29-39	26-37	24-36	21-36	19-34	16-33	14-32	12-31
	Face	64-75	61-70	59-67	57-66	56-65	55-64	54-63	52-60	50-59	49-58	47-57	46-55	43-53	40-50	38-48	37-47	37-46	35-45	34-43	33-41	32-39
Substantial success	Head	76-84	71-79	68-77	67-76	66-75	65-74	64-73	61-70	60-69	59-68	58-67	56-65	54-63	51-61	49-60	48-58	47-58	46-56	44-55	42-53	40-52
	Sword arm	85-92	80-87	78-86	77-85	76-84	75-83	74-82	71-79	70-78	69-77	68-76	66-74	64-73	62-71	61-69	59-68	59-67	57-66	56-65	54-64	53-63
	Other arm	93-97	88-95	87-94	86-93	85-92	84-91	83-90	80-87	79-86	78-85	77-84	75-83	74-81	72-79	70-77	69-76	68-75	67-74	66-73	65-72	64-71
	Guts	98-103	96-101	95-100	94-100	93-99	92-98	91-97	88-94	87-93	86-92	85-91	84-89	82-88	80-86	78-86	77-85	76-84	75-83	74-82	73-81	72-80
Total success	Right leg	104-108	102-106	101-105	101-105	100-104	99-103	98-103	95-100	94-99	93-98	92-97	90-95	89-95	87-93	87-92	86-91	85-90	84-89	83-89	82-88	81-87
	Left leg	109-112	107-110	106-110	106-110	105-109	104-108	104-107	101-107	100-106	99-106	98-103	96-103	96-102	94-101	93-100	92-99	91-99	90-98	90-98	89-97	88-96
	Throat	113-114	111-113	111-113	111-113	110-112	109-111	108-111	108-110	107-110	107-110	104-109	104-109	103-109	102-109	101-108	100-107	100-107	99-106	99-106	98-105	97-105
	Heart	115	114-115	114-115	114-115	113-115	112-115	112-115	111-115	111-115	111-115	110-115	110-115	110-115	110-115	109-115	108-115	108-115	107-115	107-115	106-115	106-115

Note: As the blow improves so your chance of missing a passive shield increases. Charge attacks (i.e., using charge bonus into combat) and lunge attacks add 15% to the die roll. Anyone who charges or lunges may not parry, dodge or disengage in next "flurry" of combat.

points damage will either cause your opponent to stagger back, disengaging (0-33 on percentage dice), double up (34-66 per cent) or collapse (67-100 per cent), either of the latter two circumstances giving you a free hack. On an arm, 3 points damage causes any weapon or shield to be dropped. On a leg, 5 points damage will cripple; 3 points will lame (half movement rate thereafter).

Parry, dodge or disengage

Instead of attacking, either you or your opponent may shield parry, weapon parry, dodge or disengage, and this intention must be declared before combat takes place. Calculate all relevant factors as under combat procedure for "all other weapons," including mêlée factors, then further add or deduct according to the following list. Finally, refer to the striking table and throw two percentage dice to see whether you achieve total, substantial or partial success, or fail in your attempt to parry, dodge or disengage.

Room to maneuver: large (50+ sq ft) +2; moderate (30-49 sq ft) +1; medium (20-29 sq ft) 0; small (15-19 sq ft) −1; cramped (14− sq ft) −2. (You cannot disengage other than in a large or moderate area; you cannot dodge other than in a large, moderate or medium area.) Achieved substantial success in last "flurry" +4; achieved partial success in last "flurry" +2.

"Miss/shield or trunk if unshielded" counts as a failure for parry/dodge/disengage. "Trunk/face" counts as partial success. "Head/sword arm" counts as substantial success. All other results count as total success.

PARRY, DODGE, DISENGAGE EFFECT

Effect on opponent's blow	Parry	Dodge	Disengage
Failure	No effect	No effect	No effect
Partial success	−2 points	−2 points	−2 points
Substantial success	Shift 1 column left* −3 points	Shift 1 column left* −4 points	Shift 2 columns left* −4 points
Total success	Take damage on your weapon	Opponent misses you	Opponent misses, you are out of range and he must close again

* On striking table.

Effects of a successful parry on weapons and shields

If damage is greater than the defensive value of a shield, or scores higher than a roll using the combat dice of the opposing weapon, then the shield or the losing weapon is checked on the following table.

WEAPON BREAKAGE

Result	Excess damage						
	1	2	3	4	5	6	7
All OK	0–90	0–84	0–72	0–56	0–46	0–34	0–22
A drops, B, C OK	91–94	85–90	73–80	57–65	47–57	35–45	23–41
A breaks, B drops, C OK	95–97	91–93	81–87	66–75	58–62	46–55	42–53
A, B break, C drops	98–99	94–97	88–92	76–82	63–78	56–65	54–55
All break	100	98–100	93–100	83–100	79–100	66–100	56–100

Large scale combat

A simple definition of large scale combat is one in which the number of men fighting is such that playing them as individuals would be too unwieldy and time-consuming. Exactly where this break is reached depends on a wide variety of factors, including the number of players in an adventure, the number of characters each controls, how many characters are being controlled by the GM and the time available to the players. A reasonable average is probably any combat involving more than 20 or so characters. However, because it *is* flexible, we have opted to provide a variable character-to-figure ratio, by means of which the majority of large scale battles can happily be concluded in a reasonable time. Needless to say, a pocket calculator is virtually indispensable!

Before going on to the rules, however, a few words about preparation are needed. Most wargamers who fight battles in the Ancient and medieval periods understandably make use of the

WEAPON TABLE: DARK AGES

Number	Weapon	Physique needed to use effectively	Agility needed to use effectively	Dice & adds for combat	Weapon factor for parry	Effective length/range	Encumbrance if using other weapon (− on agility)	Dense formation combat alteration	Room needed to wield	Time needed to make ready	Where carried normally on the person	Weight	Class of weapon for breakage & loss	Cost Florins	Special factors
1	Long thrusting spear	13	13	D4+4	No parry	6'	−2	+2	4' behind	Ready	Hand	6 lb	B	20	
2	Thrusting spear	12	12	D4+3	No parry	5'	−2	+2	3' behind	Ready	Hand	5 lb	B	20	
3	Javelin	12 (13)	12 (13)	D4+1 (D4)	No parry	3'6" (60 yds)	−1	+1	2' behind (same)	Slow	Back	2½ lb	A	4	
4	Dart	10 (11)	10 (12)	D4 (D4)	No parry	2' (40 yds)	None	None	1' behind (same)	Medium	Back of shield	1 lb	A	3	
5	Francisca	12 (12)	13 (13)	D4+2 (D4+1)	−2	3' (40 yds)	None	None	None	Quick	R. Hip	2½ lb	B	4	
6	One-handed axe	12	11	D4+3	−1	4'	None	−1	None	Medium	R. Hip	4 lb	B	25	
7	Two-handed axe	14	13	D4+8	−1	6'	−3	−2	3' above or to side	Quick	Hand	8 lb	C	36	
8	Long one-handed sword	12	13	D4+3	+2	5'	−1	−2	2' above or to side	Slow	Back	5 lb-8 lb	C	60	
9	Short sword	11	12	D4+2	+2	4'	None	None	None	Quick	L. Hip	6 lb-8 lb	B	30	
10	Seax	10	11	D4+2	+1	3'6"	None	None	None	Quick	L. Hip	4 lb-6 lb	B	20	May not be used as main gauche

Number Weapon	Physique needed to use effectively	Agility needed to use effectively	Dice & adds for combat	Weapon factor for parry	Effective length/range	Encumbrance if using other weapon (– on agility)	Dense formation combat alteration	Room needed to wield	Time needed to make ready	Where carried normally on the person	Weight	Class of weapon for breakage & loss	Cost Florins	Special factors
11 Dagger	9	10	D4+1	+1	2'6"	None	+1	None	Quick	R. Hip	¼lb-1lb	A	18	May not be used as main gauche
12 Mace	14	13	D4+4	-1	4'6"	None	-1	1' above or to side	Medium	Belt	8lb-9lb	C	30	
13 Club	11	9	D4+1	-1	4'6"	-1	-1	1' above or to side	Ready	Hand	1lb per 2 Phys	B	Free	Find a hefty tree branch
14 Quarterstaff	9	12	D4	+3	2'6"	-2	-2	2' either side	Ready	Both hands	8lb-10lb	B	8	
15 Spiked shield	15	12	D4	Treat as shield	2'6"	None	None	None	Ready	L. Hand	6lb	C	14	+2 strike probability (surprise): no blow with main weapon
16 Light lance	14	14	D4+4	No parry	8'	No other weapon usable	None	None	Ready	Hand	6lb	C	37	Cavalry only
17 Short bow	10	11	D4+3	No parry	(220 yds)	-1	None	None	Slow*	Back	2lb	No breakage or loss	14	
18 Crossbow	12	11	D4+4	No parry	(280 yds)	-2	None	None	Very slow*	Hand	4lb-10lb	No breakage or loss	28	
19 Sling	9	13	D4+1	No parry	(120 yds)	None	-2	2' behind & above	Slow*	Belt	Negligible	Loss	3	

*Unless ready-loaded: then quick. Bracketed numbers are if thrown. "Dense formation" covers warriors similarly armed fighting side by side with 2' or less between them.

WEAPON TABLE: MIDDLE AGES

Number	Weapon	Physique needed to use effectively	Agility needed to use effectively	Dice & adds for combat	Weapon factor for parry	Effective length/range	Encumbrance if using other weapon (– on agility)	Dense formation combat alteration	Room needed to wield	Time needed to make ready	Where carried normally on the person	13lb-15lb	Class of weapon for breakage & loss	Cost Florins	Special factors
20	Heavy lance	15	14	2D4+2	No parry	10'	No other usable	None	None	Ready	Hand	13lb-15lb	B	40	+1 damage when used from horseback
21	Two-handed sword	13	13	2D4	+1	6'	–2	–1	3' all round	Quick Slow	Back	7lb-10lb	B	36	
22	Pole arms (thrusting)	13	12	D4+4	+2	7'	–2	–1	4' all round	Quick Slow	Back	6lb	B	Average 28	+1 if charging into combat
23	Pole arms (slashing)	13	12	D4+2	+3	7'	–2	–2	5' all round	Quick Slow	Back	7lb	B	Average 20	
24	Flail/Morning Star	11	12	D4+2	No parry	5'	–1	–2	3' all round	Quick Slow	Back	9lb	A	32	
25	Pike	13	12	D4+4	No parry	12'	–3	+3	None if trained, 2' if not	Quick	Hand	7lb	A	20	
26	Falchion	10	11	D4+2	+2	4'	None	None	None	Quick	L. Hip	6lb	B	30	
27	War Hammers/Mauls, etc	12	11	D4+3	+1	4'	–1	None	None	Quick	Hand	4lb-5lb	B	30	
28	Stiletto	8	10	D4+2	+1	3'	None	+1	None	Quick Slow	Hand Hidden	¾ lb	A	26	
29	Cinquedea dagger	9	9	D4+2	+1	3'	None	None	None	Quick Med	Belt	1½ lb	B	32	
30	Longbow	14	14	2D4	No parry	(280 yds)	–1	+2	3' all round	Quick	Hand	4lb	A	18	
31	Heavy crossbow	12	11	D6+4	No parry	(280 yds)	–2	+1	4' all round	Medium Slow	Hand Back	8lb-12lb	A	60	
32	Handgun	9	9	2D4	+1	(120 yds)	–3	+1	4' all round	Medium Slow	Hand Back	8lb-12lb	B	60	***

• 5% chance per hit with Morning Star to tangle around opponent's body.

•• Remember the actual length is about 14'-16'. Watch the tight corners!

••• 10% chance of misfire, 2% of explosion in hand, 1 full turn to reload, – on morale of opponent if they do not have guns: treat as hostile magic of higher level.

ARMOR, HELMETS AND SHIELDS

	Type of equipment	Physique needed to use	Agility needed to use effectively	Reduction on agility if worn or carried	Protection afforded (on area covered)	Weight	Cost in Florins	
Armour	1 Scale armor	11	—	–1	4	30 lb	100	**for parry**
	2 Lamellar armor	11	—	–1	4	30 lb	100	
	3 Short mail hauberk	10	—	—	4	20 lb	60	
	4 Long mail hauberk	11	—	–1	5	30 lb	90	
	5 Metal-reinforced leather/cloth (jacket)	9	—	—	3	10 lb	40	
	6 Leather/padded cloth (full suit)	8	—	—	2	5 lb–10 lb	80	
	7 Wolf or bearskin	10	—	–2	2	5 lb–10 lb	Free, but you've got to get it!	
	8 Plate armor (partial)	12	—	–2	6	30 lb	160	
	9 Arming doublet	8	—	—	1	2 lb	9	
	10 Full plate armor	14	—	–3	6	60 lb	240	
Shields	11 Small round shield (Buckler)	10	13	–1	3	4 lb	About 7	C
	12 Large round shield	11	11	–2	4	8 lb	About 10	A
	13 Kite shield (Norman & Byzantine)	11	11	–2	4	8 lb	12	A
	14 Flat-topped knight's shield	10	12	–1	3	6 lb	9	B
	15 Pavise	12	10	–4	5	14 lb	15	A
Helmets	16 Reinforced leather helmet or mail coif	—	—	—	2	1½ lb	15	**Defensive value**
	17 Leather cap	—	—	—	1	½ lb	3	
	18 Metal cap	—	—	—	3	1½ lb	12	
	19 Nasal or faced helmet	—	—	–1 if faced	4	2 lb	17	
	20 Boar-crested helmet	—	—	–1 if faced	3	2¼ lb	16	
	21 Kettle hat, etc	—	—	—	4	2 lb	17	
	22 Full helms	—	—	–1	5	4 lb	About 22	

Note: For items not mentioned check material used in construction against Nos 3, 5, 6 & 8.

widely available and popular playing rules published (now in their 6th edition!) by the Wargames Research Group. As a result, although our actual playing rules differ from theirs, we have decided to stick to the same base sizes so that fantasy wargamers do not need to rebase their figures in order to use these rules.

Close order infantry 15mm; close order cavalry 20mm; open order infantry and cavalry 30 mm; light chariots and wagons, etc., 40 mm.

If your fantasy figures are not already mounted on bases (which can be simply cut out of stiff cardboard and painted to resemble "ground") it is not a bad idea to do so, as it not only means they are then ready for large scale combat, but also makes them easy to pick up without ruining the work you have put into painting them. The above measurements for base sizes refer to the *width;* items like chariots (or dragons) will obviously need a great deal more depth, and the only criterion is that depth should never be *less* than width.

Close order troops are defined as those accustomed to fighting in dense formations; open order troops are usually skirmisher types—javelin men, light archers, slingers and the like—whose main function is to harass the enemy rather than closing in on unequal terms with his two-handed axemen or pikemen.

The way in which our variable character-to-figure ratio works is quite simple. A model figure who, in a normal adventure will just represent himself, is said to have a character-to-figure ratio of one-to-one (1:1). In a large scale battle with, say, 500 men on each side, a ratio of 10:1 might be adopted, in which each model figure *represents* ten men dressed and equipped in similar fashion. If there were 5,000 men on each side, a ratio of 50:1 or 100:1 could be used.

The one thing which is obviously also affected by figure scale is ground scale. A single figure on a 15 mm base representing one man would be occupying a frontage of maybe three feet; if the figure ratio was 10:1 the same 15 mm would represent 30 feet, and so on. To simplify calculation, the accompanying graph cross-references figure ratios with the distance scale.

In the event that all the above is gibberish to you, we regret that space precludes our explaining here all the basics of "ordinary" wargaming. An excellent primer to this is the *PSL Guide to Wargaming,* which explains how wargaming works and gives more background military information on the Ancient and medieval periods (as well as others).

Initial procedures

When a battle appears imminent, and the numbers involved are too great for you to use the group combat rules, the first thing to do is count up the number of model figures of suitable types you have to represent your army, then divide that into the number of actual troops required. Say, for example, that you want to represent a Norman army of 2,400 men, but have only 30 suitable figures available. 2,400 divided by 30 gives a character-to-figure ratio of 80:1, each model representing 80 real men. If your opponent's army should number, say, 2,000 men, divide by the same factor (rounding to the nearest fraction, if necessary): this would mean he should use 25 figures against your 30. It may on occasion be necessary to "fiddle" the figures slightly but you should be able to settle on a ratio which suits the models available. In the unlikely event that neither you nor any other players have any figures available, simple counters cut from cardboard can each be marked with a number indicative of troop type and used instead.

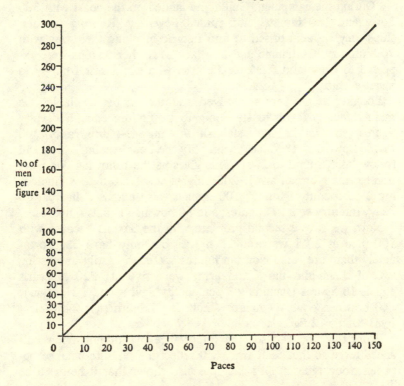

Use above with 20, 25 or 30 mm figures; double with 15 mm figures or smaller; always shift to the multiple of 10 to the left when checking ground scale.

Setting up the game

Now that you know how to set the armies up, let us introduce to-day's contestants: Leofric, a Saxon; and Guillaume, a Norman. Leofric is charged with guarding a section of the English coast and Guillaume fancies a quick raid to collar some loot. The figures each player has available, backed up by those owned by the GM, are as follows.

Saxon troops. 3 personality figures, on foot and mounted; 12 Huscarls; 6 bowmen from the Fyrd; 12 spearmen from the Select Fyrd. *Norman troops.* 2 personality figures, on foot and mounted; 10 Norman and Breton knights; 6 heavy infantry; 6 archers; 6 light cavalry.

"During the campaign, Guillaume landed on the coast with 300 horse and 160 infantry and raided Pevensey. Retiring to their ships they were surprised to find Leofric blocking their way with 700 infantry. Guillaume had to attack as further Saxons were expected to come and reinforce Leofric, who was himself happy to await events."

Looking at the forces involved and the figures available, the main difficulty is obviously going to be finding enough cavalry figures, so *that* has to establish the man-to-figure ratio. 300 divided by 16 is 18.75 so, to simplify the bookkeeping which will follow later, round to 20:1. This gives us the following composition for the Norman army: 200 knights equals 10 figures (including 2 personality figures); 100 light cavalry equals 5 figures; 80 heavy infantry equals 4 figures; and 80 bowmen equals 4 figures.

Now, we have a second problem with the Saxons because with 700 men at 20:1 we need 35 figures but only have 33. Fortunately there are some Norman figures spare, so hastily impressing two of them into the Saxon army we arrive at: 320 Huscarls equals 16 figures (including 3 personality figures and 1 Norman); 140 bowmen equals 7 figures (including 1 Norman); 240 Select Fyrd equals 12 figures.

From this you can see the importance of building up a balanced force so that each army will reflect the real-life balance between troop types.* This example also shows that it helps to be

---

* The observant reader will note that the proportion of Huscarls to Fyrd in this particular scenario is rather higher than normal!

prepared to swap among players since, without the two Norman "recruits," the man-to-figure ratio would have had to have been higher and the number of figures used smaller.

Now it is time to set up the table for the game. The GM will have decided beforehand, or helped the players decide, where the battle will be held. Terrain features such as hills, streams and woods can simply be chalked on the table or, for a better visual appearance, proprietary model trees and river lengths plus hills cut from polystyrene ceiling tiles, painted green, could be used.

"Leofric, after consulting the local people in his army, decided to delay the Normans at the col above the bay where Guillaume had arranged to be met by his ships."

Using the ground scale decided by referring to the preceding graph, you can see that the Saxons might just be able to hold the gap between the trees. "Leofric combined his 560 Huscarls and Select Fyrd and placed them in the gap with his 140 archers split and hidden in the woods at either side. Guillaume, impatient to reach the bay, formed his 200 heavy cavalry in line, supported by his 100 light cavalry. His 160 infantry were split to either side." Here we must leave them while we summarize the rules.

The rules are split into four sections, each of which is taken simultaneously by both forces. If you trust your opponent to play fairly you can simply run through each section as it occurs, or to prevent arguments you can write out secret orders for each move

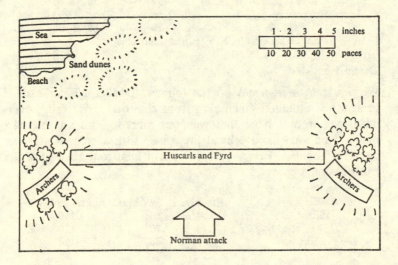

beforehand. The four sections in each move are: *movement* (including compulsory movement); *distant combat* (i.e., with bows, slings, etc.); *close combat;* and *morale.*

Movement

Movement depends on troop type, the action being taken and the terrain over which the movement takes place. However, basic movement rates are:

Troop type	Normal move	Charge bonus
1 Close order infantry	60 paces	25 paces
2 Close order cavalry	100 paces	40 paces
3 Open order infantry	80 paces	30 paces
4 Open order cavalry	150 paces	50 paces
5 Chariots and wagons	80 paces	20 paces

These are subject to the following modifications.

Terrain feature or action	Troop type 1	2	3	4	5
Open woods	−10	−50	−5	−10	−30
Dense woods	−40	−80	−20	−80	Imp
Hedges	−15	−20	−5	−15	Imp
Steep hills	−40	−60	−20	−50	Imp
Slight hills	−5	−30	−5	−20	−20
River over 10′ wide	−40	−80	−30	−60	Imp
Stream under 10′ wide	−15	−30	−5	−20	−20
Earthworks	−20	Imp	−10	Imp	Imp
Using missile weapon	−30	−50	−40	−60	N/A

(Imp = impossible, N/A = not applicable.)

Distant combat

Weapon ranges in paces are as follows. Deduct 25 per cent if firing while mounted (including from chariots) or if firing overhead over troops. Note that weapons marked with an asterisk* may not be used for overhead fire, those with a cross+ may not be used mounted. Heavy crossbows and handguns may only fire every alternate move.

Weapon	Effective range	Maximum range
Sling*	60	100
Staff sling*+	80	120
Short bow	80	120

Crossbow	80	120
Longbow+	120	160
Heavy crossbow+	120	160
Javelin	15	25
Light spear	10	20
Throwing axe	10	20
Rocks	10	—
Handgun	80	120

During each move the unit using the distant weapon will inflict a basic 10 per cent of its own strength as casualties on the opposing unit, subject to the following adjustments. (Thus a force of 60 archers would inflict a basic 6 casualties on the opposing force each move, for example.)

At up to effective range +10 per cent; at between effective and maximum range —5 per cent; firing at close order troops +10 per cent; firing at open order troops —5 per cent; opposing troops unarmored +5 per cent; opposing troops in mail armor —5 per cent; opposing troops in plate armor —10 per cent; opponents using shields —5 per cent; using favored weapon (e.g., English yeoman with longbow) +5 per cent.

Note that there is no deduction for mail and only 5 per cent for plate when firing bows, crossbows and staff slings at less than half effective range.

Having calculated your basic percentage, throw an ordinary six-sided dice, deducting 10 per cent on a throw of 1 or 2 and adding 10 per cent on 5 or 6.

"Impatient with delay, Guillaume ordered forward his archers to fire at the Huscarls and Select Fyrd. They marched forward to within 120 paces of the Saxons—the maximum range of their short bows—and let fly. Plucking up their courage, they advanced to within 60 paces and let fly again."

The results were as follows. In the first firing the archers took their basic factor of 10 per cent, deducted 5 per cent for being at maximum range, added 10 per cent because the Saxons were in close order, deducted 5 per cent for their mail and another 5 per cent for their shields, and threw a 3 on the dice, giving no extra advantage or disadvantage, for a total of 5 per cent. Being 80 strong, they therefore caused 4 casualties. In the second firing all factors were the same except that instead of —5 per cent for range they had +10, for a total of 20 per cent. 20 per cent of 80 being 16, the total casualties inflicted in the two moves of firing were 20, so one Saxon figure had to be removed from the table.

Close combat

This is still calculated on a percentage basis, but slightly differently. In every case, the *smaller* force involved counts as 100 per cent, the larger being assessed in terms of this. In the following diagram, for clarity's sake the man-to-figure ratio has been taken as 10:1. Here we have 50 close order cavalry (5 figures) attacking 200 close order infantry (20 figures). The cavalry are on bases 20 mm wide, the infantry 15 mm. The shaded figures cannot take part in the first round of the mêlée as you are only allowed a one figure overlap on each flank of the smaller force. Thus you can see that there are 9 infantry figures involved (90 men) against the 5 cavalry. Since the cavalry, as the smaller force, counts as 100 per cent, the infantry therefore count as 9/5 × 100 = 180 per cent.

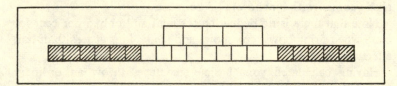

The following adjustments are then made to the percentages.

Troop types	Adjustment	1st round	2nd round
Chariots/cavalry	Long spear	+20	+10
versus	Charging	+20	—
Cavalry/chariots	Close v open order	+20	+10
	v disorganized*	+20	+20
	General with unit	+10	+10
	Opponent shielded	−10	−10
	Attacking rear	+30	+10
Chariots/cavalry	Long spear	+30	+10
versus	Charging	+30	—
Infantry	Close v open order	+20	+10
	Open v open order	+30	−30
	v disorganized*	+30	+30
	General with unit	+10	+10

	Opponent shielded	−10	−10
	Opponent has pike or long spear	−20	−10
	Attacking rear	+30	+10
Infantry	Pike or long spear	+20	+10
versus	v open order	+10	+10
Cavalry/chariots	v disorganized*	+20	+20
	General with unit	+10	+10
	Opponent shielded	−10	−10
	Opponent has long spear	−10	−10
	Opponent charging	−10	—
	Attacking rear	+20	+10
Infantry	Pike or long spear	+30	+15
versus	Close v open order	+20	+15
Infantry	v disorganized	+30	+20
	General with unit	+10	+10
	Opponent shielded	−10	−10
	No pike v pike+	−10	+10
	Opponent charging	−10	—
	Attacking rear	+20	+10

* Troops who lose the first round of a mêlée are disorganized in the second; all troops are disorganized after two rounds. To re-organize (or reform) takes a full move in which the unit may not undertake any other activities.
+ First round deduction does not apply to two-handed axemen or swordsmen.

To your total so far *add* 15 per cent if opponents have no armor or 5 per cent for leather armor, but *deduct* 5 per cent for mail, 15 per cent for mixed plate/mail and 20 per cent for full plate. Then throw a D6 as usual counting −10 per cent for 1 or 2, +10 for 5 or 6.

To calculate casualties, multiply your total score by 10 per cent of the men involved in the mêlée.

"At this point, Guillaume decided to throw in his heavy cavalry, who advanced. They took 10 casualties from the hidden Saxon archers but their morale held good [see later] and they charged home, 190 knights against 320 Saxons [base to base plus one figure overlap on each side]."

The Normans, as the smaller force, count as 100 per cent and the Saxons therefore as $320/190 \times 100 = 168$ per cent. The Norman cavalry add +30 for their long spears, +30 for charging, +10 for their general, Guillaume's, presence, −10 for the

Saxon shields and —8 for the Saxon Fyrd's long spears,* thus 100+30+30+10—10—8 = 152 per cent. The Saxons add +8 for their own spears*, +10 for their general, Leofric's, presence, —10 for the Norman shields, —10 for their long spears and —10 because they are charging, thus 168+8+10—10—10—10 = 156 per cent. Both sides are wearing mail so these scores both come down by 5 per cent. In addition, during this actual game the Saxons threw a 5 on the D6 giving them an additional 10 per cent, while the unlucky Normans scored 1 for —10 per cent.

Casualties were therefore calculated as follows: Normans 15 per cent basic, —5 for opponents' mail, —10 on the dice, ended up with 137; the Saxons 156 per cent basic came down by 5 per cent for their opponents' mail but up 10 on the dice, to end up with 161.

The Normans had 190 men so inflict 10 per cent of 190 times 137 per cent casualties on the Saxons (19 × 137 per cent = 26). The Saxons had 320 men so inflict 32×161 per cent, or 52 casualties (rounded up). The Normans, having already received 10 casualties from archery fire, have to remove three figures from play, the Saxons another one.

As the losers of the mêlée the Normans now recoil and the Saxons may follow up—but first, each side has to take a morale test.

Morale

Morale is checked at the end of each move for each unit which has an enemy unit within 10 paces, which has been under distant fire, which has been in a mêlée or whose basic morale has dropped below 80. It is also checked in the middle of a move if a charging unit comes under distant fire before making contact.

At the beginning of a game, the morale of every unit is taken as being 100 per cent, except that complete novices and untrained militia, etc., start at 90, and veterans of more than three encounters start at 110. You then make the following adjustments.

---

* Since there are 320 Huscarls armed with axes mixed in with 240 Fyrd equipped with spears, additions and deductions for the Saxon spears are only 40 per cent of ±20, i.e., 8.

Armored in mail or better	+ 10
For *each* friendly unit of the same size or larger within 100 paces	+ 5
For each *stronger* enemy unit within 100 paces (infantry menaced by cavalry — 20)	— 10
Victorious in last round of mêlée	+ 10
For each *weaker* enemy unit within 100 paces *unless* total enemy outnumber total friends	+ 5
Unit is more than half nobility	+ 20
Battle is for a religious purpose	+ 10
Troops in open order	— 5
Troops disorganized	— 20
Nearest enemy unit disorganized or retiring	+ 10
Troops impressed into army	— 10
Troops see general killed (see later)	— 20
For *each* friendly unit retiring or routing within 100 paces and in sight	— 10
Surrounded on at least three sides	— 20
General with unit*	± 15
Mercenary*	± 10

* Apply + or — to give best desired effect.

Result

Less than 0 Drop everything, scatter and run like hell (charge bonus) away from enemy.

0-20 Retire with weapons at charge speed away from enemy but break up, scatter and run if attacked.

20-40 Retire as a unit from the field, taking wounded and weapons, marching at normal speed.

40-60 Stop to catch breath for two moves; retire as above if attacked.

60-80 Stop to catch breath for one move; count as disorganized if attacked *or* retire as above.

80-140 Obey orders.

140-160 Advance towards nearest weaker enemy unit.

160-180 Advance towards nearest enemy unit.

180-220 Charge as a formed body at nearest enemy unit.

220 and over Charge as a disorganized open order mob at nearest enemy.

Returning to Leofric and Guillaume, at the end of the mêlée we thus have the following situation.

The Norman knights, being veterans, started the game at a basic morale level of 110. They are armored in mail, so +10, and have Guillaume with them, so ±15, but they are also disorganized having lost so —20 and also have a stronger enemy unit within 100 paces, so —10, giving a final result of between 90 and

WARRIOR TABLE

Culture / Type of warrior	Weapons (for meaning of numbers, see weapon table)	Armor (for meaning of numbers, see armor table)	% composition of typical army	Type of mount (if any)	Movement (per minute) Mounted	Movement (per minute) On foot	Charge bonus	Special factors
Viking								
Early chieftain (1)	2 Javelins (3), shortsword (9),	Mail corselet (4), faced helmet (16), lge round shield (11)	1 per army	H	200 yds	120 yds	50% if horsed 25% foot	7th century and before. WRG class: HI.
Early warrior (2)	1 Javelin (3), scramaseax (10)	Leather corselet (8), mail helmet (13), sml shield (12)	40-80%	None	—	160 yds	25% foot	7th century and before. WRG class: LMI/Irreg C.
Late chieftain (3)	Two-handed axe, dagger (11) or longsword (8)	Long mail corselet (5), faced helmet (16), lge rd shield (11)	1 per army	H	220 yds	120 yds	50% if horsed 25% foot	Shield is spiked and may be used offensively. 8th century +. WRG class: HI.
Huscarl (4)	Longsword (8), dagger (11), 2 darts (4), spear (2) or axe (7)	Mail corselet (3), nasal helmet (16), lge rd shield (11)	Up to 33%	M	200 yds	120 yds	50% if horsed 25% foot	Shield is spiked and may be used offensively. 8th century +. WRG class: HI/Irreg B.
Bondi (5)	Long spear (1), javelin (3), shortsword (9) or axe (6) or bow (17)	Padded leather (6), leather helmet (14), lge rd shield (11)	40-80%	Nag	180 yds	120 yds	50% if horsed 25% foot	8th century +. WRG class: MI/Irreg C.
Berserker (6)	As Huscarl or two shortswords (9)	Wolf/bearskin (9) or nothing. No helmet, shield (11) unless 2-swords	Up to 20% early & late	Nag	180 yds	160 yds	50% if horsed 25% foot	All period. WRG class: LMI/Irreg A.
Archer (7)	Short bow (17), quiver (30 arrows), scramaseax (10)	Quilted leather (6), sml shield (12)	Up to 15% early Up to 20% late	None	—	160 yds	25% foot	All period. WRG class: LI/Irreg C.

Culture	Type of warrior	Weapons (for meaning of numbers, see weapon table)	Armor (for meaning of numbers, see armor table)	% composition of typical army	Type of mount (if any)	Movement (per minute)			Special factors
						Mounted	On foot	Charge bonus	
Viking	Slinger (8)	Dagger (11), sling (9)	Leather (7), sml shield (12)	4% early 5% late	None	—	160 yds	25% foot	All period. WRG class: LI/Irreg C.
	Peasant "militia"(9)	Club (13), Javelin (3) or francisca (5)	Leather (7), sml shield (12)	Up to 50% early Up to 30% late	None	—	160 yds	25% foot	All period. Only found in armies fighting at home in Scandinavia. WRG class: LI/Irreg D.
	"Hero"(10)	Long spear (1), two-handed axe (7), short-sword (9) or axe (6), (17) or (3) or (4)	As late chieftain	—	M	200 yds	120 yds	50% if horsed 25% foot	8th century +. Before then use"early chieftain."
Anglo-Saxon	Early chieftain (1)	Light spear (2) or shortsword (9), scamaseax (10)	Mail corselet (3), boar helmet (17)	1 per army	M	200 yds	120 yds	50% if horsed 25% foot	5th-7th centuries. WRG class: HI.
	Early warrior (2)	Light spear (2), scramaseax (10)	Leather (7), sml shield (12)	40-80%	None	—	160 yds	25% foot	5th-7th centuries. WRG class: LMI/Irreg C.
	Late chieftain (3)	Light spear (2), shortsword (9)	Long mail (5), mail helmet (13), or faced (16), shield (11)	1 per army	H	220 yds	120 yds	50% if horsed 25% foot	8th century-1066.* May only be used as cavalry when pursuing a beaten foe. WRG class: HI.
	Huscarl (4)	Axe (7) or light spear (2), shortsword (9)	Long mail (5), metal helm (15) or nasal helm (16), shield (10)	Up to 25%	M	220 yds	120 yds	50% if horsed 25% foot	950-1066.* May only be used as cavalry when pursuing a beaten foe. WRG class: HI/Irreg B.
	Upper-class warrior (5)	Light spear (2), shortsword (9)	Reinforced leather (6) & helm (13), lge shield (11)	Up to 5%	M	200 yds	120 yds	50% if horsed 25% foot	8th century-1066. WRG class: LHI/Irreg C.
	"Lower-class" warrior (6)	Light spear (2), scramaseax (10)	Leather coat (7) & helm (14), sml shield (12)	Up to 25%	Nag	180 yds	160 yds	50% if horsed 25% foot	8th century-1066. WRG class: LMI/Irreg C.

WARRIOR TABLE, CONTINUED

Culture	Type of Warrior	Weapons (for meaning of numbers, see weapon table)	Armor (for meaning of numbers, see armor table)	% composition of typical army	Type of mount (if any)	Movement (per minute) Mounted	On foot	Charge bonus	Special factors
Anglo-Saxon	Select fyrdman (7)	Light spear (2), short-sword (9), javelin (3) or francisca (5)	Long mail (5), reinf. leather helm (13), lge shield (11)	Up to 75%	Nag	200 yds	120 yds	50% if horsed 25% foot	8th century-1066. WRG class: HI/Irreg C.
	General fyrdman (8)	Club (13), javelin (3) or francisca (5)	Leather armor (7): sml shield (12)	Up to 60% all period	None	—	160 yds	25% foot	All period. Home armies only. WRG. class: LMI/Irreg D.
	Slinger (9)	Dagger (11), sling (19)	None	Up to 3% all period	None	—	160 yds	25% foot	Often Welsh (in service). All period. WRG class: LI/Irreg C.
	Archer (10)	Short bow (17), quiver (20 arrows), dagger (11)	Leather (7), leather cap (14)	Up to 6%	None	—	160 yds	25% foot	900-1066. WRG class: LI/Irreg C.
	Javelin man (11)	4 Javelins (3), dagger (11)	Leather coat (7) & cap (14) sml shield (12)	Up to 6%	None	—	160 yds	25% foot	8th century-1066. WRG class: LI/Irreg C.
	Norman-style knight (12)	Lance (16), longsword (8)	Long mail (5), nasal helm (16), kite shield (10)	Up to 10%	H	240 yds	120 yds	50% if horsed 25% foot	1030-66 only. Rare. WRG class: HC/Irreg B.
	"Hero"(13)	Light spear (2) or axe (7): longsword (8)	Long mail (5), nasal or faced helm (16), kite shield (10)	—	H	220 yds	120 yds	50% if horsed 25% foot	8th century-1066. Before then use "early chieftain."
Irish	Chieftain (1)	Shortsword (9), lt spear (2), 2 darts (4)	Padded leather (6), sml shield (12), leather cap (14)	1 per army	H	200 yds	160 yds	50% if horsed 25% foot	All period. May use a light chariot in battles up to 750. WRG class: LHI.
	"Hero" or axeman (2)	Axe (7) and shortsword (9) or longsword (8)	Leather (7) & cap (14), sml shield (12)	Up to 30%	None	—	160 yds	25% foot	9th century-1066. WRG class: LHI/Irreg C.
	Common warrior (3)	Lt spear (2), shortsword (9) 2 darts (4)	None, sml shield (12)	Up to 100% all period: may use bows	None	—	160 yds	25% foot	All period. WRG class: LMI/Irreg C. Archers will be LI/Irreg C.

Culture	Type of warrior	Weapons (for meaning of numbers, see weapon table)	Armor (for meaning of numbers, see armor table)	% composition of typical army	Type of mount (if any)	Movement (per minute) Mounted	On foot	Charge bonus	Special factors
Welsh	"Hero" or chieftain (1)	Lt spear (2), shortsword (9)	Padded leather (6), & cap (14); lge shield (11)	1 per army	H	200 yds	160 yds	50% if horsed 25% foot	All period. WRG class: LHI.
	Early Welsh infantry (2)	Lt spear (2), one-handed axe (6) or dagger (11)	Leather (7) & cap (14); lge shield (11)	Up to 100%	None	—	160 yds	25% foot	500-750. WRG class: LMI/Irreg C.
	Late Welsh infantry (3)	Lt spear (2), one-handed axe (6), dagger (11)	Leather (7) & cap (14); lge shield (11)	Up to 100%	None	—	160 yds	25% foot	750-1066. WRG class: LMI/Irreg C.
	Welsh archer (4)	Short bow (17), quiver (20 arrows), dagger (11)	Leather (7)	Up to 20% early Up to 25% late	None	—	160 yds	25% foot	All period. WRG class: LI/Irreg C.
	Slinger (5)	Sling (18), dagger (11)	None	Up to 5% all period	None	—	160 yds	25% foot	All period. WRG class: LI/Irreg C.
Picts & Scots	Early chieftain (1)	Spear (1), shortsword (9)	None, sml shield (12)	1 per army	M	180 yds	160 yds	50% if horsed 25% foot	500-900. "Hero," WRG class: MI.
	Late chieftain (2)	Spear (1): shortsword (9), 2 javelins (3)	Padded leather (6), cap (14), sml shield (12)	1 per army	M	200 yds	120 yds	50% if horsed 25% foot	900-1066. "Hero," WRG class: LHI.
	Early warrior (3)	Spear (1); dagger (11) or hand axe (6)	None	Up up 100%: half may use bow	None	—	160 yds	25% foot	500-900. WRG class: LMI/Irreg C.
	Late warrior (4)	Spear (1): dagger (11) or axe (6): javelins (3) or bow (17)	Leather coat (7), sml shield (12)	Up to 100%	None	—	160 yds	25% foot	900-1066. WRG class: LMI/Irreg C.
	Pictish cavalry (5)	5 Javelins (3), shortsword (9)	Mail corselet (3), metal cap (15), sml shield (12)	Up to 20%	L	200 yds	160 yds	50% if horsed 25% foot	500-900. WRG class: LC/Irreg C.
	Scottish select warrior (6)	Light spear (2), shortsword (9), 2 javelins (3)	Mail coat (3), reinf. cap (13), lge shield (11)	Up to 40%	M	180 yds	120 yds	50% if horsed 25% foot	900-1066. WRG class: LHI/Irreg C.
	Scottish huscarl (7)	Axe (7) or spear (1): dagger (11): darts (4)	Mail coat (3), metal cap (15) lge shield (11)	Up to 25%	M	200 yds	120 yds	50% if horsed 25% foot	1010-1066. WRG class: HI/Irreg B.

WARRIOR TABLE, CONTINUED

Type of warrior	Weapons (for meaning of numbers, see weapon table)	Armor (for meaning of numbers, see armor table)	% composition of typical army	Type of mount (if any)	Movement (per minute) Mounted	Movement (per minute) On foot	Charge bonus	Special factors
Culture								
About 1100 AD								
Local militia (1)	Improvised pole arms/slings/bow	None	Up to 25%	None	—	160 yds	25% foot	Average factors, vary according to nationality.
Yeoman (2)	Bow/sword crossbow javelin/sling	Brigantine, open helmet/Aqueton	Up to 25%	Nag	180 yds	160 yds	25% on foot	Longbow, English +1SS. Only lighter troops, no "armor."
Sergeant (3)	Lance/sword, axe/mace	Mail, open helmet shield	Up to 10%	M	220 yds	120 yds	35% on horse / 15% on foot	No horse armor, probably not full mail, may be scale.
Knight (4)	As sergeant	As sergeant but full mail	Up to 40%	M	220 yds	120 yds	35% on horse / 15% on foot	Throw D6, 1-3 = "+", 4-6 = "-".
Nobleman, King's Officer (5)	As sergeant	As sergeant but full mail	Single figures	2 M	220 yds	120 yds	35% on horse / 15% on foot	Throw D6, 1-3 = "+", 4-6 = ";".
Squire, page (6)	Dagger	None	As Knight	M	220 yds	130 yds	35% on horse / 15% on foot	Knight's servant only—no combat usually.
Military Orders, Knights (7)	As Knight	As Knight	Up to 10%	M	220 yds	120 yds	35% on horse / 15% on foot	+1 on social status if going or been on Crusade.
Military Orders, other fighting men (8)	As Yeoman	As Yeoman	Up to 15%	M	200 yds	140 yds	25% on foot	

Culture	Type of warrior	Weapons (for meaning of numbers, see weapon table)	Armor (for meaning of numbers, see armor table)	% composition of typical army	Type of mount (if any)	Movement (per minute)			
						Mounted	On foot	Charge bonus	
About 1300 AD	Mercenary infantry, Yeoman, Trained Bands (1)	Bow/crossbow, pike/sword	Padded cloth, jack shield/pavise, leather buff coat, kettlehelm	Up to 25%	Perhaps Nag	180 yds	140 yds	25% on foot	English longbow +1 SS Mercenary –1 SS, +5 money
	Sergeant, Mercenary Knight (2)	Lance/sword, axe/Mace	Mail, open helm, shield	Up to 25%	M	200	100	25%	Mercenary –1 SS, +8 money.
	Knight, Nobleman, King's Officer (3)	As Sergeant	Close helm, mail hauberk, plate cuisse & greaves, shield	Up to 30%	M	180 yds	90 yds	25%	King's Officer, Nobleman +2 SS, +15 money
	Squire, page (4)	As 1100	Shield	As Knight					
	Gunners (5)	Sword, siege guns	None	5% Max	Nag	160 yds	140 yds	N/A	See rules on guns
About 1475 AD	"Regular" infantry (1)	Bow/crossbow, sword/hand gun, pike, halbards, etc.	Usually some to half plate, helmet (open), pavise, small shield	25%–40%	Nag	160 yds	100 yds	15%	If mercenary –1 on bravery +5 on money.
	Men-at-arms (2)	Heavy lance, sword, mace	Full plate, frontal horse armor	15%–25%	H	160 yds	85 yds	20% mounted 15% foot	Mercenary as above.
	Household Knights, Gendarmes (3)	Heavy lance, sword, mace	Full plate, some full horse armor	5%–12%	EH	140 yds	85 yds	20% mounted 15% foot	Mercenary as above.
	Gunners (4)	Sword, field & siege guns, halbard, etc	Some plate, open helmet	8% Max	Nag	160 yds	130 yds	N/A	Mercenary as above.
	Light horse (5)	Javelins, mace, saber	Mail, shield, splint armor, open helmet	10%–20%	L	200 yds	120 yds	25%	Skirmish-trained.
	Urban militia (6)	Pike, handgun, crossbow, halbard	Some plate mail, open helmet, pavise	Up to 50%	None	— yds	100 yds	15%	

105, depending on how they apply their general's factor, so "obey orders" is the result.

The Saxons, being mostly Huscarls and therefore also veterans, started at a basic morale level of 110 too. They are also armored in mail and have their general with them for an additional +10 ±15, but they were victorious in the mêlée, have a weaker enemy unit within 100 paces, an enemy which is also retiring disorganized, so add another 10 + 5 + 10 to end up with a morale of 130 to 145, depending on the application of the general's factor. In this situation it was up to the Saxon player whether he took the lower factor and made his troops do what he wished them to, or the higher one which would have resulted in them pursuing the Norman knights.

"The cavalry retired to think again about attacking a Saxon shield wall. The Huscarls leaned on their axes and the Fyrd on their spears, remarking among themselves what lousy opponents Normans made."

Personality and leader figures

If your personal character is fighting with the army, you must expect a chance of getting him wounded or killed. Whether you gain experience from a battle is up to the GM's decision. If you opt to fight in the front rank he will look more favorably on you, but you also double your chances of getting thumped.

To calculate the chances of your getting wounded or killed, take the number of men killed in a mêlée or firefight as a percentage of the total unit strength. If you then throw that number or less on a percentage dice you've had it. If you fight in the front rank, you must throw better than *double* that number.

In the preceding example, Guillaume was riding with his knights who lost 62 men out of their original 200, so he must roll better than 31 per cent (i.e., 32 per cent or above) to survive. Leofric was also with his troops, who suffered a total of 46 casualties from archery and close combat out of a starting strength of 320, a total of 14 per cent. Leofric thus has to throw 15 or better to emerge unscathed.

To find out whether you are lightly wounded, seriously wounded or killed, divide the percentage score thrown by five, giving you five groups of numbers. Rounding to the nearest number divisible by five makes the above 30 and 15 respectively. In the first case 0-12 would be a light wound, 13-24 a serious wound and 25-32 dead; in the second, 0-6 would be a light wound, 7-12 serious and 13-14 dead.

With a light wound you may fight on or leave the field. With a serious wound you fall to the ground and remain there until the battle is over. If you're dead you're dead unless someone works a miracle!

Active magic rules

Magic in *Fantasy Wargaming* is broadly divided into two types: the "active" and "passive" modes. "Passive magic" is the observation and detection of the magical influences at work in any given situation; it includes astrology, the tarot and other forms of Divination. In this section, we are interested in Active magic—by which Sorcerers use arcane forces to alter and shape the world around them, mainly through spells.

A spell can take many forms, requiring different types of preparation and material depending on the nature of the magic user. All, however, can be separated into two processes. The first is the establishment of a link or channel through the Ethereal plane, connecting the magic user to the target of his sorcery. This link requires great subtlety and faith, the intelligent carrying out of preparations, manipulation of the hidden forces at work in the world through magical items and the great medieval system of correspondencies, personal resilience—and luck. The second stage is a command: thought, spoken or inscribed, an act of personal willpower directed at the fabric of the universe and often at a particular, sentient or inanimate target. Once the link has been established, up to three spells (or seven absolute commands) by the Mage may be made before renewal becomes necessary, provided (a) that these spells and commands occur within 30 minutes of establishment, (b) there is no radical change in circumstances (GM's discretion).

Basic magic calculation (1): the link

Magic level of the Mage plus—
Faith: 8 or below, —2; 9-10, —1; 11-13, 0; 14-15, +1; 16-18, +2; 19-24, +3; 25 or above, +4.

Intelligence: 8 or below, —1; 14 or above, +1.

Luck: ± in the usual way.

Preparations carried out: + (add); max +4.

Enchanted devices (magical items) used to assist spell: +.

Protective devices (religious and magical items, spells, pentacles) used by the target against spells: — (subtract).

The System of Correspondencies: incidental links between the spell and situation: ± (add or subtract as appropriate).

Mage failed in his last magical operation: —1.

Availability of target: target is visible to Mage, +2; target is not visible but within 1 mile, +1; range 1-5 miles, —1; over 5 miles, —2; location/nature of target unknown, —1 (for each).

Mage's birth sign is controller/diminisher of spell: ±1.

Target's birth sign is controller/diminisher of spell: ±1.

DD (Degree of Difficulty) of spell: Halve (round *down*) and subtract.

Spell is mastered/done under instruction from a Mage, book, etc./without knowledge: +1/0/—2.

Propitious/unpropitious physical circumstances. Mage is exhausted /demoralized/wet through/isolated/badly injured/captive: —1 each up to max —3; Mage is in direct peril of his life/in a place of battle: —2/—1; Mage is at home/in a quiet and familiar place/supported: +1 each up to max +2.

Spell specialization factor: ± factor.

Add together the various factors and throw against the table below.

	0 or below	1	2	3	4	5	6-7	8-9	10-11	12-14	15-17	18-20	21-24	25 & over
							Numbers							
Link established	0-5%	0-10%	0-19%	0-28%	0-37%	0-46%	0-54%	0-62%	0-70%	0-78%	0-85%	0-92%	0-95%	0-99%
Failure of Link	6%-100%	over 10%	over 19%	over 28%	over 37%	over 46%	over 54%	over 62%	over 70%	over 78%	over 85%	over 92%	over 95%	100%

Link established. Communication between the Mage and the target through the Ethereal plane is established. Proceed to next stage. Mana loss = half DD of spell attempted.

Failure of Link. No line of communication has been established. Mage loses mana points equal to half the DD of the spell attempted (round up).

Basic magic calculation (2): "saving throw"

This stage only applies to sentient targets with faith 12+, or magic/religious level 2+. Such targets will feel a "touch" on establishment of the link. They may then *either* appeal to an Ethereal power for intervention *or* put up a quick counter-command, to desist. Since the link already exists, this counter-spell involves only an amended form of BMC(3), "command." The amendments reflect the superior position of the first Mage, who has the advantages of preparation, surprise, and a battlefield (link) of his own choice.

Magic level of Mage casting counter-spell minus—

2 × magic level of first mage: —

DD of command to desist: —3

Thereafter as per BMC(3).

If these "saving throws" are successful, the first Mage will suffer mana loss equal to the DD of the original spell attempted. The target Mage, whether successful or not, will suffer after counter-spell mana loss as per BMC(3).

Basic magic calculation (3): the command

Multiple target: 2 = —1; 3-4 = —2; 5-10 = —3; 11-20 = —4; 21-50 = —5; 51+ = —6.

2 × magic level of Mage: + (minimum +1).

Magic level (if any) of target (highest ML if many): — (but *ignore* if target wants spell to succeed).

DD of spell: —.

Faith of Mage is 3+ points higher than target (sentient targets only)/ lower than target: ±1.

Charisma of Mage, etc., likewise: ±1.

Word of command is thought/spoken/inscribed: 0/+1/+1 (accumulative).

Command is echoed by another Mage's spell*: add number of Mages up to +4.

Mage pledges (in advance!) 50/100 per cent extra mana loss: +1/+2.

The true name of the target is cited in the command: +1.

* Each Mage's spell must be gone through separately, the same + factor being added to each (if spells are simultaneous).

Add together the various factors and throw against the table below.

				Numbers						
−2 or −1 below	0	1–2	3–4	5–7	8–10	11–14	15–19	20–26	27 and above
Success 0–5%	0–15%	0–25%	0–35%	0–45%	0–55%	0–65%	0–75%	0–85%	0–95%	0–99%
Failure 6% +	16% +	26% +	36% +	46% +	56% +	66% +	76% +	86% +	96% +	100%

Success. Apply effects of the spell. *Failure.* Sorry!

Mana loss. Whether successful or not, the Mage expends mana. This is equal to the DD of the spell plus magic level (if any) of *unwilling* target plus any additions made for pledges.

Explanation of factors

Magic level. This registers the amount of magical experience accumulated by the Mage from previous operations and activities: the technical knowledge of the user. Magical experience is explained elsewhere. Magic level is especially important at the "command" stage, which is essentially a combat of magical power.

Faith. This intuitive understanding of the Ethereal plane is accordingly more important in establishing the link than enforcing the command: it helps the Mage "find his path" to the target. It is only of incidental use in overcoming the resistance of a (sentient) target.

Intelligence. Rational ability can help the Mage interpret evidence from the Ethereal plane during the link.

Charisma. The self-confidence of Mage and (sentient) target can similarly influence the impact of a command.

Luck. In magic as in all human and, indeed, divine affairs, the impact of fortune has its place.

Availability of target. Visibility enhances the Mage's ability to create an Ethereal link. Similarly, ignorance of the place or nature of the target disadvantages the Mage.

Physical circumstances. These affect the ability of the Mage to concentrate fully during the link. Since the act of command is an arcane exercise of willpower, and almost reflex, it is not affected by physical difficulties.

Failure in last magical operation. This affects the self-confidence and so the concentration of the Mage.

Birth signs. Like all creatures, the Mage—and sometimes the target—has a dominant astrological sign. Spells, by their nature, similarly come under astrological influences to increase or decrease their effectiveness. These "controllers/diminishers" are given in the spell tables.

Learned/mastered spells. Magic is partly intuitive, partly willpower—and partly the learning of formulae by which the link through the Ethereal plane is created. To master or learn a spell, the Mage must cast it three times in succession, successfully, within the space of six hours and with no intervening magical activity. His struggle is greatly aided by the possession of a book, scroll, etc., in which the spell is described, or by the help and tuition of another Mage. A powerful, highly intuitive or lucky Mage may, however, be able to find the right path through the Ethereal plane, or even establish his own, fresh channel appropriate for the spell. Mages in *Fantasy Wargaming* may therefore try to cast spells without certain knowledge of their nature.

True name. Ethereal spirits of animate beings have true names, just as their animate counterparts on Earth have names. Humans' names are usually their true names also; but some characters, especially Mages, may take a pseudonym to conceal their own true name. Inanimate objects and their spirits have no names, true or otherwise. True names may be discovered in various ways: by appeals to God and the Devil (DD6), by commanding a spirit, person, etc., to name himself (DD3), or (for the names of Higher and Lower Powers) by reading grimoires. Beware—the last may not be accurate! "The Name of a Thing is the Thing, and has the Power of the Thing."

Inscribed commands. Certain Mages, notably cabalists and runic sorcerers, can amplify or replace spoken commands with symbols and words of command—written, inscribed, drawn or carved. Inscribed commands have the benefit of permanency. A written command fastened to the target after casting will maintain the order indefinitely, until it is destroyed or removed. Carved commands on a magic item have the same effect. Symbols, words, etc., may be left as traps in an adventure, the command being triggered by *any* passing creature that looks at them. Beware: this can be costly in mana loss! The symbol provides an automatic link in these cases: simply apply BMC(3). Inscribing such commands requires Literacy, Agility of 14+, Faith and Intelligence of 13+ plus knowledge of which symbols, etc., to use. Cabalists, runic sorcerers, etc., will know automatically. Other Mages must consult them, books of magic demons, or other Powers. Notes: 1

Mana loss occurs when the command is triggered, not written; 2
the target does not have to understand the symbol or word, or
even be sentient. It must, however, be a living, Ethereal or Undead being for the "trigger" effect to occur.

The System of Correspondencies

PHYSICAL CORRESPONDENCIES

Star sign	Planet	Dates	Day	Hours of day	Element	Metal	Gem
Aquarius	Uranus	Jan 20-Feb 18	Saturday	2.0-3.0	Air	Tin	Opal
Pisces	Neptune	Feb 19-Mar 20	Thursday	3.0-4.0	Water	Bronze	Pearl
Aries	Mars	Mar 21-Apr 20	Tuesday	4.0-5.0	Fire	Iron	Ruby
Taurus	Venus	Apr 21-May 20	Friday	5.0-6.0	Earth	Copper	Sapphire
Gemini	Mercury	May 21-June 20	Wednesday	6.0-7.0	Air	Mercury	Onyx
Cancer	Moon	Jun 21-Jul 20	Monday	7.0-8.0	Water	Silver	Emerald
Leo	Sun	Jul 21-Aug 21	Sunday	8.0-9.0	Fire	Gold	Topaz
Virgo	Mercury	Aug 22-Sep 22	Wednesday	9.0-10.0	Earth	Mercury	Diamond
Libra	Venus	Sep 23-Oct 22	Friday	10.0-11.0	Air	Copper	Jade
Scorpio	Mars	Oct 23-Nov 22	Tuesday	11.0-12.0	Water	Iron	Aquamarine
Sagittarius	Jupiter	Nov 23-Dec 20	Thursday	12.0-1.0	Fire	Tin	Cornelian
Capricorn	Saturn	Dec 21-Jan 19	Saturday	1.0-2.0	Earth	Lead	Garnet

Wood	Herbs	Color	Number	Body (inc. ills and wounds)	Beasts	Type of place	Particular aspects of human life
Elm	Fumitory Mullein Barley	Transparent	4	Legs	Horses	Wetlands	Magic, treasure-seeking, friendship with comrades
Beech	Meadowsweet Rosehip Lungwort	Blue	10	Feet	Fish, frogs etc	Open water	Religion, mysticism, treachery, travel
Oak	Rosemary Marjoram Cowslip	Green	1	Brain	Sheep	Hills	Individual combat, deeds of strength & valor
Hornbeam	Mint Thyme Tansy	Black	6	Head	Cattle	Fields	Health & curing, endurance, leisure
Willow	Dill Parsley Lavender	Violet	11	Chest	Deer	Woods	Communications, gathering of knowledge, concealed things
Thorn	Balm Agrimony Daisy	Pink	8	Guts	Shellfish, insects	Underground	Fortune, madness, rational thought
Mistletoe	Bay Rue Saffron	Yellow	12	Heart	All cats	Plains	Worldly power, justice, leadership
Pine	Fennel Valerian Savory	White	7	Sex organs	Unicorn rodents	Heaths	Love, sex, language, worldly knowledge
Yew	Yarrow Violet Dandelion	Red	2	Hips	All dogs	Towns	Peace, cooperation, commerce, organisation
Fir	Basil Nettles Tarragon	Orange	5	Stomach	Scorpion, snakes	Deserts	War, vengeance, evil deeds, scheming
Poplar	Sage Chervil Samphire	Grey	3	Arms, hands	Birds bats	Highlands	Humor, teaching, resurrection, defense
Ash	Comfrey Sorrel Beet	Brown	9	Lungs	Goats	Icy wastes	Death, failure, old age, destruction

Astral signs six places on from each other are opposite: e.g., Aquarius and Leo.

Mana loss. Mana—the emanation of the Ether Elemental by which all operations in or involving the Ethereal plane take place —is accumulated and concentrated in the Mage by various techniques and preparations. Mana is difficult to handle: there is a maximum which any Mage can accumulate ($16 \times$ magic level), while normal operating level is half this. Mana is expended by active magic, during the link as well as in command. To pledge extra mana in advance of command is to determine on a crushing act of willpower that will leave the Mage drained. Lost mana returns to the Ether Elemental.

The System of Correspondencies: explanation

The System of Correspondencies is the central element in medieval arcane thought, and therefore in *Fantasy Wargaming*. It can be defined as the system of invisible levers by which the physical universe is run—by God, the Devil, the "Primum Mobile," or whomever. At its heart are 12 Ethereal forces, the Signs of the Zodiac. These are linked to physical phenomena: times of day, days, dates of the year; colors, numbers, types of place; animals, parts of the human body, aspects of human life; gems, metals, elements, plants, trees—and many more not covered in the accompanying chart. By affecting one or more of these phenomena, magically, you can influence the whole system and so alter the nature of the universe. That same universe, including your own surroundings and body, are similarly affected by the action and interaction of the Ethereal forces.

The system was used both for passive magic—divination—and for active. The former use will be explained in more detail later. In active magic—Sorcery—the system has two main effects. One is in the creation of magical devices; the other is its incidental use during the establishment of a link.

Most places and situations are influenced more or less indifferently by every Ethereal force; but a few may be under the particular influence of one or more sign. In designing his adventure, the GM should use the Correspondencies, creating places and scenarios under such influence. Players should similarly try to assess what influence is present at each stage in their progress, by comparing the Correspondencies on the chart with the visible world around them. Both GM and player should note the changing pattern of influences with time. The GM must decide whether to allow his players *carte blanche* to detect influences, or to restrict such detection to those whose characters might reasonably by expected to look out for the arcane. The latter adds authenticity. Purists may wish to apply the following calculation for players claiming to have detected an influence, or asking if their characters could do so:

Detection of Ethereal influences

Magic level of Mage plus—
Faith: 8 or below = —2; 9-10 = —1; 14-16 = +1; 17-19 = +2; 20+ = +3.
Intelligence: as faith.
Number of common factors present: 3-4 = +1; 5-7 = +2; 8-11 = +3; more = +4.
Luck: ± in the usual way.
Mage is a specialist Diviner/Astrologer = +1/+2.

Multiply by six and throw under with percentage dice for successful detection.

The number of Correspondencies determines the extent of the Ethereal influence. There must be at least three common factors for any influence to exist. An open field with cattle and a hornbeam is under the minor influence of Taurus; the same field will show much more influence if there are six hornbeams and cattle, if there are large patches of mint in one corner, and if it is 5:30 on a Friday in late April! The rule is the same in detection, Sorcery and the creation of magical items: 3-4 common factors = +1; 5-7 = +2; 8-11 = +3; 12 and over = +4. GMs should be discreet in identifying or accepting "common factors": one swallow does not make a Sagittarius! The birth sign of the character *is* a factor.

Use of factors in Sorcery. Spells are controlled and diminished by different signs. The birth sign of the Mage or target can therefore affect their performance. Similarly, a spell controlled by Taurus will be more effective in the field above than elsewhere. A spell diminished by the Bull will be correspondingly *less* easy to cast. The ± figures above are simply transplanted into the calculation of the link.

Use of the System in non-Magical operations (Optional). GMs may at their discretion wish to use the System of Correspondencies for other purposes: e.g., arguing that a warrior born under Taurus might function more effectively in a place or situation governed by that sign, and one born under Scorpio (the opposite sign) less effectively. No more than ±1 should, however, be assigned for such effects, in any calculations.

The creation of magical devices

Almost anything can be a magical device: a twist of wool, a wax image, a cup, a bunch of herbs, a thorn branch, a place or an animal. To those who have studied the System of Correspondencies, the reason will be clear. A magical device is a physical object into which has been bound by Enchantment a small part of one or more of the Zodiacal forces. Once created, the device is a repository of those bound forces, and an aid usable by the Sorcerer in casting a spell controlled by the relevant star sign. A wand of Taurus (made of hornbeam, painted black, with six copper bands and a sapphire set therein) thus enhances the link of spells controlled by the Bull. Devices may also be created to aid a limited number of spells only, at very powerful effect, or to protect the possessor against the use of magic. Mages may also create Enchanted items meant not for the casting of spells but for physical purposes—combat being the most obvious example. All this is done through the System of Correspondencies.

The more Correspondencies or common factors linked in the device, the greater its potency in establishing the link. The wand of Taurus above thus has five Correspondencies, giving +2; if it was enchanted at the correct time, day and date, however, in an open field, it would have nine common factors and a potency of +3 (see above). Devices can be created covering more than one star sign; but what they add in versatility, they more than lose in strength.

Stages of creation

Assembly of the item. Note: if the device covers two or more star signs, it must have the same Correspondencies from each. A seal of fire might thus have a gem, metal and color from each of the fire signs—Aries, Leo and Sagittarius. Note: human and animal effects—e.g., the heart of a lion—may only be used after their death and dismemberment. Otherwise it is Conjuration.

Enchantment. This is the process by which the appropriate Ethereal influences are fixed and bound into the device. It is in itself a piece of active magic requiring preparation, the establishment of a link, and command—in the usual way. Note: the spell of binding has no particular controller or diminisher, and so no alterations in the link should be made for the System of Correspondencies, or the birth sign of the Mage and his target, or for the use of enchanted devices. The DD of the spell is equal to the number of *physical* Correspondencies in the device, plus 1. The +3 wand of Taurus has five physical Correspondencies and so a DD of 6; so, coincidentally, has the +2 wand enchanted in a less propitious time and place. The seal of fire described above has three physical Correspondencies from three signs, giving a DD of 10 for three separate effects of +1!

The use of Enchanted devices in Sorcery

The main use is to enhance the link when casting a spell controlled by the same star sign as that in the device: simply add the +factor to the BMC. Be careful, though! Each spell has its diminisher as well as its controller; if you have in your possession (on you or nearby) other devices of the diminishing sign, you must *subtract* their +factors from the enhancement! Enhancement may never be less than −2 or more than +5, however many devices are used. The law of diminishing returns is enshrined in the Ethereal plane, as on Earth!

Enchanted devices can, however, be directed or channelled to have narrower, more potent effects in Sorcery and everyday life, as devices of protection, single-spell devices or magical swords, keys, etc.

Devices of protection (*amulets*). An amulet is an Enchanted device whose potency for active magic has been switched into a protective mode. It cannot be used to enhance a link, but will be carried by its possessor to prevent a link being established with him as the target. The transference into the protective mode is carried out after Enchantment (and before any other magical use

of the device) by a single command, "Protect"—DD being equal
to the + factor or (e.g., seal of fire) sum of +factors of the device. The amulet will then provide the same —factor in the
BMC(1) for spells against the Mage *diminished* by the amulet's
star sign as it would a +factor for spells by him *controlled* by the
sign. The same limits on protection as enhancement apply. Protective devices of the spell's controlling sign will *aid* the spell!
The range is therefore —5 to +2.

Relics, objects of worship/ceremonial, crosses, etc., have minor
protective power against magic, being invested with part of the
Divine campaign and intervention to eliminate all sources of potency save the Christian God. Count a —factor of 1 in BMC(1)
per item, max —3.

Single-spell devices. These are enhancing Enchanted items in
which one—or, exceptionally, more—spells have been fixed. In
so doing, their power to enhance the link for other spells of the
same star sign is halved (round *down!* +½ = 0!). A spell
is fixed into the device by casting successfully three times in
succession with its aid. The Mage may continue to fix spells
into the device in this way provided: that there is no failure in
the link or command—which stops the sequence but does not
wipe clean other spells fixed into the item, and that he does
so within a single six-hour period, without casting any spells
(fixed or unfixed) between the series of three. The enhancement
given to fixed spells by the item is 3 × the original +factor up to
a max of +8. Fixed-spell devices reduce enhancement on spells
for which their sign is a diminisher at the half original level explained above.

Single-spell amulets could only be created by following the
command "protect" with three spells cast at the Mage by another,
all successfully repelled. Procedure and effects as above.

Magical swords, shields, keys, etc. Any physical item can be
Enchanted. Magical devices intended to enhance and protect in
arcane spell-weaving tend to have no purposeful shape—the
wand or staff is *not* a quarterstaff or walking stick, the "seal"
could not be used as such, and so on. Magical swords, shields,
keys, cups, etc., are rather different. Their practical purpose im-
pedes their use for the enhancement of the link. (This is why so

many magical items are in the shape of jewelry, which has no practical purpose.) Their magical ability to enhance and protect is limited to ± 1, however many Correspondencies have been built into the device. A magic sword will, however, carry up to $+4$ when used in combat, on all relevent equations: $+$factors as per System of Correspondencies. A magic shield will similarly aid its user by up to ± 4—reducing hits against the shield by a further four points, reducing its encumbrance similarly so that the owner may dodge and disengage more easily. Magic keys will help open locked doors and chests, lock open ones.

With the System of Correspondencies, any number and variety of magic items can be created, and their effects explained! No separate list of magic items is therefore included in *Fantasy Wargaming*.

Your magical item and you

The difference between a Conjured and Enchanted creation is only that the latter is dead. This makes some considerable difference. The Ethereal spirit of an inanimate object is generally torpid; that of a living or once-living creature is not. Both spirits wish to return to the Ethereal plane, from which you have dragged them. Both are bound to you by your superior exercise of magic. A number of effects follows:

A Mage is in contact with his device, even when physically apart. If someone else picks it up, attacks it, or throws a spell at it, he will get a "touch." Action taken is up to the Mage: but his contact with the device means an automatic link between him and his target.

There is no such contact between the device and anybody but the original enchanter. A thief, or a warrior using a magic sword, will not feel any "touch." A Mage obtaining a device not of his own manufacture can only use the item magically after issuing a command to obey: this being a DD equal to the $+$factor or sum of $+$factors in the device, plus 1. Only then (if successful) will the Mage achieve contact with the device, learn its full nature, etc.

An item will, or may, resist use by a thief: the magic sword may slip in the hand and cut you! This will not apply to magical swords, keys, etc., honestly acquired . . . unless, of course, you bought them from a thief! GM's discretion can be the only guide to such lesser treacheries. Beware items inscribed with runes, symbols, or language you cannot understand. These may be commands to the item enjoining faithful and diligent service, which will include resistance to thieves!

The Ethereal spirit in an item may try to escape back to the other plane, if its owner weakens ($\frac{1}{2}$ EP or less). 01-75 per cent, no attempt, 76-100 per cent, attempted escape. Apply BMC(3) with $+1$ for previous obedience: target item has magic level equal to $+$factor. DD $= 5$ ("obey"). Item may try again at EP3 or below—no $+1$ for previous obedience, 67-100 per cent, attempt will be made. The spirit *will* escape if the object in which it is contained is broken.

Preparations for Sorcery/the accumulation of mana

Humans have a limited number of magical activities by which they may prepare themselves for the exercise of active magic, increase their personal store of mana—or, for that matter, create mana for their deities through the exercise of worship. These activities all rely on the heightening of consciousness and concentration in the individual—and are generally the same across different cultures, types of religious or magic users. The principal activities are incantation, ululation (including singing), shamanistic or rhythmic dancing, deep meditation and study, self-denial through fasting and sexual abstinence. A bloodthirsty alternative is the destruction or sacrifice of living beings, by which part or all of the mana stored in them is transferred to the celebrant.

Ritual and magical preparations (excluding sacrifice)

By indulging in the following activities, Mages will create mana for themselves and prepare themselves for the exercise of Sorcery. The same activities, ritualized into equivalent religious ceremonies, will similarly create mana for transference to the god in worship: and it is upon this table that the mana rates given in each of the ceremonies (see Religion Rules) is based. All preparations can be carried out "on the move," but the first three are interrupted by combat or any physical obstacle/situation requiring concentration by the Mage. Only fasting may be combined with other preparations.

Magical Activity	Equivalent religious rites	Time spent per point of mana gained (basic rate)	Maximum duration of activity	+ Factor for the link
Incantation & ululation	Mass, High Mass, Ordination, Investment, preaching: Black Mass, Feast.	8 mins	96 mins	Mana ÷3
Shamanistic dancing, frenzy, etc	Orgy, Dance	4 mins	60 mins (see fatigue rules)	Mana ÷4
Deep meditation or arcane study	Confession, Veneration	12 mins	120 mins	Mana ÷2
Fasting (includes sexual abstinence)	Fasting	8 hours (do not count normal "fasting" during a night's sleep!)	Indefinite (but see fatigue rules)	Mana

Notes

Magical activity. Any of these preparations can be used to boost the likelihood of establishing a link for any spell. However, certain activities are more closely associated with particular types of magic user than others.

Religious dance. The witches' dance and orgy, unlike the feast and Black Mass, is not an act of worship, although taken part in by the coven as a whole; it is in fact a means by which the witches raise mana for their own use, and not for transference to the Lower powers.

Time spent per point of mana gained (*basic rate*). Low-level Mages carrying out preparations under unpropitious circumstances gain mana at this basic rate. Mages with higher faith, magic levels or more likely situations can accumulate mana at an accelerated rate, having more ability to concentrate on the arcane forces within themselves.

Accelerated accumulation of mana

Add the following factors:
    Magic level.
    Faith: 8 or below, —1; 14-15, +1; 16-17, +2; 18+, +3.

Secondary characteristic (shamanistic dancing = agility, meditation, etc. = intelligence, fasting = endurance, incantation = charisma): 8 or below, —1; 14-17, +1; 18+, +2.

Mana is below/above normal operating level (8 × magic level): ±1(*).

Physical circumstances, as BMC(1) (optional, GM's discretion).

System of Correspondencies: Mage is in place or situation influenced by his own sign/by the opposite sign = ±1.

Results. 0-2: basic rate. 3-5: time reduced by ⅛. 6-8: reduction by ¼. 9-11: reduction by ⅜. 12+: reduction by ½. Retain fractions. Reductions also apply to the 16-minute inter-preparatory time.

These calculations should also be used for individual accumulations of mana by clerics, etc., for transference to their powers. Substitute religious for magical level and ignore (*). Note: only ¼ of the mana gained reaches the deity. The remainder is lost.

Maximum duration of activity. Self-explanatory. The duration is *not* reduced by the factors above: high-level Mages therefore accumulate mana faster, and to a greater maximum. The activity may not be resumed until a mandatory 16-minute inter-preparatory time has passed.

+*Factor for the link.* Preparations concentrate the mind as well as mana; and at different rates. Divide the mana gained by the appropriate figure, round down, and use as a +factor in the next link (BMC(1)) calculation only. Max: +4.

The gaining of mana by sacrifice

Certain Mages may decide to accumulate mana by the ritual destruction of a living being, usually accompanied by cannibalism (e.g., of the heart, brains of the victim). Murder of this kind releases mana latent in the victim which was never tapped or utilized. Animals and non-sentient monsters will have 1-6 points of latent mana, humans and sentient creatures 7-12 points (a six-dice +6). But consider your piety! (Human sacrifice is murder *and* Black Magic. Animal sacrifice for non-religious purposes is Black Magic.) Note also: sacrifice does *not* carry +factors in establishing a link.

Mana limits

No earthly being may concentrate more than a certain level of usable mana in himself. This limit is equal to $16 \times$ his magic level. Normal operating level is half this limit. Ethereal beings may concentrate mana up to $32 \times$ their magic level.

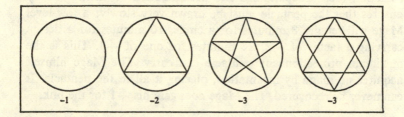

Pentacles

Pentacles are protective designs drawn or inscribed, usually on the ground, to defend objects and persons inside them from magic or (under certain circumstances) assault. They are particularly useful in combats of Sorcery, and in Conjuration.

A pentacle may be of any shape or size. It must be closed, symmetrical and so "perfect." The simplest pentacle is a single circle. Above are various designs.

Drawing the pentacle

The pentacle must be drawn continually, without pause, lifting the implement or retracing any line. There must be no gaps. A flawed pentacle is imperfect, and affords no protection. The passage of a physical object or person across the design will break the magical protection if (and only if) it breaches the design. Drawing the pentacle can fail; apply the following calculation below: add magic level, faith and agility points over 10, luck (in the usual way). Multiply by 5 and throw under with percentage dice.

Protection vs magic

The —factors under each pentacle above go forward into BMC(1) for spells aimed at Mages, etc., inside the pentacle.

Spells cast from inside the design suffer no such diminution. The pentacle is a repository of mana. While drawing the pentacle, the Mage makes an incantation: he must finish each part of the design and the relevant incantation simultaneously. Each crossing line between the outside and the center is a barrier with a factor of −1, junctions being −2. The length of time needed for the incantation (see "Preparations and accumulation of mana" above) ensures that the pentacle must be drawn very slowly: a low-level Mage will require 8 minutes for a circle, 16 minutes for a design carrying a factor of −2, 24 minutes for one of −3. This is the maximum protection any pentacle can carry. The Mage himself acquires no mana by incantation, placing it all in the pentacle. It can never be recovered. The Mage *does* gain his +1 for the link.

Protection vs assault

This can be added by inscribing symbols, words or names in the outer segments. The symbols and words are inscribed commands (e.g., "die," "go away," "desist"). When the assaulter reaches this point, he triggers the command and a BMC(3) (no need for link) takes place. The Mage may back the written command with a verbal order also. The Mage suffers mana loss in the usual way.

Names of power are rather different. They are usually the true names of Higher (or, exceptionally, Lower) powers, of opposite alignment to the assailant: typically, names of God and the Archangels being used to ward off demonic attack during Conjuration. If the attacker enters that segment, he automatically invades the preserve of the true name, which then appeals to its Higher power for intervention: appeal factor +5, no reduction for resistance of Higher power, defender to choose the miracle asked for. Note: it is the name which is appealing, not the defender. And beware: putting down the name of God may not cost you mana, but it sure as Hell (sic) involves loss of piety— counting as blasphemy (Class 2 Sin) or Black Magic (Class 3), at the GM's discretion!

The effects of symbols, words and names continues even after the design has been breached, and the magical protection of the pentacle ended.

Conjuration

Conjuration is the use of arcane forces to summon an Ethereal being on to the Earthly plane—and, by extension, to control, bind and compel such beings. This element of compulsion separates conjuration from appeal, and makes it a very powerful but extremely hazardous branch of Black Magic. No Ethereal spirit— with the possible exception of damned souls burning in the pit of Hell—likes being forced out of its natural plane, or ordered by lesser beings than themselves. Demons and other Higher/Lower powers consider it particularly irreligious, and disrespectful. All conjured beings will resist the Mage, as far as possible and at all times, seeking to escape back to the Ethereal plane. Many may seek to exact vengeance on the Mage for their humiliation.

Beings which can be conjured: Demons and all Lower powers; Angels and all Higher powers; other gods, demigods, etc.; spirits of living creatures and persons, present or not; souls (ghosts) of dead persons, whether in Heaven, Hell, Purgatory, Valhalla or wherever—this branch being known as Necromancy; Elementals, including Ether (just try it!).

Beings which cannot be conjured: Living creatures and persons in their bodily form; dead persons likewise; beings who have united their physical and Etheral forms by self-conjuration (e.g., Elves and other beings in Faery); Zodiacal forces (see Enchantment).

Stages in Conjuration

The most basic form of Conjuration is simply to establish a link with the Ethereal target (BMC(1)), and then command it to "appear" (DD4). All but the most reckless and/or powerful Mages, however, think it advisable to prepare defenses first.

Construction of a circle of appearance. This is a simple but "reverse" pentacle invested with 1 mana point (by simultaneous incantation) protecting those *outside* from magic thrown by the being when within. An inscribed command to appear is usually written in the circle. This ensures a +1 in BMC(3), and that the being appears *inside* the circle. The actual protection offered by the circle is small; its main function is to warn you if the conjured being gets out of control. A being that moves out of the circle is automatically out of control, unless acting under orders! Time: 6-12 minutes. Note: more complex "reverse pentacles" cannot be created.

Construction of a pentacle of protection. Time: 6-84 minutes depending on complexity of the pentacle and ability of Mage. A single Mage constructing a circle of appearance and a pentacle of protection will need to allow 20-40 minutes between operations as inter-preparatory time.

Commanding the being to appear. BMC(1-3), with a DD of 4. Note the probability of the being having a "saving throw," particularly if a Higher or Lower power.

The appearance of the being should not necessarily be taken as proof of successful conjuration. Demonic powers in particular may appear voluntarily, to punish the Mage or trap him under the pretense of being conjured. Nor does the appearance of a being under conjuration prevent it from attempting magic or assault against the Mage—though the circle of appearance will prevent the movement of a conjured being. This stage is therefore often followed by:

Commanding the being to obey. BMC(3) only, if within 30 minutes of the link being established. DD = 5. Obedience is temporary only, unless reinforced by inscribed commands, etc. (GMs) throw a six-dice and multiply by 10 minutes for approximate length of obedience. Obedience may also cease (GM's discretion) if the position or capacity of the Mage(s) drastically weakens. Remember: powers may only be pretending to obey! Those desiring permanent obedience must bind the demon, etc., by successfully repeating the command of obedience two more times, without intervening magical activities of any kind. Bound spirits may attempt to escape if their master weakens, and need further command. See "Your magic item and you" for procedure. Bound spirits and demons will carry out one suitable service a day, at order.

Reasons for Conjuration

Conjured beings may be used for many purposes. If magical, they may teach the Mage new skills, reveal new spells, or carry out magical operations on the Mage's behalf. (Beware what you ask it to do! I once asked a bound demon to "create light": it exploded a ball of fire 20 feet across in a 10-foot room, and my Mage went straight to Hell!) All beings are useful sources of knowledge about the Ethereal plane, and sometimes about events on the Earthly plane as well. They can thus be used for divination. Bound beings can prove useful physical servants; a Necromancer can with luck build up groups or small armies of Undead, by Conjuration. Conjured Elementals can be used to lessen the DD of active magic involving Air, Earth, Fire, Water and Ether. Few branches of the arts are as potentially rewarding—and disastrous—as Conjuration!

Special factors

Demonology. The true names of demons are mostly to be found in grimoires. They are not necessarily accurate (0-90 per cent accuracy). Demons are exceedingly treacherous and unreliable—as the above shows! It is wise to fasten inscribed commands upon even a bound demon, and to expect diabolic intervention after a year and a day unless you free the demon at that time. Demons will carry out orders by the letter, so think carefully what you say; they will, however, perform in battle, etc., at full efficiency. Conjuring demons is Black Magic, and a Class 3 Sin.

Angelology. Conjuring the Higher powers is a challenge to God's claims of ultimate mastery; it is therefore a Class 1 Sin. Conjuring other spirits under God's control—in Heaven, Purgatory and Hell—is Class 3.

Self-conjuration. Faery is created by the self-conjuration of the inhabitants. This requires a Mage to summon his own spirit (ML = Mage's ML +3), reduce it to binding, and then unite it in himself. It is a Class 1 Sin (implications of godhead), and requires a special entering (DD 6) command to achieve. This command needs no repetition for permanency. There is a high chance of madness resulting: 60 minus 5 per cent for each magic level above 4, each faith and intelligence point over 14, minimum chance 10 per cent. Throw a six-dice. Madness will last (1) a day, (2) a week, (3) a fortnight, (4) a month, (5) six months, (6) permanently. The self-Conjured being exists in both planes simultaneously; he cannot be Conjured, he has an automatic link in magic, can vanish into the Ethereal plane at will (up to 3 turns), gains 2 magic levels immediately (with attendant increases in characteristics) and can acquire mana up to $32 \times ML$.*

Spirits of living persons and creatures. ($ML = $ those of person or creature $+ 3$.) Once reduced to obedience, or placated after appearance, these can reveal the innermost secrets of their Earthly avatars. You can also conjure the spirit and body together—but why make another so powerful? A witch in particular, however, may conjure the spirit of a small animal into its body, and bind it to obedience. The resultant "Familiar" will carry out simple commands and errands, visiting places and returning to report telepathically (no spell needed).

Necromancy. Class 3 sin. Necromancy can be either the summoning of dead souls, as ghosts, or their binding and unification with whatever remains of their physical bodies. The latter involves only the disinterment of the body, skeleton, skull, bone or whatever of a person or creature, the conjuration of the spirit ($ML = ML$ of dead person $+ 3$) in a circle of appearance containing the relic, its binding through commands of obedience, and an order to occupy and remain within the relic. The result is Undead: a skeleton, ghoul (embodied corpse), mummy, singing bone, etc. Possession of the relic gives an extra $+1$ to $+3$ in establishing the link, depending on the freshness and completeness of the physical remains. Beware! You may fail to conjure a dead spirit and still find what appears to be one in front of you. Demons frequently (0–15 per cent) appear and pretend to obey necromancers, "re-animating" the corpse under a semblance of binding. In these cases, their purpose is your own soul!

Elementals. These are Ethereal powers of immense level (Earth, Air, Fire, Water $= 24$, Ether $= 25$), concerned intimately with the running of the Ethereal and Earthly planes. They can appear in any size, their power partly being determined by that size: so keep your circles of appearance small, if you fear vengeance! The entire Elemental can never be Conjured, without

---

* The spirit may only try to escape if the being goes down to 3 EP or below; see "Your magical item and you" for details. Magic level of spirit = ML of being. Roll for madness if escape is successful.

destruction of the Earthly or (Ether) Ethereal plane. The level of the Elemental varies directly with the diameter of the appearance circle, at ½ ML per foot. Elementals rarely (0-15 per cent) attack Conjurers after appearance, but will violently resist binding. Their main use is to carry out Elemental magic with the Mage. Appearance: the Air Elemental appears as a mini-tornado, the Fire Elemental as an uneven pillar of flame, the Earth Elemental as a single huge rock and Water as a shifting wave. Ether is invisible. Bound Elementals must be stored in jars, under compression.

Joint conjuration. Conjuration is one of the few occasions in which more than one Mage may cooperate in a magical operation. In basic sorcery and divination alike, the Mage must plough a solitary course—making his own link and command. Since pentacles of protection, etc., however, protect anybody therein, it is possible for one Mage to expend time and mana on the pentacle and circle of appearance while another handles the commands and negotiations with the Conjured being. To a lesser extent, the same is true in combats of Sorcery involving pentacles. In other cases, examples of apparent joint exercise of magic are entirely explained by simultaneous *preparations* for a spell followed by two separate attempts at its casting. Magic is a solitary business!

Possession. This is the counterpart of Conjuration—when a Demon takes power and occupation of a living person or creature. Only Demons will do this, and humans of PB 0 or above are protected by the probability of Divine Intervention. Possession occurs very simply; the Demon appears, commands you three times to yield—BMC(1-3) and then 2 × BMC(3) in succession; if unsuccessful, he will depart. If successful, he will have power over you, and may if he wishes take possession. The possessed creature has the physical attributes of the host, the mental and personality factors of the demon. Possession can only be overcome by exorcism.

Spells

Spells are the building blocks of active magic, as well as its most spectacular manifestation. They play a fundamental part in the more complicated exercises of magic, like Conjuration and Enchantment of objects. The range of spells is enormous. Most fantasy games present the player with a limited list of spells, each with invariable effects. This bears little relationship to the enormous variety of magical effects reported in medieval and earlier sources. Nevertheless, such a list is one inevitable element in a game, and a selection will be included later. Before then, however, we will examine certain broad categories of spell, between them amounting to a range of possibilities. In these categories, the main concerns are to arrive at the Degree of Difficulty (DD) of a spell—and, if possible, to lay out rules by which the inventive Mage can devise spells fitting into the range.

Spells of curing/disease and death

To calculate the DD of a spell, one must know the number of different parts of the body affected, as defined on the System of Correspondencies, and the amount of change the spell is designed to make: the more dramatic the recovery, the higher the DD. Add:

Number of parts of body (as defined on System of Correspondencies) affected: 1, +1; 2, +2; 3, 4, +3; 5, 6, 7, +4; 8+, +5.

Condition of patient. Slightly injured (lost less than ¼ EPs), —1*; seriously ill (¼-½ EPs lost), 0; grave (over ½ EPs lost), +1; desperate (EP 3 or below), +2.

Degree of cure sought. Gradual cure (patient will lose further EPs before disease goes) equals minus number of further EPs to be lost (max —4); cure (no further EP loss), +1; gradual recovery (immediate cure: patient restored to full EPs at twice normal recovery rate), +2; immediate recovery to full EPs, +3.

Controllers. Taurus, Aquarius; *Diminishers.* Capricorn.

The DD calculation for spells of sudden death, wasting death, heart attack, disease and magical wound, etc., are very similar: *number of parts of body*—as above. *Degree of harm sought.* Gradual wasting = + (number of EPs to be lost each day, max +3) +2 (if intended to lead to death); immediate damage = + half number of EPs to be lost immediately (and +2 if designed to cause death).

---

* Minimum DD of 1 for any spell.

Controllers. Capricorn, Aquarius; *Diminishers.* Taurus.

From these guidelines, you can work out any number of interesting ways to kill, maim and heal people: magical wounds in the guts or brain, gradual decay in the mind/legs/sex organs, niggling headache, etc. The amount of damage absorbable by different parts of the body is defined in the combat rules.

Spells of illusion

DD depends on the size of the image, its monotony, its degree of animation and movement:

Size of the image. Occupies under 1 per cent of the field of view, —2; under 5 per cent, —1; over 10 per cent, +1; over 20 per cent, +2; over 40 per cent, +3; over 80 per cent, +4; the entire field of view (e.g., illusory landscape), +5.

Monotony of image. A uniform image, —1; one involving two or three colors and patterns, +1; many patterns, pieces, colors, +3.

Type of image. Inanimate, —1; mixed, 0; animal or monster, +1; human or Ethereal spirit (including Undead), +2.

Mobility of image. Immobile, —1; moving, +2.

Familiarity of image. Common sight, —1; unusual, +1; totally new, +2.

Involves other senses as well as sight. +1 per extra sense deluded.

Controllers. Pisces, Gemini; *Diminishers.* Cancer, Aquarius.

Example: a "fieldmouse" running through a real landscape, twittering as it goes, is an illusion of DD1: —1 (size), 0 (monotony—neither completely uniform nor truly varied), +2 (moving), —1 (common sight), +1 (hearing illusion).

No spell may be under DD1. Illusions may engage in combat but not exercise religious or magical powers. Any creature, monster, spirit, etc., may be presented in an illusion.

Spell As per BMC but add intelligence of target: below 8, +1; 14-17, —1; 18+, —2.

If the spell is successful, the illusion will be real for the target (inflicting ⅓ × real damage in combat) until "circumstances change," e.g.: a new sense must be deluded—e.g., if you touch a visual image; you come in close proximity (2') of image at eye level; you engage in physical combat with the illusion; a previous still illusion "moves"; you are informed that the object is illusory.

A "saving throw" of 01-12 per cent will then break the illusion. Three unsuccessful saving throws make the illusion permanent.

Detection of illusion. Is handled through Divination.

Dispelling an illusion. Targeted not at the illusions, but the believers: DD = DD of illusion; Controller = Cancer, Aquarius; Diminisher = Gemini, Pisces.

Non-visual illusion. Illusions without any visual element involve only familiarity or "image" and other sense aids. Controllers and diminishers, etc., as visual illusions.

Blurred image. Blurring or distorting the image of a real object has a DD = half DD of a comparable illusion (round up). Attempts to hit, catch, etc., the blurred image are at −2 efficacy. Controllers and diminishers as illusions.

Concealment. A real object may be concealed by a superimposed illusion, using the equation above. The DD depends on the uniformity, etc., of the false image. The spell can be "triggered" by inscribed commands, in the usual way.

Permanent illusion. Successful repetition of the spell three times running (no intervening use of magic) renders the illusion permanent, for the victims. It will never be disbelieved, even after the death of the Mage.

Spells of protection from magic

Spells of protection from physical dangers come under the heading of absolute commands. This section covers spells of protection from active and, indeed, passive magic.

Spells of magical protection work much in the same way as amulets, namely by the System of Correspondencies. The Mage simply relinquishes certain mana points by casting a command of resistance upon himself, under BMC(3), DD of spell = number of protection points = number of mana points given up (unless pledges are made). The controller of the spell is whatever sign(s) the Mage chooses for the area of protection. The diminisher is the opposite sign(s). If more than one sign is chosen for protection, it is the sum of all the protection points. The protection covered will only apply to spells of the controlling sign—but will not, however, amplify spells of the diminisher. Up to 3 points' protection may be given to any one sign, fading at 1 point per hour (can be topped up). Mage may alternatively choose one spell or type of spell (curing/disease and death, illusion, fire/earth/air/water, absolute commands, divination/detection): protection as above, but fading at 1 point every 3 hours. If types of spell are chosen for protection, there must be the same number of protection points in each of the controllers cited in the section (e.g., Capricorn, Aquarius for disease and death protection, Aries, Leo and Sagittarius for fire protection).

Notes: Mage loses mana points for casting the spell as well as in laying down protection; you cannot protect yourself from spells of protection; one protection point gives a —1 factor in the link that the other Mage tries to fasten upon you: accumulative.

Spells of absolute command

All spells involve command, as we have seen. Absolute commands are, however, overwhelming orders delivered by a Mage in the normal way (BMC(1-3)) against a living, Ethereal or Undead creature. This spell is characterized by the short and explicit nature of the instruction. It is the very stuff of magical combat, when done in earnest. For the best results, absolute commands should be readily comprehensible to the target, and backed by a public superiority in will. Commands can, however, be made to distant targets, just like any other spell. Absolute commands are carried out via BMC(1-3), like the other spells. However, up to seven commands can be funnelled through the link, using BMC(3), before a link has to be re-established. No other types of spell or magical activity may be done in the period, and the commands must, of course, all be to the same target.

Apply the following special factors in BMC(3): target is insentinent, —2; target is sentient, but deaf or unable to hear command, —1; target hears but does not understand command, +1; target hears and understands command (i.e., command is in a language understood by him, or in Hebrew, language of magic), +2; target has obeyed/disobeyed previous commands in the sequence, ±1 for each obedience/disobedience.

Types of absolute command. These may crudely be divided into commands of movement and action, on the one hand, and commands of personal behavior on the other. Except where otherwise stated, the commands can be used to all living, Ethereal and Undead creatures. However, you may only command something which the creature can do, physically or emotionally. It is no use demanding that a man should fly. Commands of movement and action have an immediate application, stopping once the maneuver is completed. Commands of long-term behavior last one turn, except as otherwise stated, and can be made permanent by repetition under the three-times rule.

DD	Movement/action	Longer-term behavior
1	Eat, drink; defend yourself; move, stop moving.	Like, dislike, ignore; be happy, be sad.
2	Walk (trot, slither, fly, etc.—i.e., normal mode of movement); come here (can be used for distance summoning of persons, beasts, etc.), go away; turn (left, right, back, etc.); stumble; pick up, drop; stand, sit, lie; speak, shut up; wake.	Feel cold/hot/wet/dry/comfortable/uncomfortable; sleep; keep moving (or any action already in progress).
3	Run (etc.—accelerated movement); fall over; follow; stop attacking; tell (me, him, truth, untruth, etc.); believe (me, him, this, etc.), disbelieve.	Love, hate; never tell; be frenzied/panicky/calm; be blessed/cursed (as clerical benediction and malediction; no ± factor for appeals).
4	Climb, swim, jump, ride, etc. (abnormal movement mode); grovel; perform (this) deed; freeze (stand rigid: up to 10 minutes); disobey; name another (true name); appear, disappear/vanish (Ethereal spirits); forget.	Alteration of characteristics.*
5	Attack, kill, hurt, defend (me, etc.); destroy (thing); obey, surrender, yield; name yourself.	Alteration of characteristics*; be blind/deaf/senseless; be furious (berserk rage); be stunned (coma).
6	Worship (it, me, etc.); kill yourself; enter me (self-conjuration).	Alteration of characteristics*; go mad.

* Alteration of characteristics. Bravery, greed, selfishness, lust, intelligence, charisma, leadership, agility, physique and endurance, can all be altered up or down by up to 3 points (DD = Degree of Alteration +3) by commands to be: brave/fearful; greedy/restrained; lustful/uninterested; selfish/selfless; intelligent/stupid; self-confident/lackluster; masterful/unimpressive; agile/clumsy; strong/weak; tireless/fatigued. The effect is temporary (1-6 hours) unless the command is made permanent by double repetition (i.e., three commands in all). The figure altered is the basic factor, as amended by adds for levels; such a factor may only be altered magically twice—once in either direction. Altering the endurance of an injured man will not cure him or speed his recovery; it is the basic factor, not the present level, which is altered.

A target moving or acting under command is an automaton, who will not even defend himself if attacked. However, targets may be programmed to act normally as part of your instructions after a command to obey. Such *instructions,* unlike absolute commands, involve no loss of mana. The only time when an obedient target need be commanded again magically is in self-conjuration ("enter me").

Controllers. Aquarius, Leo, special controllers[1]; *Diminishers.* Cancer, Sagittarius, special diminishers[2].

[1] Move, stop, walk and all commands of movement—Pisces. Commands of battle—Aries. Sleep, wake, betterment of characteristics, pleasant feelings, calmness, blessing—Taurus. Naming, telling, being silent, forgetting—Gemini. Unpleasant feelings, destruction of inanimate things, worsening of characteristics—Capricorn. Like, love, hate, dislike—Virgo. Obey, surrender, yield, worship—Leo. Ethereal commands—Pisces.

[2] Special diminishers are the opposite sign in all cases.

Spells of Elemental matters (Fire, Earth, Air, Water)

There are two methods of carrying out Elemental magic. One is to conjure an appropriate Elemental, force him to obedience (or binding), and then order him to carry out the magic. An Elemental may also be used as a "store" of material. Spells involving the creation or destruction of matter violate the laws of physics, and so have a very high DD—as will be made clear below. An Elemental can be used to supply the new or absorb the old matter, shrinking or growing in the process. (Note: the magic level of the Elemental will fall or rise accordingly, and the spirit may try to escape or use magic against you.) This reduces the DD of the spell by 1 point per 2 magic levels of the Elemental before casting. The same reduction applies when the Elemental is doing spells of creation/destruction. These uses only apply to spells involving their own element: an Earth Elemental cannot carry out or assist Water spells, but can assist spells mixing Earth and Water.

The remainder of this section is given over to spells of Elemental magic, without assuming the presence of an Elemental. This is an enormously large and important area of Sorcery, covering everything from combat and adventure movement to control of the weather.

To arrive at the DD of the spell desired, add:

Nature of the element. Fire, 0; Air/Water, 1; Earth, 2. (If more than one Element is involved, add the factors.)

Size of material involved. (Amplification/diminution: count *highest* factor applicable): a fragment (under 3 cubic inches), 0; a piece (up to 1 cubic foot), 1; a block (up to room size—10 ft cube), 2; a mass (up to 100 ft cube), 3; a mountain (anything bigger), 4.

Spell involves. Movement: slow (up to 3 mph), 0; medium (3-30 mph), 1; fast (30+), 2. Change in shape: Fire, 0; Air/Water, 1; Earth, 2. Defiance of gravity or other physical law: +1 per turn (20 minutes). "Animation" of material (i.e., giving it an appearance of life, purposive movement, sensory response, etc.), +3 per turn.

Construction of a wall, wave or concrete form from raw and disintegrated material/disintegration of concrete form into raw material: +2.

Repair of a breach/opening a breach or split: +2.

Creation of new matter out of nothing/annihilation of existing matter: +3.

Amplification or diminution of existing matter: +2.

Spells are carried out normally through BMC(1) and (3). Elemental material, unlike Elemental spirits, has no magic level. Some things you can do with Elemental magic include the following examples. Erecting a wall of rock: from lying earth (DD6); from a large block of rock, by change of shape (DD6); by enlargement or creation (DD7). Implanting a dart-shaped rock in a man's heart by creation (DD6). Covering a lake 50 yards across with a sheet of ice 1 in thick, by removal of heat (fire) (DD6). Lighting a fire: by creation (DD3); by movement of fire (DD0). Open up a man-size corridor through 20 ft of solid rock by breach (DD6); through 20 ft of fire (DD4); water (includes defiance of gravity—DD6 for 20 minutes, DD7 for 40 minutes, etc.). Turning a clearing 20 ft across into a mudpool 6 ft deep by creation or enlargement of water (DD7 or 6). Hurling a sphere of rock or a fireball 3 ft across at an opponent (DD5/3 if no creation, amplification or shape change needed). For all damage done by Elemental missiles, add Element, size and speed factors, and multiply by 5; but fire burns! Killing a man by holding a sphere of fire, water or (removal of) air about his head (DD4, 6, 6—includes +1 for defiance of gravity).

Weather control. There are far too many variables to give definite DDs here. Weather is mainly affected by Water and Air, in large quantities, giving a basic DD6 plus movement for storms, fogs, mists, etc. High winds involve only Air (DD5 + movement), tidal waves only Water (same). Fine weather can be brought by blowing away clouds, mist, etc.; a hot spell by heating the air with fire, etc. Small areas of "weather" can also be created. Magical weather lasts 1 hour: for 1-3 hours, +1DD; 3-8 = +2DD; 8-24 = +3DD.

The range of magical effects using Elemental magic is enormous. Be inventive! Fires can be extinguished by the creation or movement of water, or earth, or by the movement/annihilation of air. Armor on a man's body can be heated to an intolerable level by creation of fire. People can be desiccated or frozen solid, blinded by dustblows, etc. Traps can be formed, or evaded and escaped. It is for the player to suggest spells, and the GM to accept or reject them.

MISCELLANEOUS SPELLS

Name of spell	Effects	Maximum duration	Astrological Controllers	Astrological Diminishers	Witch	WW/CM	Wizard	High Sorcerer	Cabalist	Notes
Flight	Air movement of self, other creature or object: twice normal ground speed	1 turn (20 mins)	Pisces Sagittarius	Virgo Capricorn	3	6	5	4	3	DD + 1 for object.
Levitation	Vertical ascent and floating: up to 50 ft, controllable at will. Soft descent guaranteed.	10 mins	Aquarius Libra	Virgo Capricorn	4	6	5	4	3	
Lethargic/ rapid movement	Halves/doubles speed of movement on ground or in water.	1-6 turns (dice)	Virgo/ Pisces	Pisces/ Virgo	2	4	3	3	2	
Teleportation	Instantaneous transportation through Ethereal plane; destination must be known.	Instan-taneous	Aquarius Pisces	Cancer Leo	7	9	7	6	5	Can also be used to teleport objects and persons from a known, distant location to the Mage: +4 DD. Targets: human only.
Giant leap	Increases bounding power to 1 yard per physique point.	1 leap	Leo	Scorpio	2	3	3	2	2	Range: 30 ft.
Climbing	Subject of spell obtains physique and agility of 20 during his climb.	1 turn	Leo Capricorn	Libra Scorpio	4	6	4	4	3	
Invisibility	(a) Personal invisibility (can still be heard or touched); (b) Invisibility for all persons, objects in a 10 ft cube area.	1 turn	Gemini Pisces	Taurus Capricorn	3	5	4	4	3	Area = +4 on DD (and ignore multiple target section of BMC(3)).
Absolute darkness	Unnatural darkness, oppressive (−1 on morale throws). Will snuff out natural sources of light.	1 turn	Gemini Aquarius	Leo Cancer	3*	4*	3*	3*	2*	* Darkness covers 10 ft cube. Increase DD by 1 for each doubling in size. Penetrated by fire spells or by "Light."

DD

Name of spell	Effects	Maximum duration	Astrological Controllers	Astrological Diminishers	Witch	WW/CM	Wizard	High Sorcerer	Cabalist	Notes
Night vision	Subject can see through any *natural* darkness as if fully lit. Range: natural horizon.	1-6 turns (dice)	Cancer Leo	Pisces Aquarius	2	2	2	2	1	Does not penetrate Absolute Darkness—see "Light".
Telescopic vision	Subject can zero in on distant events, as if happening 10 ft away. Range: natural horizon.	1-6 turns (dice)	Sagittarius Aquarius	Gemini Pisces	3	4	3	2	1	
Through vision	Subject can see through up to 3 layers of solid matter, in perfect clarity.	10 mins	Taurus Sagittarius	Aries Capricorn	4	5	4	4	3	
Ethereal vision	Subject can observe spirits, etc, on Ethereal plane or spy on events anywhere in the Earthly plane.	5 mins	Pisces Libra	Cancer Aries	5	7	6	5*	4	* DD6 for Runic Sorcerers.
Telepathic communication	Subject can 'talk' to another's mind (living creatures only) or listen in unobserved.	1 turn	Gemini Aries	Scorpio Capricorn	4	6	5	4	3	+2 DD with animals, monsters, spirits. There is a "natural" telepathy between witch and familiar, needing no spell.
Animal speech	Subject understands speech of any living creature, and can converse in it. Language forgotten afterwards.	1 turn	Gemini Virgo	Leo Aries	3	3	4	3	2	
Gift of tongues	Subject can read/write any unknown language or script. Forgotten afterwards.	1-6 turns (dice)	Gemini Virgo	Aquarius Pisces	4	6	5	3	2	
Silence	Artificial silence in a 10 ft cube, smothering all natural noises. Cube moves with subject of spell.	1 turn	Capricorn Scorpio	Virgo Libra	2	3	3	2	2	

MISCELLANEOUS SPELLS, CONTINUED

Name of spell	Effects	Maximum duration	Astrological Controllers	Astrological Diminishers	DD Witch	WW/ CM	Wizard	High. Sorcerer	Cabalist	Notes
Bolt of lightning	Visible lightning streak from above Mage's head directed at target by arms. 3-18 (3 6-dice), damage points inflicted.	Immediate	Leo Aries	Libra Sagittarius	4	6	5		3	
Gentle nudge	Invisible push (up to physique 6) on an object, person etc. No gesture by Mage.	Immediate	Sagittarius Pisces	Libra Capricorn	2	3	2	2	1	
Bolt of force	Invisible bolt of force by Mage (no gesture), 4-24 (4 6-dice) damage.	Immediate	Aquarius Virgo	Leo Sagittarius	5	8	7	5	4	
Weapon-wield	Increases *or* decreases agility needed to wield a particular weapon. Targeted at weapon only.	1-6 turns (dice)	Aries, Scorpio/ Libra, Sagittarius	Sagittarius Libra/ Aries, Scorpio	1*	3*	2*	1*	1*	* + number of points difference to be made in agility needed. Runic Sorcerers start from base DD 0.
Weapon-power	Likewise, strength needed.	1-6 turns (dice)			1*	3*	2*	1*	1*	* + number of points difference to be made in strength needed. Runic Sorcerers start from base DD 0.
Armor strength	Increases *or* decreases protection of a shield, helm, suit of armor	1-6 turns (dice)	Sagittarius, Aries/ Scorpio, Capricorn	Capricorn, Scorpio/ Sagittarius, Aries	1*	3*	2*	1*	1*	* + number of extra (or lower) protection points. Altering shield, armor *and* helm is an extra + 2. Runic Sorcerers start from base DD 0.

Name of spell	Effects	Maximum duration	Astrological Controllers	Astrological Diminishers	DD					Notes
					Witch	WW/CM	Wizard	High Sorcerer	Cabalist	
Open/lock door	Will open any locked door, lock any open one.	1-6 turns (dice)	Aquarius, Libra/ Scorpio, Leo	Pisces, Leo/ Aquarius, Libra	2	2	2	2	1	Mage stores mana in the door, to 'lock' it. Mana fades at 1 point per turn. Door can be opened magically by another Mage, spending extra mana on an open spell to surpass that in door.
Create poison	Poisons liquid, food, vegetable or animal matter; poison removes 2 EP at once, then 1 EP per hour.	Immediate (poison is indefinite)	Scorpio Capricorn	Taurus Cancer	4	3	5	4	3	+ 3 DD for an 'instant-death' poison.
Purify food and water	Removes all poison, germs, etc, from food and water.	Immediate	Taurus Virgo	Scorpio Capricorn	4	2	4	3	2	+ 2 DD to remove 'instant-death' poison.
Earthquake	Will collapse stone/timber buildings, forests, shake caverns, etc. Shaking itself causes 1-2 EP loss.	Immediate	Earth signs	Water signs	7	9	8	7	6	GM must check effects of falling masonry, etc, on party.
Psychic disruption	Reduces intelligence and other personality factors (*not* class) of target to 3.	Immediate	Aquarius Capricorn	Cancer	4	6	6	5*	4	Target recovers at 1 point on all factors per hour. • DD6 for a Runic Sorcerer. • DD3 for a Runic (Dark Age) Sorcerer.
Water breathing	Target can breathe and operate happily under water.	1-6 turns (dice)	Pisces Cancer	Virgo Capricorn	5	4	5	4*	3	Likewise.
Soft landing	Ensures damage-free landing from any height/at any speed.	Immediate	Leo Gemini	Aries Capricorn	4	6	5	4	3	
Suspended animation	Target is dead to all appearances but conscious, alert and in command of his senses.	Up to 1 day	Sagittarius Capricorn	Taurus Cancer	5	3	4	4	3	

MISCELLANEOUS SPELLS, CONTINUED

Name of spell	Effects	Maximum duration	Astrological Controllers	Astrological Diminishers	DD					Notes
					Witch	WW/CM	Wizard	High Sorcerer	Cabalist	
'Stoppage of Time'	Stops time (and all movement, action etc) within a 20 ft cubic area about Mage. Affects others entering area.	1 turn	Aquarius Virgo	Leo Capricorn	7	8	7	6*	6	* DD7 for a Runic (Dark Age) Sorcerer.
Destruction of magic	Dispels any spell currently in operation within a 30 ft cubic area about Mage.	Immediate	Cancer Aries	Aquarius Pisces	*	+1*	*	*	-1*	* DD equal to that of spell they are trying to dispel—except as marked in columns.
Shape-changing	Target can assume any animate or inanimate form. Mental attributes remain the same, personality and physical attributes alter.	Up to 1 day	Aquarius Pisces	Taurus Cancer	7	9	7	7*	6	+5DD if object/creature turned into has ± 25% mass of target. * But DD4 for Dark Age Runic Sorcerers.
Light	A cold light, moveable at will of Mage, the size of a tennis ball: lights a 10 ft cube magically.	1-6 turns (dice)	Cancer Leo	Taurus Capricorn	2	2	2	2	1	+2 for an area or wall of light will break a spell of Absolute Darkness.
Pain	No EP loss, just pain: take bravery from 20 and equal/throw over with a six-dice to avoid surrender*	1-3 turns (6-dice ÷ 2)	Scorpio Pisces	Taurus Libra	3	3	5	4	3	* Surrendering means curling up (no action possible), begging for relief. Relief at Mage's will. Resistors: -3 in calculations.
Evil eye	1 EP loss. -1 on all luck throws.	1 month	Scorpio Cancer	Sagittarius Leo	2	3	4	4	4	Can be removed by removal spell (same DDs) or by scratching the Mage to draw blood.

Controllers and Diminishers. Air signs (Aquarius, Gemini, Libra) control Air spells. Opposite (Fire) signs are their diminishers. Likewise for other Elements. In multi-element spells, the controllers are Aquarius and Libra: the Diminishers are Aries and Virgo.

Spells of complex matter

All other material objects and forms of matter are created from the four terrestrial Elements. (Ether is, of course, immaterial.) The balance between the four elements determines how resistant to magic the material is: *Metals* Mercury $= 0$, gold/silver $= 1$, lead/iron $= 3$, all others 2; *gems, crystals, etc.,* 1; *Salts, other minerals* 2; *Glass, pottery* 3; *Vegetable matter* (wood, thorns, bark, flowers, stems, etc.) 2; *Animal matter* Blood, flesh, innards, 1, hair wool, etc., 2, bone 3; *Liquids, gases* (including poisonous), 2.

The same calculation for DD applies with complex as with Elemental matter—these factors taking the place of the Element factor. Again, the range of things which can be done with these spells is enormous—far greater than the effects allowed for in an ordinary spell list. Consider, for example, sinking a ship or boat by opening a breach in the wooden hull (DD5); erecting a wall of thorns from a bush, by amplification (DD6); instant plant growth or shrinkage; repair of a sword, glass vessel or pottery beaker/breakage of the same (DD6 in each case); or animation of a table or other object—making it behave as if alive.

Transmutation

Fantasy Wargaming ignores the alchemist, as a class of Mage; he occurs too late in the period, and has too little place in the average adventure, to be examined here. Nevertheless, it is possible to find Sorcerers of all types indulging in transmutation between forms of matter—though *not* between Elements. The classic spells of petrification—turning a creature to stone, giving life to a statue—are an example. The procedure for transmutational spells between types of complex matter, and between matter and a single Element, is the same, and based on the DD calculations above. Add the factors for *both* the forms involved (e.g., flesh $+$ stone $= 3$). Add size factor for the object or material. If the transmutation involves a change in shape $(+1)$ or size as well as in type of matter, apply the relevant additions. Then add 3 for transmutation. Apply BMC(1) and (3) as usual.

Passive magic

Active magic occurs when a Mage manipulates arcane forces to change all or part of the fabric of the universe. This is known as Sorcery. Passive magic is rather different, and summed up under the general heading of divination/detection. This merely seeks to observe the workings of the universe in action, to understand what occult forces are affecting the Mage and his surroundings, to detect influences and gather knowledge. Although widely regarded in the Middle Ages as a separate branch of the magical arts, divination was widely practiced by Sorcerers of all types. The main differences between the two branches in *Fantasy Wargaming* are: that in certain types of divination, intelligence is as important as faith in obtaining success; and that in all passive magic, there is less mana lost than in Sorcery. This, after all, reflects the magical process itself; the diviner establishes his own special kind of Ethereal link, but does not issue a command. In other respects, there are considerable areas of overlap. Diviners use the same preparations as Sorcerers—meditation and deep study being most important for some, incantation, ululation or frenzy for others. The System of Correspondencies is naturally exploited, in the former case; but there also were diviners who sought to obtain the secrets of the Ethereal plane directly, by an act of will.

This is, in fact, the great difference within divination. On the one hand, there are sophisticated techniques explicitly geared into the System of Correspondencies. The main examples are astrology and tarot, each card in a tarot pack having its own astrological implications. These techniques were mainly confined to Cabalists and High Sorcerers—and entirely so in *Fantasy Wargaming*. The witches, wizards, wise women and cunning men had their own forms of divination, relying on different items. Crystal balls, pools of ink or the entrails of a sacrificial animal became a focus through which the Mage could concentrate his powers, and "see" into the Otherworld. Between the two traditions lies the Runic Sorcerer of the Dark Ages. His divination too required magic items—but in this case, the objects (carved rods) were

Enchanted, and inscribed with runes. Each rod is treated in *Fantasy Wargaming* as a single astrological influence, and their pattern when cast links the Runic Sorcerer directly into the great System. Each technique—the astrological and the focus—has its advantages and disadvantages. The second is often more accurate, or at least easier and quicker to perform. It requires more of the diviner, however, and so uses more mana. The first is much more economical, and painstaking.

Finally, one must not forget divination through dreams—sometimes voluntary, sometimes a gift from the gods. That too is covered in this section.

Calculation of divination

Apply BMC(1) in active magic *except* for the factors below. Apply the *whole* DD of the question (see below).

Intelligence. 8 or below, −2; 9-10, −1; 11-13, 0; 14-15, +1; 16-18, +2; 19-20, +3.

Agility. 8 or below, −1; 14 or above, +1.

Note: if a "spell" (i.e., act of divination) is made without any of the appropriate equipment (an ephemeris for astrology, a full tarot pack, a full set of Runic rods, a crystal ball, etc.) it counts as "without knowledge," and so −2.

Tables for divination

Consult the table for BMC(1) to see whether a link has been established. (Mana loss = ½DD rounded up, as usual.) Note: the GM must do the rolling here, and keep the result secret. If a link has not been established, the GM must give an answer to the player's question—for all acts of divination are attempts to get information out of the GM!—that is totally or partially misleading. If a link has been well established (i.e., percentage die roll is under half that required for success in BMC(1)), the GM should give a fairly precise and complete answer to the question asked of him, without if possible giving away any fundamental secrets. If a link has been tenuously established (percentage roll over half that required), the GM should give an incomplete answer, or one including a certain measure of untruth.

The most difficult question to deal with is the one dealing with future events—a staple element not only in astrology, but in all systems of divination. Classic examples are: "If I go down this tunnel, will I get out alive?"; "If I challenge Hrothgar for leadership, will I win?"; or "Will I be able to do what I want to do without getting VD?"

If possible, GMs should try to fit the question into one of the "standard categories" on the following table. The last could, for example, be partially answered by a "detect disease." Most, however, can't; and it would ruin the atmosphere to limit artificially the questions that a character can ask of his diviner. Historically, diviners were called on to handle an enormous variety of queries, of all kinds. The answer is to reduce every question asked to one requiring either a *yes* or *no* answer. Throw to establish a link, then throw again for the result: 0-60 per cent = yes, 61+ per cent = no. However: "The Stars incline, but do not compel." Since all equations and calculations in *Fantasy Wargaming* involve the intervention of that most medieval goddess, Fortune or Luck, the solution is obvious: during relevant calculations (e.g., a combat calculation in the tunnel but not on the other side), alter all die rolls for luck by ± 1. This includes calculations by others against the questioner. Do not allow the questioner to repeat his piece of divination; it is not historical, and exploits the differential.

Creation of Runic rods

There must be 12 rods, of wood banded with metal and set with runes. They should each be enchanted up to at least $+1$ factor, in the usual way. The runes carved upon them are astrological symbols, not symbols of command. These rods can be used individually to aid Sorcery, like other enchanted items. No other divinatory equipment in either tradition is Enchanted.

Questions which can be asked

These are innumerable—certainly far too many to enumerate here. Within the guidelines above, the GM should be willing to accept—and answer, more or less truthfully—any question asked of him. However, certain types of query did predominate historically, and indeed are also likely to be those asked by any suitably cautious adventuring party. These are set out below, together with the astrological controller/diminisher for each (for these too are affected by the Great System) and the DD for each in either tradition.

Controller	Diminisher	Question	Astrology, etc		Peasant tradition	
			Time needed	DD	Time needed	DD
Sign of person	Opposite sign	Detect general character (at least 5 characteristics) of a person or sentient being	15 mins	3	25 mins	4
Sign of person	Opposite sign	Detect (a) religious alignment/(b) deepest secret of a person or sentient being	8 mins/ 10 mins	2/3	10 mins/ 12 mins	3/3
Sign of person	Opposite sign	Detect the time *or* place *or* manner of a person's death	12 mins	2	12 mins	3
Own sign/ Gemini	Opposite sign/ Sagittarius	Detect whereabouts of (a) the caster/(b) other creatures, plants, places, objects, etc	4 mins/ 6 mins	2/3	3 mins/ 5 mins	2/2
Taurus	Scorpio	Detect (a) the nature/ (b) the cure for a particular illness	12 mins/ 15 mins	2/4	10 mins/ 10 mins	3/3
Aquarius	Leo	Detect (a) the use/(b) the nature of magic in a given place, person, object, etc	2 mins/ 8 mins	3/5	3 mins/ 6 mins	4/4
Gemini	Sagittarius	Detect the concealed presence nearby of (a) a person/(b) metal/gem/ wood, etc	3 mins/ 4 mins	3/3	3 mins/ 3 mins	2/2
Pisces	Virgo	Detect what is happening up to 200 yards away (behind obstacles) (a) by sight/ (b) by ear	3 mins/ 5 mins	4/4	2 mins/ 3 mins	3/3
Sign of spirit	Opposite sign	Detect possession of a person by an alien spirit or by his own conjured spirit	5 mins	4	4 mins	5
Own sign	Opposite sign	Detect presence of enemies (a) inside/(b) outside the party	4 mins/ 8 mins	3/5	4 mins/ 8 mins	4/4
Sign of day	Opposite sign	Detect weather during ensuing 48 hours (if successful, GM must give details)	10 mins	3	6 mins	2
Cancer	Aquarius, Gemini	Detect illusion/traps/ poison	3 mins	5	2 mins	4
Signs of Element	Opposite signs	Detect Fire, Earth, Air, Water	4 mins	Element Factor* +1	3 mins	Element Factor* +1
Sign of material	Opposite sign	Detect specific metal/ gem/wood/other complex material	5 mins	Material factor** +1	6 mins	Material factor** +1
Libra	Pisces	Detect an untruth/ theft/thief	3 mins	3	2 mins	1

* Element factor: see spells of Elemental matter.
** Material factor: see spells of complex matter.

Preparations. Astrology and tarot—deep meditation/study only; Runic divination—incantation; other techniques—any preparation.

Dreams and visions

Any character with a high faith may have a prophetic or meaningful dream. Some characters with high intelligence are able to interpret their own and other's dreams. Throw for a dream at any convenient time during the night. Characters with faith below 14 should not throw for meaningful dreams. Characters capable of a dream should add faith points above 14, half their magic and half their religious level (round up either case), and luck. If the place or situation is under an Ethereal influence, add up to +4 (usual way) for System of Correspondencies. Mages and clerics may boost their chances by preparations: two points for every point of mana accumulated through prayer/meditation/study, ceremonial and magical incantation/ululation, devilish and shamanistic dance /frenzy, fasting, etc. Throw percentage dice under this figure for a memorable dream.

Interpretation. Repeat addition above, ignoring Ethereal influences and preparations, adding intelligence points of interpreter over 12. GM's throw. If the throw is well inside (i.e., under half percentage required), the dream is highly meaningful, and the GM should reveal a major secret of the adventure (or of another character). If the throw is above half percentage required, reveal a minor detail. If the throw is above percentage required entirely, invent something—as wildly misleading as you like!

All Mages and clerics satisfying the criteria may apply once a day for a vision, on the same basis. Dreams and visions lose 1-3 mana points, or 1-2 endurance points.

Magic users: class, preparations, etc.

Transition from one Mage type to another. As a cunning man gathers experience and social class, he comes closer in knowledge and techniques to a wizard. A wizard, similarly, may develop into a High or Runic Sorcerer; while any Mage may enter a coven and thereby develop into a witch. Such development, however, means

Min/Max social class

	Landowning & warrior classes	Clergy	Townsfolk	Rural dwellers	Preparations for spell & mana accumulation	Main Correspondences used in Enchantment	Notes
Wise woman or cunning man	—	9-12	4-9 (Rural immigrants)	4-13	Incantation & ululation	Herbs, woods, times of day/week/year, parts of animal bodies	Level 4 and above: may elect to become a wizard if minimum social class is satisfied.
Witch	A witch may be of any class or type—united in diabolic service. Covens will, however, tend to be rural, rather than urban or nobility				Incantation/ululation, Shamanistic dancing	Herbs, woods, times of day/week/year, parts of animal bodies, place, colour	Other Mages (level 2 and above/ may become witches by joining a coven, retaining their other specializations.
Wizard	9-13	9-13	6-13	12-14	Incantation/ululation, deep meditation/study (Above level 4 only)	Metals, herbs, woods, times of day/week/year, parts of animal bodies, place, color	Level 4 and above: may elect to become a High or Runic Sorcerer if minimum social class is satisfied.
High or Runic Sorcerer	13+	13+	13+	—	Incantation/ululation, deep meditation/study	Metals, gems, times of day/week/year, color, number, place, woods	—
Cabalist	—	—	12-16	—	Incantation/ululation, deep meditation/study, fasting, etc.	All	Cabalists must be Jewish or Mohammedan. No entry to Christians.

unlearning much that has already been garnered. The Mage making the transition will thus retain the best of both worlds, in his spell specialization factors, choosing whichever factor is higher; he must, however, drop a magic level in transition (e.g., a 4th-level wizard will become a 3rd-level High Sorcerer or witch). This does not require any reduction in characteristics, or in use of preparations or materials for Enchantment.

Min/max social class. This applies only at the start of your character's career, when you are choosing a father for him. The class figure is that of the father—whether the latter is a Mage or not.

Spell specialization. The table above tabulates some of the magical differences between the types—notably in preparations and enchantment. The miscellaneous spells tables give different DDs by Mage type. Below is a brief table showing the variations between the types in the main categories of magic: the "spell specialization factors." These ± factors apply in BMC(1) in spells belonging to the main categories.

Spell specialization: factors and notes

	Inscribed command? (yes/no)	May practice Conjuration (yes/no)	Curing	Illusion	Disease &death	Protection	Absolute commands: movement & action	Absolute commands: behaviour	Absolute Elemental matter	Complex matter	Divination: Aristocratic mode	Divination: Peasant mode
Wise woman or cunning man	No	No	+2	+1	-1	—	-1	—	—	-1	-1	Yes
Witch	No	No	+1	+2	—	-1	+1	+1	—	—	—	Yes
Wizard	No	Yes (above level 4)	+1	—	+1	.—	+1	—	—	—	Yes (above level 4)	Yes
High or Runic Sorcerer	Yes	Yes	+1 (but Runic Sorcerer zero)	+1	– (but Runic Sorcerer +1)	—	+1	+1	+1	+1	Yes	—
Cabalist	Yes	Yes	+1	+1	+1	+1	+2	+2	+2	+2	Yes	—

Magical experience

Experience is acquired through the casting of spells, the accumulation of mana in preparations, the carrying out of divinatory magic, and the correct evaluation of astrological and other magical influences at work in different situations within the adventure. The calculations below are meant only as the roughest guidelines: GMs must also take into account the circumstances (physical and Ethereal) within which the Mages were operating, to arrive at a suitable figure.

Casting spells. Record the percentage probability of success in BMC(1) and (3). Add together, subtract from 200 and halve for basic experience points (if spell was successful).* If the link only was successful, experience will equal mana points expended.* If spell involved BMC(3) only, subtract percentage probability from 100 for experience.

Preparations. 4 mana points gained in preparations will give one experience point. Max 6 a day.

Resisting counter-magic (BMC(2)). Subtract your percentage probability of success in command "desist" (BMC(3)) from 100 for experience, if successful. If unsuccessful, subtract this probability and halve.

Divination BMC(1). Subtract percentage probability of success from 100, if successful. If the answer is completely accurate, this is the Mage's experience gained. If answer is of mixed accuracy, halve for experience. Inaccurate answers gain no experience.

Detection of Ethereal influences. Subtract the number of Correspondencies under the Ethereal influence in the place or situation from 12; this is the Mage's experience.

Religion rules section one:

Appeals, intercessions and miracles

The routine "magical" activities of the cleric and coven member are carried out by the delegated powers in section three. More important or unusual "magic" requires a different course, appealing to one of the Higher (or Lower!) powers for action. *Anyone* may appeal; a cleric or coven leader is more likely to have his appeal answered, other things being equal, but a common worshipper with the right piety or a special link to a power may also have regular success. Appeals can be to any power, supreme or lesser. An appeal to a lesser power may be valuable even if the latter does not himself have the ability to carry out the miracle asked for. In such a case, the lesser power will contact another being higher in the host and intercede on behalf of the appellant. This is the second calculation. The third stage is to calculate the success of the power in carrying out the miracle.

Appeal to a Higher or Lower power

Faith of the appellant: 14 or above, +1; 8 or below, −1.
Divine Grace/Devil's Favor of the appellant: Add the religious level, rank and piety/(piety) band of appellant together.
Subtract the resistance of Higher/Lower power to appeals.
Halve the degree of difficulty of miracles asked for (rounded up) and subtract.
Proofs of serious intent:
  Instant appeal: mental only, −1; spoken, 0.
  Appeal supported by prayer/meditation: for each 60 mins add +1 (max +2).
  Appeal supported by all-night vigil: +3.
  Appeal supported by fasting: first day +2; subsequent days +1 each (max +5).
  Appeal supported by sacrifice or gift: candles, +1; money, +1 per 5 per cent of total income up to +3; animal sacrifice, +1; human sacrifice (Lower powers only), +2 (+3 for virgin or unbaptized child).

Appeal supported by religious ceremony: +2.

Piety points dedicated by the appellant in advance: +1 per 10 points up to max +3.

Luck (calculate as usual).

Astrological factors: Appeal is made in a situation or place governed by the birth sign of the power/opposite sign: +1/−1.

Special relationship between appellant and power:

Power is the appellant's patron or special protector: +1.

Appellant is using a relic of the power, or appealing at a shrine/church dedicated to the power: add appeal factor.

Power is an unrecognized Saint: −1.

Appellant is inspired/has been blessed: +3/+1.

Target of the proposed miracle:

Is in good standing (piety band 2+) with the power: subtract piety band.

Is in good standing (piety band 2+) with the enemy power: add piety band.

Interest of the power appealed to:

Intervention indirectly/directly in power's interest: +1/+2.

Intervention indifferent to/opposes power's interest: −1/−2.

Communal appeals are handled as individual appeals by the man with the highest Divine Grace/Devil's Favor but with factors for communal support:

For each appellant in good standing with power: +1 (but clerics +2).

For each clerical appellant not in good standing: +1(up to max +5).

Appeal lies in an area specialized in by the power appealed to: +2.

Appellant has appealed to a power that day already:

Per unsuccessful appeal: −1.

Per successful appeal: −2.

Special circumstances (see below). At GM's discretion, he may apply any factor between −2 and +2.

Notes

Faith. Your instinctive appreciation of the Ethereal plane helps contact with the power. Faith is, however, less important here than in the exercise of magic itself.

Divine Grace/Devil's Favor. In the unlikely event of a Devil worshipper or impious person appealing to God, or someone with positive piety appealing to the Lower powers, the figure must, of course, be subtracted in this equation.

Degree of Difficulty of miracles. Most miracles are in fact magical spells carried out by Higher/Lower powers, and so can be found in the Magic Rules. There are, however, a number of special miracles dependent totally on the powers, which are essentially appeals for favor: see below for details.

Proofs of serious intent. The ceremonies, etc., carried out in support of the appeal confer no piety on the appellant—because they are expressly done with an ulterior motive.

Dedication of piety points. "Lord, that Thou has lovest me before, and shown me grace; lettest Thou carry out this Appeal, though Thou thinkest less of me for it." Piety points "spent" here are over and above any that may be specified on the table of success.

Special circumstances. For example, where an appellant in good standing is threatened with loss of life, etc. Use sparingly! For extra period flavor, subtract —1 for every magical device worn by the appellant!

Communal appeals. For composition of an undifferentiated congregation, see "inspiration" in section three.

Repetitive appeals. Persistent appeals (more than two a day) will count as a class 4 sin, except under the most extreme of circumstances. It is as disrespectful to the powers as omission of religious observances.

Add all the factors together and apply on the table below, rolling %ge dice.

	—5 or below	—2 to —4	—1	0	1	2–3	4–5	6–7	8–9	10–11	12–13	14–19	20–24	25+
Success without penalty	1%	1–4%	1–7%	1–10%	1–15%	1–22%	1–30%	1–40%	1–50%	1–60%	1–70%	1–80%	1–90%	1–94%
Success with penalty	2–5%	5–9%	8–15%	11–24%	16–34%	23–44%	31–54%	41–65%	51–74%	61–79%	71–84%	81–90%	91–95%	95–98%
Failure without penalty	6–15%	10–20%	16–33%	25–45%	35–60%	45–70%	55–78%	66–85%	75–90%	80–93%	85–96%	91–97%	96–98%	99%
Failure with penalty	16+	21–99%	34–99%	46–99%	61–99%	71–99%	79–99%	86–99%	91–99%	94–99%	97–99%	98–99%	99%	—

Meanings

Success without penalty. You have won the support of the power. Well done!

Success with penalty. You have his support, but lost goodwill. See below.

Failure without penalty. The power was out at lunch—or didn't want to know. Sorry.

Failure with penalty. The appeal has failed, *and* lost you goodwill. Throw a ten-sided dice and reduce your piety by the percentage indicated there—rounding up. "He whom the Gods wish to destroy, they first drive mad."

Intercession

Double the "rank in host" of the power whose support has been gained by appeal. Subtract the "rank in host" of the power with whom he is interceding, and half (rounded up) the Degree of Difficulty of the miracle asked for. Add/subtract luck as usual. Miracle asked for lies in second power's area of specialization: +1. Zero or above = automatic success in obtaining support; —1 to —3 = 0-50 per cent chance of success. Roll percentage dice; —4 to —6 = 0-25 per cent chance of success. Roll percentage dice.

Execution of the miracle

You now have a Higher or Lower power primed to execute the miracle. No calculation is necessary if your power is God himself, in any part of the Trinity, or (at the GM's discretion) the Devil. Otherwise, treat the execution of the miracle as a magical spell carried out by the power. Since Ethereal powers of this magnitude have no problems in locating their targets, however, ignore the "Communication" section and apply only the "Command" calculations (BMC2-3).

There are a number of "miracles" which, while best handled under the appeals system, need no execution calculation. These are appeals for information and appeals for favor, listed below. The Degree of Difficulty here refers not to difficulty at all, but to the unwillingness of the powers to upset the balance of the universe by interference. This figure should be halved before being used in the equations above.

Appeals for information

Concerning the whereabouts of the appellant: DD4; ditto in relation to other specified persons, places, objects, etc.; DD6.

Concerning the future state of the weather: DD4.

Concerning the present state of your soul (i.e., to reveal your piety): DD6.

Concerning your future in the adventure/a general prediction of what may befall you in the near future: DD2 per piece of information asked for; a specific prediction revealing plans already under way, GM's secret, etc.: DD4 per piece of information.

Concerning the nature of a wound or illness: DD4; concerning the cure for the same: DD8.

Concerning future behavior: DD2 if general; DD6 if specifically geared to success or survival in the adventure.

Others: at GM's discretion.

Appeals for favor

For forgiveness (i.e., for an increase in piety to make up for losses on specified sins): DD4 if the appellant is totally isolated; DD12 if there is a cleric anywhere nearby and available for confession.

For protection from unseen assault or magic in the ensuing period: DD8 per 12-hour period asked for; from temptation or the wiles of the enemy powers: DD6 per 12-hour period asked for; from all dangers: DD10 per 12 hours. Effect: factors in any relevant calculation can be varied by up to ±2. Defensive calculations only.

For assistance in the exercise of combat: DD8; in the exercise of magic: DD14; in the exercise of clerical duties (*not* further appeals): DD4 per 12 hours asked for. Effect: as per protection, but offensive and executive calculations only.

For a personal appearance by the power: DD here is *twice* his resistance to appeals.

For inspiration of yourself or of a community or group: see section three.

For resurrection of a dead person, etc.: DD16 if temporary (1–6 turns); DD20 if permanent. Note: a resurrected person is truly alive, not Undead.

Other appeals: at GM's discretion.

Holy relics, shrines, churches and coven sites

Relics, shrines, churches and coven sites can be used by men to further their appeals. In the great majority of cases, relics and shrines will belong to only one Higher or Lower power, and can therefore benefit only appeals to him. Churches and coven sites are similarly dedicated to Saints and Demons respectively, and so further primarily appeals to the patron. Churches with multiple dedications—e.g., St. Paul and St. Lawrence, or All Saints—will carry smaller + factors in appeals. These factors—for relics, shrines, churches and coven sites alike—will normally be between +1 and +5.* Churches and coven sites will, however, carry also +1 factors in appeals direct to God and the Devil respectively. Crosses, and images of particular Saints, count as minor relics, with small + factors.

Relics, shrines, etc., may be desecrated if they fall into the hands of an enemy power or its Earthly servants. Since they are not themselves sources of magical power, they can only resist desecration or offensive magic by an appeal to their Higher power/ Lower power. In such an appeal, make no deduction for resistance of the power appealed to. A desecrated object or place ceases to have any link with the power until solemnly reconsecrated. Christian reconsecration involves ritual purification, benediction, exorcism and veneration—the last being replaced in the case of a church by the saying of a Mass. Diabolic reconsecration requires only purification and veneration. The reconsecrated relic, etc., will carry only half (rounded up) its previous + factor in subsequent appeals.

Possessors of Holy relics and objects of Christian ceremonial worship carry some minor defensive power against offensive magic. This is explained in the Magic Rules.

Religion rules section two:

Divine Grace/Devil's Favor

Divine Grace defines the degree to which you are regarded by God as a loyal and trustworthy servant, deserving His support.

* The higher factors should be reserved for major relics—e.g., a fragment of the True Cross—or an important shrine or center of the religion. False relics and shrines can never have more than +2 in appeals: they only get that as objects through which the Higher power has been venerated.

Devil's Favor is the diabolic equivalent. All clerics, and all laymen with piety over 0, possess at least some measure of Grace; all coven members and contracted devil worshippers, together with others whose piety lies under 0, possess Favor. It is an absolute figure, varying according to behavior and success, known by the player only approximately, and guarded by the GM. Like faith, your instinctive appreciation of the Otherworld, it influences the success of your appeals and other calculations involving your relations with the Higher/Lower powers. Lastly, it is a composite figure made up of three parts. One of these, piety, has already been mentioned and is treated below at some length. The other two parts are: firstly, your religious experience level; and secondly, your rank within the religious hierarchy. The former is explained in the experience rules; the latter, here.

Rank within the religious hierarchy

The table below shows the rank factor of different positions held within the hierarchy of the secular and monastic Christian Churches, and of the Diabolic covens. Note: a contracted Devil servant automatically holds the rank of coven member. Contracted servants participating in a coven hold the rank of assistant coven leader.

| | Christian Church | | | | |
Rank	Secular clergy	Monks & monastic canons	Friars	Religious Knights	Devil Worshippers
1	Unordained clergy	Novice	Novice	Knight	Coven member
2	Priest	Monk	Friar	Knight-Commander	Assistant coven leader
3	Dean	Prior	Friar	House Master	Coven leader
4	Archdeacon	Abbot	Friar	Provincial Commanders	Coven leader
5	Bishop	Abbot of a Mother House	Head of Order	Grand Master	Master of the High Coven (13 covens)
6	Archbishop	Abbot of a Mother House	Head of Order	—	Master of the High Coven
7	Primatial Archbishop	Abbot of a Mother House	Head of Order	—	Master of the High Coven
8	Cardinal	Cardinal	Cardinal	—	Master of the Grand (13 × 13) Coven
9	Cardinal	Cardinal	Cardinal	—	Master of the Grand Coven
10	Pope	Pope	Pope	—	Anti-Pope

Promotion in the hierarchy depends on many factors. Religious experience is marginally the most important of these, and it is at level breaks that promotion takes place. However, social class is also of great importance (Christian hierarchy only). Normally, the individual will ascend the ladder step by step. However, a character with social class of 16 may at any level break "apply for promotion" to any rank in his column up to 4: those with social class of 17 up to 5, of 18 up to 6, and of 19 up to 7.

Add religious experience level plus—

Social class below the norm*: *Subtract* difference; at the norm: 0; above the norm*: *add* difference.

Piety band: halve (rounding down) and add.

Add rank held.

Subtract rank desired.

Charisma, intelligence, leadership: Below 8, —1; 14 or above, +1; 18 or above, +2, for each factor.

Luck (in the usual way).

Multiply the resulting factor by 5 per cent and try to throw under the indicated percentage. Note: GMs may care to make an allowance (up to +4) for money spent on bribes.

Piety and (piety)

The two other parts of Divine Grace/Devil's Favor vary only at set points, and upwards. They are also figures well known to the player concerned. Piety is rather different. It reflects absolutely the degree to which your power *wants* to support you, rather than merely feeling obliged to do so to maintain the position of his Church. It rises and falls according to your behavior, and the attention you pay your god. Behavior can be divided into virtues, which bring an increase in Christian piety, and sins, which bring about a corresponding decrease. For the Devil worshipper, the position is exactly reversed. The Devil is concerned to build up a body of servants on Earth bound to him by their own awareness of being damned sinners. Each sin they commit removes them further from Divine Grace, and therefore increased the Devil's Favor. Virtuous deeds bring corresponding changes in the other direction. Of equal importance, however, is the service you do your power. By carrying out ceremonies, by conversions and

* See "Social class and background: character generation" table.

other religious duties you increase His majesty, His mana. By frustrating the plans of His enemies on Earth, and serving His own designs diligently, you increase his temporal power. Both bring goodwill upon you, from your own power—and thereby automatically damn you further in the eyes of the other.

The quantification of piety and its diabolic equivalent, impiety or (piety) is difficult and requires sensitive treatment by the GM. The figures below are only guidelines. GMs should be careful to avoid wild fluctuations in a character's piety, by interpreting every little mistake as a sin or every casual alms as proof of virtue.

Piety is quantified in points, and divided into certain bands. It is the piety bands/(piety bands) which contribute most ± factors to other calculations in the book; the points are only important in determining to which band the character belongs. Thus:

Piety points 0-09 = Piety band or PB 0.
Piety points 10-39 = Piety band or PB 1.
Piety points 40-79 = Piety band or PB 2.
Piety points 80-129 = Piety band or PB 3.
Piety points 130-189 = Piety band or PB 4.
Piety points 190-259 = Piety band or PB 5.

Etc.—width of band increasing by 10 each time. The band breaks for (piety) are at the same minus numbers, PB0 therefore spanning piety points −9 to +9.

Piety is lost by sinning. For quantification, sins are divided into seven classes, of descending magnitude. Class 1: murder (but see class 6 below), act of worship to other gods or the Devil, denying god. Class 2: incest, homosexual activity, other sexual perversion, blasphemy. Class 3: adultery, fornication, lust, practice of Black Magic, assault, rape. Class 4: theft, greed, usury, omitting religious observances (including tithes), anger, practice of magic (other), atheism, false evidence against a neighbor. Class 5: hypocrisy, practice of White Magic, dishonoring your parents or the Sabbath, covetousness, meanness. Class 6: pride, cowardice, passing judgement upon others, manslaughter in fair combat, selfishness, breach of promise. Class 7: laziness, lying to strangers, gluttony, drunkenness.

The following table gives a range of piety points lost for sinning, in each piety band. Obviously, God expects more of those in high piety bands, and so finds sinful behavior on their part more shocking than those below PB 0. However, in deciding on a suitable deduction, GMs must take other factors into account. Firstly, there is the victim of the sin. If the victim is a poor person, or someone in good standing with God, the sin is the greater —and still more if it offends the Church or God Himself. On the other hand, a sin committed against an enemy of God may be almost no sin at all. Secondly, there is the magnitude of the sin: an unprovoked assault is more heinous than a provoked one, and murder of a hundred persons more sinful than of one. Finally, a sinning cleric is more of an abomination to the Lord than a sinning warrior! This is why each compartment of the table carries only a range of deductions, for the GM's choice.

Piety points lost for sinning in different piety bands

Left group columns (7–1) are labelled **(Piety bands) or (PB)s**; right group columns (4–7) are labelled **Piety bands or PBs**.

Class of sin	Below 7	7	6	5	4	3	2	1	0	1	2	3	4	5	6	7	Above 7
1	5–	5–	6–	6–	7–	7–	8–	10–	13–	15–	25–	35–	45–	55–	65–	75–	85–
	10	12	14	16	18	20	22	25	30	35	45	55	65	75	85	95	105
2	2–	2–	3–	3–	4–	4–	5–	5–	6–	8–	13–	18–	23–	28–	33–	38–	43–
	4	5	6	7	8	9	10	12	14	17	22	27	32	37	42	47	52
3	1–	1–	2–	2–	3–	3–	4–	4–	5–	5–	8–	12–	15–	18–	22–	25–	28–
	2	3	3	4	5	6	7	8	10	12	15	18	22	25	28	32	35
4	1	1–	1–	2–	2–	2–	3–	3–	4–	4–	6–	9–	11–	14–	16–	19–	21–
		2	3	3	4	5	6	7	8	9	11	14	16	19	21	24	26
5	—	1	1–	1–	2–	2–	2–	2–	3–	3–	5–	7–	9–	11–	13–	15–	17–
			2	3	3	4	5	6	6	7	9	11	13	15	17	19	21
6	—	—	1	1–	1–	2–	2–	2–	3–	4–	6–	7–	9–	11–	12–	14–	
			2	3	3	4	5	6	6	7	9	11	13	14	16	18	
7	—	—	—	1	1–	1–	2–	2–	2–	2–	3–	5–	6–	8–	9–	11–	12–
				2	3	3	4	5	6	6	8	9	11	12	14	15	

Increases in piety are more difficult to quantify, since virtue in Christian terms lies mainly in the absence of sin. *Fantasy Wargaming* allows players a certain, automatic increase of 30 piety points per game day, for all the times when you had the opportunity to sin and did not take it. Days spent in circumstances allowing no opportunity to sin, and non-gaming days in campaigns, do not accumulate piety points. Additionally, the GM should award points for definite virtues of commission. These again fall into seven classes, descending in importance: and the table above can be used to register increases as well as deductions in piety. Simply use the equivalent band on the *opposite* side (a character with PB3 showing mercy looks under (PB)3 and class 2 sin for his piety gain). Class 1: defending God or His interest against His enemies. Class 2: mercy, staunchness in the service of God in adversity, performance (or being the subject) of a religious ceremony. Class 3: resisting sexual temptation, private religious observance, charity to the poor or the Church, attendance at a public religious ceremony. Class 4: resisting financial or other temptation, humility, selflessness. Class 5: charity to other persons, forgiveness of wrongs done to you, act of peace under provocation, act of brotherly love. Class 6: honoring your parents or the Sabbath, telling the truth when inconvenient, bravery. Class 7: moderation in food and drink, activity (i.e., not laziness).

Additionally, the GM should take care to consider the interests of God and the Devil at all times. If a character does anything which tends to the interest of his power, but does not fit into the scheme above, piety points should still be awarded. If he opposes in any way that interest, a corresponding deduction should be made.

The dangers of impiety

To be pious ensured God's goodwill, increased the chances of a successful appeal, and boded well for your soul after death. It also meant strict restraints on your behavior, and passing up great opportunities for self-advancement. To many players, as indeed to most of the medieval characters they manage, piety could be done without—the candle, so to speak, was not worth the game. Even clerics might feel that way. Piety left their routine ceremonial and disciplinary powers unaffected; medieval theologians and modern scholars like Keith Thomas agreeing that "The Sacraments worked automatically, regardless of the moral worth of the officiating priest." In *Fantasy Wargaming,* the use of such powers by clerics not in good standing with God brings further loss of piety—but so what?

Yet dangers did exist for the layman or cleric whose piety was low. These dangers are again related to particular piety bands. Persons in PB2 or above are in good standing with God. On reaching PB2, the person receives an ex gratia grant of 30 piety points "for encouragement." All clerics are expected to have this standing. Below PB 0, in the negative piety bands, a person is officially considered impious by God: and at (Piety band) 2, he becomes in peril of his soul. These are the only times at which

God of his own urging gives an indication of a character's piety—when it falls below PB2, PB0, or to (PB)2. The indication will be in the form of a warning or a punishment: a dream of hellfire, for example, for the former, a sudden misfortune or illness for the latter. GMs should be inventive, but not too destructive, here!

Below PB2, clerics are penalized for exercise of delegated powers or appeals. This exercise counts as a Class 4 sin, piety loss for appeals being additional to any specified by the appeals table. If his fall from Grace becomes known to his ecclesiastical superiors, he may be disciplined with a penance.

Below PB0, clerics and laymen face possible excommunication by the church. Continuing exercise of delegated powers and appeals now count as a Class 3 sin. Only characters below PB0 may be possessed.

At (Piety band)2, characters *will* receive an awful warning from the Higher powers. At (PB)3, they *may* also receive a visitation from the Devil, claiming their soul. This is already forfeit, so the Devil need do no more than kill your Earthly body to collect. However, the Lower powers are concerned to build up a body of devoted servants on Earth. The Devil may therefore "merely" bind you to his service. In this case, He will appear and use magic to demonstrate your powerlessness; e.g., by a command to yield. Performing this command three times will bind you to Him. Magical and religious defenses may be used against Him, including appeals to the Higher powers for help or forgiveness. These will probably not succeed. Having obtained power over you, the Devil may then demand a contract of service, with your life and soul as the forfeit. The terms of the contract lie between the GM and player—and should be very much one-sided! This is in great contrast to the other kind of contracted servant, who has made a pact with the Devil of his own free will in return for knowledge, wealth or power—in short, Faust. The latter contracts may involve no service or worship to the Devil, although again the life and soul of the man will be forfeit after a specified number of years. And God help Faust and those like him if they fall into (PB)3! A free-will contract may come about either by conjuration of the Devil/subordinate Demon or by an appeal for personal appearance.

Diabolic visitation may again occur at any downward piety

band break after (PB)3. The Devil frequently avoids an appearance at (PB)3 deliberately, to lure the character into further iniquities and remove him further from the Grace of God.

After death/the state of your soul

Characters in *Fantasy Wargaming* should live their lives in continual awareness of salvation and damnation. The state of your soul was a preoccupation of all religious people, and many more who were not as religious as they should have been! The Divine Grace rules above cover this in life. They would, however, be incomplete without an indication of the soul's future after death. Indeed, players may need to know where a dead man's spirit is located in the Otherworld, for conjuration purposes.

Characters who die in good standing with God—i.e., in Piety band 2 or above—go automatically to Heaven. Similarly, those in (Piety band)2 or below are damned into Hell. Between these two lies Purgatory, where a spirit must purify itself of sins committed during the life of its Earthly body, before entering Heaven. This is, however, only stage one of the process. For most souls in Heaven or Hell, this is their final destination; but a few especially gifted and pious or impious spirits may be selected to continue in the service of their powers, as Saints or Demons. Similarly, a calculation is needed to decide how long a soul in Purgatory remains there before being sufficiently purified for Heaven.

Becoming a Saint or Demon

Add Divine Grace/Devil's Favor of character at death plus—
Circumstances of death:

Character killed in service of God/the Devil, +1;

Character martyred for serving God/the Devil, +2 (accumulative).

Faith: 8 or below, −1; 14 or above, +1; 18 or above, +2.

Social Class of 18 or above, +2.

Luck, as usual.

Below 15: failure. 15-19: enrolment of the spirit as a minor Saint/Demon, Grade 7. 20-24: enrolment as a medium Saint/Demon, Grade 6. 25 or above: enrolment as a major Saint/Demon, Grade 5.

Enrolment is immediate upon death—although powers will not

normally allow the new Saint or Demon to continue action in the particular adventure. However, the history of the medieval church shows that it took great time for recognition on Earth of sanctification: major Saints 1-50 years: throw percentage dice and halve; medium Saints: 1-100 years: throw percentage dice; minor Saints: 5-500 years: throw percentage dice and multiply by 5. Unrecognized Saints carry an extra minus factor in appeals.

Passage of a soul through Purgatory

Piety band/(Piety band) of character at death, +/—.
Religious experience level of character at death, add half (round up).
Faith: 8 or below, —1; 14 or above, +1.
Luck, as usual.
Propitiation by relatives: for each 20 GS spent by relatives or others in prayers, alms, benevolences, indulgences or religious ceremonies, etc., for the state of the soul, +1 (max +4).
Per 50 years spent in Purgatory so far, +1.

This calculation should be made each 50 years; or repeatedly at death, until success. Success is achieved by a score of 10 or above, and brings final admittance into Heaven.

Religion rules section three:

Delegated, ceremonial and routine clerical powers

The great majority of spectacular religious interventions in an adventure will come by appeal: the channelling of help down from a Higher power, to meet particular dangers or needs of people on Earth. Appeal, as we have seen, can be made by anyone who is actually a worshipper of the deity, although clerics and coveners have an advantage. There are, however, also a number of powers which the clerical servants of a deity, and particularly the Christian God, may exercise without appeal. These are the main subjects of this section. The powers are not uniform in type or effect. Some are ceremonies, a few not. Some have an effect that is totally explainable in psychological terms: they raise the morale of worshippers, and give them a chance of becoming inspired with the awe and majesty of their deity. They also increase the piety of worshippers, as we have seen in section two, counting as a Class 3/4 virtue. Some of their effects, however, are truly magical, requiring the use of Supernatural power. This does not mean that the cleric is carrying out magic himself. Instead, he is achieving magical effects in the normal way, through an appeal to his Higher powers—but an appeal which those powers will *always* answer, no matter what the circumstances or piety of the appellant. They thus remain to an extent dependent on Divine goodwill and Grace. The Higher power will grant the "appeal" automatically—but may think less of you thereafter, if you have misused the powers in your trust. Misuse brings loss of piety. Exercising powers when not in good standing with your god is misuse. So is their use to benefit persons whom you *know* to be worshippers of no or another power, to have been expelled or suspended from the body of worshippers, or to be rank offenders against the behavior expected of a worshipper. The last means any Christian in a negative piety band, any Devil worshipper in a positive one. All such misuse is a Class 4 Sin—though in the case of a coven master, it is uniquely a sin which *reduces* his (piety)!

Magical and psychological effects apart, there are also routine clerical powers with a disciplinary and punitive effect. Again, these are particularly strong in the Christian community, where the priest and his superiors have powers to punish violations of the Christian code of behavior among laymen and clerics alike. These powers are covered either below or in the section on the law and justice.

Finally, religious ceremonies increase the power of the being worshipped, through transference of mana. This is an inefficient process, and ¾ of the mana accumulated by the incantations, etc., of the worshippers is lost during transference. The mana gains set out in the lists below fit squarely with the "Accumulation of mana/preparations for Active magic" section.

Christian ceremonies and powers

*Mass.** Duration: 1 hour. Celebrant: Abbot, Ordained Priest or above. Ceremonial morale factor: +3. Process: a Mass is the principal religious rite of the Church, commemorating the sacrifice of the flesh and blood of Christ. It celebrates this sacrifice through the taking of bread and water, changed magically into the very being of the Savior, and the saying of prayers and hymns. Counts as a ceremony for appeals and piety purposes. Must be heard in a church or sanctified place. Mana: 2 points to God per worshipper. Experience: 10. Adds for appeal: +2 on defensive dice rolls within hour.

*High Mass.** As Mass. Takes 1½ hours, is usually said at midnight, or on a Sunday/Holy Day. CMF: +4. Mana: 3 points per celebrant. Experience: 15. Adds for appeal: +2 on defensive die rolls within 1½ hours.

*Benediction: formal.** Duration: 2 minutes. Celebrant: any cleric. CMF: +2. Process: sprinkling with holy water and the saying of holy words and blessings. No accumulation of mana. Experience: 4. Adds for appeal: +2 on all defensive die rolls within following hour. Negates a magical command of cursing. Formal Benediction brings 5 per cent increase in piety.

*Benediction: informal.** Duration: 1 minute. Celebrant: any cleric. CMF: +1. Process: as formal Benediction, but applied generally to a group. No mana or experience effects. Adds for appeal: +1 on defensive rolls within following turn.

Malediction (*curse*).** Duration: 2 minutes. Celebrant: Ordained clergy and Abbots. Process: a solemn prayer to God to remove his Grace from a single identified person. Morale: Malediction has a CMF of 2—calculate as for Benediction but treat results on morale table as *negative*. No mana. Experience 4. Piety results: To be formally cursed involves a 5 per cent loss in piety (but 5 per cent increase if curse is by a cleric of opposite alignment). Magic results: —2 on all appeals, and on defensive die rolls within hour. Negates a magical command of blessing.

*Ordination.** Duration: 1 hour. Celebrant: Bishops. CMF: +3 for the new Priest, +1 for the Bishop. Process: the novice Priest is solemnly introduced to the duties of an Ordained Priest and blessed. Mana: 2 points per celebrant. Experience: 40 for Priest, 40 for Bishop. Magical effects: as per formal Benediction. Piety effects: automatic +10 per cent on piety, over and above participation in ceremony. Adds for appeal. Gives the man extra clerical rank, therefore benefiting appeals; gives him delegated powers of Ordained Clergy. Normally followed by new Priest saying Mass.

Investment.* Duration: 2 hours. Celebrant: Archbishop or two Bishops. CMF: as Ordination. Process: the new Bishop is blessed, enjoined to obey the duties of a Bishop fully, amid rejoicing, procession and singing. Followed by Mass or High Mass (included in time). Mana: 3 points per celebrant. Experience: 40 for Bishops, 40 for Archbishop. Gives access to episcopal powers and status, etc. Piety effects: as per Ordination. Magical effects as per formal Benediction.

Confession. Duration: 10-90 minutes, depending on sins! Celebrant: Abbots, Ordained Priests. CMF: +2. Process: Confession is not a ceremony, and so has no adds for appeal purposes or die rolls. It is simply the procedure by which a character details his sins to the cleric since last Confession, and is forgiven. The forgiveness will restore 10-60 piety points (six-die × 10) and will normally be followed by a penance imposed by cleric. The size of that penance will vary to follow number of PP restored. Typical penances involve payment of GS to church, saying of religious formulae (e.g., Hail Mary, Paternoster, etc.) or restitution to the persons wronged. Note: imposing too light a penance counts as a misuse of powers, as does hearing confession from a character more than twice a week. Failure to carry out penance is a Class 2 Sin. Mana: 1-2 points for the penance. Experience: 2.

Final Absolution. Duration: 10 minutes. Celebrant: Abbots, Ordained Priests. CMF: +3. Process: Not a ceremony, simply an acknowledgement of the immediacy of death and holy words absolving the sufferer of sins. Absolution will restore 20-120 piety points (two six-dice × 10). These will be lost if the character recovers, unless he voluntarily carries out a penance/donation (as for Confession). Experience: 4.

Excommunication: formal.* Duration: 30 minutes. Celebrant: Bishops or above. CMF: +4 but morale results are negative, as for Malediction. Excommunication cuts off the character from all benefits derived from ceremonies of the Church, from appeals to God, etc. Piety automatically reduced by a third. All pious members of the Congregation—PB2+—will refuse to have anything to do with the character, even to supplying him with the necessities of life. Character also ineligible for Confession, penance, etc., unless received back by Excommunicating cleric. Experience: 8.

Excommunication: informal. Duration: 5 minutes. Celebrant: Abbots, Ordained priests. CMF: +2 but results negative. This is simply the process by which a Priest refuses to admit a worshipper to Communion. Unless coupled with Malediction, it has no magical or piety effect; the character will not necessarily be barred from other clerics, either for ceremonies or confession. Social effects as per formal Excommunication. Experience: 4.

Interdict. Duration: 1 hour. Celebrant: Primatial Archbishops and Popes only. CMF: +3 on all members of the nation—and the effect permanent till Interdict removed—with results negative. Interdict suspends the religious life of the nation; only clerics themselves will be eligible for ceremonies, confession, appeals, etc. Misusing powers of Excommunication or Interdict is a Class 1 Sin. Experience: 16.

*Baptism.** Duration: 30 minutes. Celebrant: Ordained clergy. CMF: +1 on Christian parents of baptized child, or on adult being baptized after conversion. Baptism involves the sprinkling of holy water over the child or convert, to admit him into membership of the Christian community. Prayers are then said, and hymns sung. Piety of a convert increases one piety band. No mana. Experience: 6 for priest, 20 for a baptized convert.

Marriage. Duration: 1 hour. Celebrant: Ordained clergy. CMF: +3 on wedding couple, +2 on relatives, +1 on others. Marriage involves the exchange of vows, gift of a ring, and solemnization of the couple's junction. Matrimony is a holy state, the only one in which sexual acts are not a sin in God's eyes. Piety: one piety band increase for the couple. 1 mana point per member of audience. Experience: 8 for priest, 20 for the couple. Adds for appeal.

*Purification of water and materials.** Ceremonial purification of materials for use in rites. This is done by veneration and benediction, taking ten minutes in all. Celebrant: Abbot or Ordained clergy. Ritual materials of this kind, after veneration, have some magical protective powers. Purified ("Holy") Water is also a target for Devil worshippers, who use it in desecration. No CMF, piety, mana or experience. (Mana is drained into the materials, and does not pass to God.)

*Veneration of image or relic.** Duration: up to 2 hours. Celebrant: anyone. It is an act of worship through the image or relic to the Higher or Lower power it came from. Mana: 1 point per worshipper per 40 minutes passes to the Power. Experience: 1 point per mana point. Piety: Class 3 virtue. CMF: +1. Increases chance of an appeal.

Preaching. Duration: up to 96 minutes. Celebrant: anyone, but usually Ordained clergy, Friars. It is a peroration to the greater glory of God, an exhortation to the faithful and an attempt to convert the faithless. Chance of conversion by persuasion. CMF: +2 (but +1 if it goes over the hour). Piety as per Class 2 virtue. Mana up to +3, from celebrant only. Experience: 12 points.

Exorcism. Duration: 20 minutes. Celebrant: Ordained clergy. Exorcism is really an appeal to God for the exercise of magical powers to expel a Demon from a place, person, etc. Only Demons can be exorcised; attempts to expel Norse deities, elves, etc., fail. The Demon is powerless to resist exorcism after the initial holy words have been spoken. He is expelled into Hell. No CMF, but 50 piety points and experience points. No mana transfer.

Funeral rites. Duration: 45 minutes. Celebrant: Ordained clergy, Abbot. Interment and Last Rites in a Christian graveyard cuts ten years off a soul's passage through Purgatory. An interred soul has an extra resistance of 1 when being conjured by a Necromancer. CMF: +1. No mana transfer. 20 piety points for relatives. 8 experience points for celebrant.

Devil worship: ceremonies and powers

The Devil imitates, and does not invent. Most of the ceremonies and powers used by the Christian Church—those asterisked in the list above—have their exact or approximate equivalences: "mockeries." Thus *Ordination* and *Investment* become the ceremonies creating a coven leader and Master of the High Coven, respectively. They last the same time, have the same effects ("Piety" of course, being negative throughout), and involve a travesty of the Christian ceremony. The same is true of *Baptism:* the liquid used being blood rather than holy water. *Benediction* and *Malediction* (curse) have the same magical effects on die rolls, and on appeals to the Lower powers. The piety effect of blessing by a witch is, however, again to remove the subject further from God—to increase his negative piety. Cursing has a corresponding effect in the other direction. Blood is again the medium, rather than "unholy water." *Veneration*—essentially a magical process for transferring mana to the power—is identical. *Excommunication*—removing the victim from Communion—is in fact only one of a variety of coven punishments. The coven leader (Priest equivalent) exercises the strictest discipline over his members, with the power of corporal punishment and of life and death. Violating the interests of the coven will bring more than ostracism, in many cases! Diabolic "Excommunication" has, however, no wider social effects, among the Christian community—and will decrease his negative piety by a third.

The main imitative ceremony of the Devil worshipper is the *Black Mass* and *High Black Mass*. The former may be celebrated at any time, the latter usually once a quarter by a High Coven on Lammas (July 31), All Hallows Eve (October 31), Candlemas (February 2) and Mayday. At its simplest, the *Black Mass* is just a foul travesty and mockery of a *Mass,* with the Communion being a ghastly concoction of rotten food and blood, the desecration of a cross, candle and cup (e.g., by use in sexual act), and the "hymns" either obscene or ritual praisings of Lucifer. The *Black Mass* is, however, often associated with a *Sacrifice*—as below.

Some holdovers from the pagan traditions of the witches did, however, survive, as ceremonies and acts of worship to the Devil. In particular:

Feast. Duration: 1 hour. Celebrant: coven leader. CMF: +2. Process: the taking of food and drink in honor of the Devil. The meal is in silence, except for a continual low hum of concentration—a form of ululation. Adds for appeal, +1 on offensive die rolls within 1 hour. Mana: 2 points to the Devil per worshipper. Experience: 8.

Sacrifice. Duration: ¼ hour. Celebrant: coven leader. CMF: +1. Sacrifice involves incantation and the ritual slaughtering of a creature or person (preferably an unbaptized virgin Christian—as desecration) to the Devil. Special adds for appeal. Mana: ½ point per worshipper, +4 for the victim (+9 if human).

Black Masses, feasts and *sacrifices* are often followed by a "sacred" dance and orgy. These are, however, not diabolic ceremonies, in that they involve no worship. They are instead means by which witches build up their own mana shamanistically, for magical use. The dance or orgy is often followed by a spell-teaching and -practicing period, in which spells are mastered or magic carried out by the coven cooperatively.

Morale

Worshippers attending a religious service or ceremony dedicated to their deity are both confirmed in their beliefs and strengthened to meet the challenges of life. The former is handled through piety. To calculate the increase in morale that comes through a service or ceremony, make the following calculation.

Add ½ Divine Grace/Devil's Favor of cleric (rounded *up*) plus—

Piety band of worshipper (double).

Worshipper was only passively attending service, —1.

    Actively participating, +1.

    Officiating (i.e., the leading cleric), +2.

Ceremonial morale factor (see above).

Faith of worshipper: 8 or below, —1.

    14 or above, +1.

Luck: as usual.

Finally, subtract number of other religious ceremonies attended in last 24 hours.

Dice throw	5 or below	6–7	8–9	10–11	12–13	14–15	16–17	18–19	20 or above
1	—	—	—	—	—	+1	+2	+3/20%	+3/26%
2	—	—	—	—	+1	+2	+2/14%	+4/24%	+4/26%
3	—	—	—	+1	+2	+2/10%	+3/16%	+4/26%	+4/28%
4	—	—	+1	+1	+2	+2/12%	+3/20%	+5/26%	+5/28%
5	—	+1	+1	+2	+2/10%	+3/16%	+3/22%	+5/28%	+5/30%
6	1+	+1	+2	+2/10%	+3/16%	+3/20%	+4/24%	+5/30%	+6/33%

Notes

Increases in morale due to ceremonies fade away at the rate of 1 MP each 6 hours. Only those in positive piety bands who are communicant Christians will receive any morale advantage from Christian ceremonies; similarly, only bound Devil worshippers who are also in negative piety will gain from Diabolic ceremonies.

Attendance at a ceremony of another religion to your own may lower your morale. Carry out the calculation above *subtracting* your PB or (PB) × 2 and treat all figures on the table as *negative*. Treat "inspiration" percentages as percentages for conversion. For mass increases of morale: apply the calculation using PB zero and faith 10.

Inspiration. "+3/25%" on the table above means an increase in morale of 3 and a 25 per cent chance of inspiration. See next section. Only those in good standing—PB or (PB)2 or above—are eligible for inspiration.

Inspiration

Inspiration is the process by which a worshipper is suddenly filled with the awe and majesty of his deity—God or the Devil. The effects of Inspiration are:

Your piety is automatically increased by the width of a piety band—i.e., by 50 PP if you are in PB3, by —60 if in (PB)4, etc.

You will take all morale tests at +2 as long as inspiration lasts.

You will not suffer from fatigue until twice the recognized period/EP damage has occurred.

Your physique is increased by 1; likewise your endurance, bravery, charisma and faith. Your agility and intelligence are reduced by 1.

You take all control tests at +2, +3 if facing a danger from enemies of your deity.

You carry an extra +3 factor in appeals.

The following are not eligible for inspiration: those between (PB)2 and PB2—i.e., not in good standing with their deity; persons who are demoralized, exhausted or badly injured (lost ½ EPs); non-worshippers, whatever their PB. Inspired characters lose their inspiration immediately on attaining any of these states, or on a 5 per cent die roll at the end of each day. Loss of inspiration reverts you to previous factors.

Spontaneous inspiration. Inspiration through attendance at religious ceremonies is covered in the previous section. Additionally, a character satisfying the criteria for eligibility may become inspired spontaneously in a number of different circumstances:

Facing danger or threat from servants/powers of a different

religion: for the first time, +3; subsequent times, +1.

Seeing a successful appeal: your own, +2; someone else's, +1.

Being rescued from death, +3; injury or captivity, +1, by intervention of your deity; from diabolic Possession, +2.

Characters in PB/(PB)5 or above only: after *any* notable victory, success, relief from danger, illness, etc., whether brought about by intervention/appeal or not, +2.

Other: (at GM's discretion).

Add circumstance factor plus—

2 × PB/(PB)

Faith: 8 or below, —1; 14-17, +1; 18+, +2.

Religious Experience Level: add half (rounded up).

Subtract rank in Church.

Luck (in the usual way).

Character has been inspired before: +1.

Character is usually inspired: +3.

Multiply the result by 3 and throw under on percentage dice to be inspired.

Inspiration by appeal. Individuals and communities or groups may also achieve inspiration by an appeal for favor to their Higher powers, by the procedure laid out in section one. This avenue to inspiration is normally followed by those who are not eligible for inspiration through normal ceremonial or spontaneous channels—because of injury, fatigue or above all because of unworthy piety.

The "Degree of Difficulty" in such appeals is a measure of the Higher powers' reluctance to extend especial treatment to those who have not proved themselves worthy.

Degree of Difficulty for an individual appeal: 10 + 4DD for each PB/(PB) below 2.

Degree of Difficulty for a communal appeal:

Add basic DD plus—

Size of group: under 10, 0; 11-20, +1; 21-50, +2; 51-200, +3; 201-500, +4; per subsequent 500, +2.

Piety: most of group lies under PB/(PB)3*: +4.

Public confession by all members of unworthiness and statements of penance**: —4.

*In an undifferentiated congregation, there will be 2 characters with PB/(PB)3+ per 50 members, 6 × PB/(PB)2, 14 ×

PB/(PB)1 and 28 with PB zero. Those with figures above 0 will be divided equally between PB and (PB)—i.e., 7 in PB 1 and 7 in (PB) 1.

** Five minutes per person. 10 per cent chance of persons worshipping other powers being identified by those around him during confession.

Members of an inspired group—a community turned to God or the Devil—have all the characteristics of individual inspiration. There will be 5 per cent dropout rate per day; when more than a third of the group have lost inspiration (i.e., after one week), the community as a whole automatically loses inspiration.

Religion rules section four:

Ethereal hosts and hierarchies

Angels, Demons and Norse deities belong to different hosts within the Ethereal plane—known as Heaven, Hell and Valhalla respectively. The Christian and Diabolic hosts in particular may be compared to armies, or bureaucracies: divided into firm ranks with recognized chains of command and communication. The success of your appeal, and of any intercession that may result, depends to a considerable degree on the rank of the power appealed to within the host. The higher up the host, the more resistant to appeal the power usually (not always) is: but once won over, the power will carry more weight in intercession and will have more magical ability to spare in spells on your behalf. Promotions within the host are possible, but normally take decades if not centuries to achieve. To stand any chance of promotion, the power must achieve a magic level and store of mana equal to that of the worst or lowest power in the rank above his own. His promotion chance then depends on the number of powers in that next rank. If there are four powers of that rank, his chance is 1 in $4 = 25\%$: if 10 powers, it will be only 10 per cent, and so on. If the power is not promoted, but gradually builds up his level and mana to pass other powers of the next rank up, other calculations may be made each time he equals or passes a power. Count the number of powers equalled or surpassed, turn them into a percentage of the rank as a whole, and try to throw under. There is a straight 10 per cent chance that if successful, you will "dislodge" or demote the lowest of the powers in your new rank to your former rank. Mana is built up primarily by worship, but magic level requires the garnering of experience through action in the usual way.

Comparative ranks within the Ethereal hierarchies

Rank in host	Christianity	Devil worship
9	Father, Son and Holy Ghost	Lucifer
8	Virgin Mary	Beelzebub
7	3 Archangels	Ashtaroth, Belial, Lucifuge Rofocale
6	12 Apostles	Arch-Demons
5	Evangelists, Doctors and Major Saints	Major Demons
4	Saints	Demons
3	Minor Saints	Minor Demons
2	Unacknowledged Minor Saints	Incubi and Succubi
1	Cherubim and Seraphim	Imps, Gargoyles, etc.

The tables on the following few pages list the hierarchies and the individual attributes of the powers in them.

Notes

The tables include all powers in a religious supernatural hierarchy from the Supreme God to the lowest cherubim or imp. However, factors may be rather few at the top end—God Himself, for example, having infinite intelligence ("Omniscience"), strength/ constitution ("Omnipotence") and piety, but no greed, selfishness, lust at all ("Omni-benevolent"). At the lower end, *Fantasy Wargaming* treats cherubims, imps, etc., as clones from the same mold and includes factors for them only as a class. Players may, however, create individual characters by use of luck rolls to alter characteristics.

Special characteristics. These are greed, selfishness, lust, anger, piety band, charisma, bravery. All Christian Higher powers are assumed to have greed, selfishness and lust of 5, PB 8, charisma and bravery of 12. All Demonic powers ("Lower powers") similarly are assumed to have greed, selfishness and lust of 13, (PB) 6, charisma and bravery of 13. Individual variations on these figures for character appear in this section of the table.

Areas of special interest and disfavor. These affect both appeals

HIGHER POWERS

Name of power	Astrological controller	Combat level	Intelligence	Endurance	Agility	Physique	Mana	Magic level	Faith	Resistance to appeals	Rank in host	Areas of interest and patronage	Areas of disfavor	Special characteristics and notes
God	Leo	24	40	?	?	?	?	?	?	7	9	Creation, dominance	Rebellion	Three persons. Can operate independently
Virgin Mary	Virgo	10	28	26	32	24	384	24	34	5	8	Virginity, motherhood, forgiveness	Sex	
Michael	Aries	22	28	35	34	34	368	23	33	7	7	Demon slaying	Peace	Captain of Heavenly host (all forces)
Gabriel	Gemini	21	26	34	34	33	368	23	33	6	7	Communication, dreams	Plant control	Messenger of God
Raphael	Taurus	20	23	34	34	33	368	23	33	6	7	Healing the sick	Death	
Andrew	Pisces	9	24	33	32	34	336	21	31	5	6	Fishing, food	Writing	
James the Great	Scorpio	10	25	31	31	30	336	21	31	5	6	Crusades, pilgrims, Spaniards	Illusions	
James the Less	Gemini	8	24	26	27	26	320	20	30	5	6	Brotherhood, unity, family	Division	Brother of Christ
John	Sagittarius	23	25	33	32	31	352	22	32	5	6	Apocalypse, The Last Battle	Love, peace	Commander of Lesser Saints
John the Baptist	Aquarius	7	23	32	31	32	336	21	31	5	6	Conversion, monks and nuns	Active magic	Guardian of Purgatory
Jude	Cancer	8	22	29	27	28	336	21	30	4	6	Desperate, hopeless emergencies	Death	
Peter	Libra	7	24	30	27	29	336	21	30	5	6	Judgement, entrances	Backsliders	Guardian of the Gate of Heaven
Philip	Taurus	5	23	30	26	30	304	19	29	4	6	Feeding, bread, cookery	Wasting death	
Paul	Pisces	7	22	26	27	27	320	20	30	5	6	Journeys, water, robbery, fatigue	Women	

Name of power	Astrological controller	Combat level	Intelligence	Endurance	Agility	Physique	Mana	Magic level	Faith	Resistance to appeals	Rank in host	Areas of interest and patronage	Areas of disfavor	Special characteristics and notes
							Factors							
Thomas	Sagittarius	8	17	28	27	28	320	20	29	4	6	Construction, builders, waverers	Destruction	
Matthias	Scorpio	8	18	28	26	27	304	19	28	4	6	Africa, deserts, southerners	Water	
Bartholemew	Taurus	7	19	26	27	26	304	19	29	4	6	Animals, butchers, tanners	Undead control	
Anthony	Pisces	6	26	25	25	25	304	19	29	4	5	Study, meditation, occult	Worldly affairs	
Augustine	Leo	7	24	25	24	25	304	19	29	4	5	Justice, the law, judgement	War	
Christopher	Virgo	7	19	27	26	27	288	18	28	4	5	Journeys by land	Journeys by sea	
Francis of Assisi	Sagittarius	4	20	23	26	25	304	19	29	4	5	Bird control, poverty, Friars	Wealth, treasure	
George	Aries	17	16	26	25	26	288	18	28	5	5	War, Englishmen	French	
Gregory the Great	Leo	10	17	24	24	25	272	17	27	4	5	Slaves, missionary expeditions	Heathens	
Joseph	Virgo	6	20	25	25	24	272	17	28	4	5	Parenthood, children, carpenters	Sorcery	
Joseph of Arimathea	Capricorn	6	22	24	24	25	272	17	27	4	5	Guardianship, the young	Death	
Lawrence	Cancer	6	23	23	24	23	272	17	28	4	5	Alms, beggars, poor	War	
Mark	Aries	11	24	24	25	26	288	18	28	4	5	Fire, light	Water	
Luke	Taurus	10	24	25	27	23	288	18	28	4	5	Healing, physicians, doctors	Combat	
Nicholas	Libra	7	22	24	24	24	272	17	28	4	5	Sailors, merchants, thieves	Divination	
Jerome	Cancer	7	25	26	22	23	272	17	27	5	5	Thought, argument, persuasion	Sex, love	
Matthew	Leo	7	23	23	24	24	272	17	26	5	5	Money, taxes, civil officials	Disorder	
Catherine	Taurus	6	20	23	25	23	272	17	27	3	5	Death, health, nursing	Prophecy	
Patrick	Scorpio	13	20	24	25	24	288	18	27	5	5	Snakes, magic, Irish	Earth	
Sebastian	Sagittarius	13	18	24	26	24	256	16	26	4	5	Archers, soldiers, homosexuals	Persecution	

HIGHER POWERS, CONTINUED

Name of power	Astrological controller	Combat level	Intelligence	Endurance	Agility	Physique	Mana	Magic level	Faith	Resistance to appeals	Rank in host	Areas of interest and patronage	Areas of disfavor	Special characteristics and notes
							Factors							
Agatha	Gemini	6	19	23	24	23	240	15	25	4	4	Air, disease	Fire	
Agnes	Leo	7	19	23	22	23	240	15	26	3	4	Weather	Sex	
Aidan	Sagittarius	7	22	23	23	23	240	15	26	3	4	Teaching, learning, literacy	Evil deeds	
Barbara	Cancer	12	18	24	23	24	256	16	26	3	4	Lightning, gunners, miners	Peace, love	
Columba	Pisces	11	16	22	23	22	240	15	25	3	4	Journeys by sea, sea monsters	Journeys by land	
Cuthbert	Pisces	9	21	22	22	21	256	16	26	3	4	Prophecy, foretelling	Worldly knowledge	
David	Aquarius	8	17	20	20	20	240	15	24	3	4	Welsh, temperance	Alcoholism	
Dunstan	Aries	14	19	21	22	21	272	17	27	3	4	Metal-working, Demon-slaying	Gambling, luck	Commander of Cherubim (12,500)
Faith	Virgo	10	18	20	21	19	240	15	26	3	4	Prisoners, pilgrims	Confinement	
Giles	Taurus	9	17	21	21	20	256	16	26	4	4	Cripples, lepers; healing	Destruction	
Isidore	Cancer	8	22	20	20	20	256	15	27	3	4	Maths, philosophy, theology	War	
John Chrysoston	Leo	8	20	20	20	20	240	16	26	3	4	Oratory, persuasion	Sex	
Leonard	Virgo	9	18	20	19	19	240	15	26	3	4	Childbirth, sleep	Trade, industry	
Margaret	Scorpio	13	19	24	23	22	256	16	25	3	4	Dragon and Devil combat	Love	Commander of Seraphim (12,500)
Martha	Capricorn	7	17	20	18	19	224	14	25	2	4	Service, slaves, women	The rich	
Martin of Tours	Sagittarius	10	17	21	18	19	256	16	26	3	4	Resurrection, destruction of evil shrines	Warriors	
Mary Magdalene	Virgo	6	18	18	21	18	256	16	26	3	4	Fallen women, forgiveness	Hypocrisy	
Procopius	Taurus	8	20	22	20	22	240	15	25	3	4	Exorcism, recovery from wounds	Poison	

Name of power	Astrological controller	Combat level	Intelligence	Endurance	Agility	Physique	Factors: Mana	Magic level	Faith	Resistance to appeals	Rank in host	Areas of interest and patronage	Areas of disfavor	Special characteristics and notes
Remigius	Gemini	7	20	17	18	19	240	15	25	3	3	Astral visions, poets	Business	
Stephen	Capricorn	7	18	17	13	18	240	15	25	2	3	Earth	Fire	
Hilda	Leo	5	20	15	15	17	224	14	24	3	3	Politics, government	Magic/mysticism	
Eloi	Leo	6	18	16	16	18	224	14	24	2	3	Gold working, sacred objects	Use of Sorcery	
Julian	Aquarius	5	17	17	19	17	208	13	23	2	3	River-crossings, travellers	Darkness	
Brendon	Libra	5	16	18	18	17	208	13	23	2	3	Discovery, direction, Irish	Lies	
Dympna	Cancer	4	18	16	18	15	224	14	23	3	3	Madness, fits	Divination	
Elmo	Sagittarius	5	20	18	17	18	224	14	24	2	3	Supernatural fire, protection	Water	
Hubert	Gemini	9	17	18	18	19	208	13	23	3	3	Hunting, woods	Animal control	
Denys	Aries	8	16	17	18	16	208	13	23	2	3	Frenchmen	English	
Menas	Scorpio	7	18	19	15	18	208	13	23	2	3	Deserts, camel drivers	Sea journeys	
Moses	Pisces	8	16	17	16	18	208	13	23	3	3	Thieves, robbery, raiding	Possessions	
Nino	Gemini	4	17	16	17	16	224	14	23	2	3	Finding the true way	Theology	
Odile	Taurus	3	20	15	14	17	208	13	22	2	3	Sight, blindness	Light	
Rupert	Cancer	5	19	17	17	17	224	14	22	2	3	Mines, underground, Germany	Love	
Vitus	Taurus	3	17	16	16	17	208	13	22	2	3	Frenzy, health	Witchcraft	
Swithin	Scorpio	4	19	16	15	16	208	13	23	2	3	Weather, storms	Construction	
Valentine	Virgo	3	20	16	17	14	224	14	22	1	3	Love, lovers	War, hate	
Lesser Saints	—	5	20	16	17	14	208	13	21	6	2	—	—	Up to 15,000: armed as Knights
Cherubim/ Seraphim	—	18	20	18	19	18	192	12	21	7	1	—	—	Up to 25,000 (evenly split): armed as Knights

LOWER POWERS

Name of power	Astrological controller	Combat level	Intelligence	Endurance	Agility	Physique	Mana	Magic level	Faith	Resistance to appeals	Rank in host	Areas of interest and patronage	Areas of disfavor	Special characteristics and notes
Lucifer	Leo	24	30	38	32	36	400	25	35	10	9	Rulership	None	Can mobilize up to 5,000 Undead
Beelzebub	Sagittarius	23	26	33	31	34	384	24	34	9	8	Undead control	Anything else	
Astaroth	Gemini	23	26	30	31	33	368	23	33	6	7	Feelings, projection of	Rational thought	
Belial	Scorpio	23	26	32	32	33	368	23	33	8	7	Command of Demons	Anything else	Commands Demon warriors
Lucifuge	Aquarius	23	25	34	30	33	368	23	33	8	7	Treasure seeking	Women, love	
Satanachia	Virgo	22	23	29	31	30	352	22	32	5	6	Women, love	Treasure-seeking	
Agliarept	Scorpio	21	21	32	31	32	352	22	31	7	6	Battles, fighters	Peace, unity	
Fleurety	Libra	20	23	31	30	32	336	21	31	6	6	Construction	Destruction	
Sargatas	Pisces	20	25	29	31	30	320	20	30	6	6	Trickery, invisibility	Combat	
Nebiros	Taurus	19	22	30	30	30	320	20	30	5	6	Disease, healing	Fire	
Leviathan	Pisces	20	20	36	23	35	304	19	30	7	6	Strength, size, force	Active magic	
Asmodeus	Virgo	20	23	29	31	31	336	21	31	8	6	Command of Incubi & Succuba	Anything else	Commands Incubi/ Succuba (5,000 of each)
Abbadon	Capricorn	19	24	30	29	31	320	20	30	7	6	Destruction, violent assault	Construction	
Clauneck	Aquarius	20	27	29	30	29	336	21	29	7	6	Magic, Mages	Combat.	
Musisin	Leo	19	23	30	29	30	320	20	30	6	6	Earthly government, politics	Divination	
Bechard	Cancer	18	22	31	28	30	304	19	29	6	6	Weather	Communication	
Frimost	Aquarius	18	24	28	31	29	304	19	30	6	6	Charm, charisma	Conjuration	
Khil	Taurus	17	23	30	27	28	304	19	29	6	5	Earth	Fire	

Name of power	Astrological controller	Combat level	Intelligence	Endurance	Agility	Physique	Mana	Magic level	Faith	Resistance to appeals	Rank in host	Areas of interest and patronage	Areas of disfavor	Special characteristics and notes
Mersilde	Pisces	16	24	27	28	27	272	17	26	5	5	Location, transport	Animal control	
Clistheret	Scorpio	15	24	27	27	26	288	18	28	6	5	Night, darkness, evil	Air	
Sirchade	Aries	17	24	27	27	27	288	18	27	4	5	Animal control	Weather	
Segal	Pisces	15	25	26	28	26	288	18	28	5.	5	Illusions, pretenses	Creation of magical items	
Heipacht	Libra	16	25	27	28	27	272	17	28	5	5	Trade, manufacture of goods	War	
Humost	Gemini	16	26	27	26	26	272	17	27	5	5	Writing, reading, letters	Sex, love	
Frucissiere	Capricorn	18	24	28	27	28	304	19	28	6	5	Life and death	None	
Guland	Cancer	15	22	27	28	27	288	18	27	6	5	Light, energy	Earth	
Surgat	Pisces	16	23	27	26	27	288	18	28	6	5	Prophecy, the future	Memory	
Frutmiere	Taurus	16	18	28	26	28	272	17	27	4	5	Food, drink	Disease	
Huictrigara	Taurus	17	19	27	27	26	272	17	27	4	5	Sleep	Ressurection	
Essas	Aries	14	20	26	27	26	272	17	26	5	5	Time, travel	Death	
Celsus	Gemini	14	21	26	28	26	304	19	28	6	5	Ethereal plane control	Worldly affairs	
Acaos	Virgo	16	19	26	28	27	288	18	27	5	5	Gambling, luck	Water	
Cedon	Scorpio	16	20	26	26	26	288	18	28	6	5	Possessions, theft	Divination	
Munkir	Cancer	14	24	26	26	26	288	18	27	5	5	Mind, thought	Travel	
Baal	Pisces	15	21	26	25	25	256	16	27	5	4	Theology	Poison	
Agoras	Gemini	15	20	24	25	24	240	15	24	4	4	Languages, communication	Light	
Vassago	Gemini	14	16	24	25	24	240	15	26	3	4	Sound, hearing	Sight, light	
Gangyn	Cancer	15	17	25	25	24	240	15	26	4	4	Insect control	Bird control	
Morbas	Aries	18	18	26	26	26	256	16	26	4	4	Individual combat, fighters	Peace	
Valefor	Libra	15	20	23	24	25	256	16	25	4	4	Business, theft, thieves	Travel	
Amon	Libra	16	19	26	25	26	256	16	27	4	4	Hunting	Curing	Controls Hellhounds

LOWER POWERS, CONTINUED

Name of power	Astrological controller	Combat level	Intelligence	Endurance	Agility	Physique	Mana	Magic level	Faith	Resistance to appeals	Rank in host	Areas of interest and patronage	Areas of disfavor	Special characteristics and notes
Barbatos	Gemini	14	20	24	25	24	256	16	26	5	4	Communication	Destruction	
Buer	Taurus	13	17	25	25	24	240	15	23	6	4	Healing, curing	Death	
Sytrye	Leo	12	16	24	25	25	240	15	24	5	4	Taste, scent	Undead control	
Beleth	Aquarius	12	18	24	23	24	240	15	24	4	4	Plant control and use	Battles	
Eligor	Capricorn	13	17	25	23	25	256	16	25	5	4	Youth and age, young men	Worldly affairs	
Botis	Aries	18	17	24	26	25	256	16	27	4	4	Swordsmanship, duels	Curing, healing	
Bathsin	Taurus	14	16	26	23	25	256	16	25	4	4	Physical effort, endurance	Thought, mind	
Purson	Cancer	13	21	23	24	24	256	16	26	3	4	Memory, the past, thinkers	Unity, brotherhood	
Glasylabolas	Scorpio	12	16	23	24	23	272	17	27	5	4	Murder, foul deeds	Love, sex	
Ipos	Gemini	12	17	22	23	22	224	14	25	4	3	Locks, hidden things	Construction	
Ronóbe	Pisces	12	19	22	22	22	224	14	24	4	3	Truth and lies	Disease	
Bune	Capricorn	13	18	23	20	23	240	15	24	4	3	Sudden death	Prophecy	
Berith	Sagittarius	12	19	22	21	22	240	15	26	4	3	The Afterlife	Resurrection	Supervisor of Hell
Stolus	Aquarius	11	19	20	22	21	224	14	23	3	3	Astrology, divination	Active magic	
Phoenix	Sagittarius	12	17	23	20	22	224	14	24	4	3	Fire, resurrection	Water	
Halpas	Libra	12	16	21	22	21	224	14	24	3	3	Air, flight, refugees	Earth	
Raum	Scorpio	11	17	20	22	20	224	14	25	2	3	Poison, creeping death	Sudden death	
Vine	Aquarius	12	18	21	21	20	224	14	24	2	3	Witchcraft, covens	Treasure seeking	
Procel	Pisces	12	17	19	20	19	208	13	23	2	3	Water, travel, seafarers	Land travel	
Ose	Gemini	14	18	19	22	19	224	14	22	3	3	Shape changing	Animal control	
Furfur	Aries	15	18	20	19	18	208	13	23	3	3	Land warfare	Sea warfare	
Stax	Taurus	10	17	18	17	17	208	13	23	2	3	Sight, blindness, the blind	Prophecy	
Vaal	Scorpio	12	18	19	18	18	208	13	24	1	3	Deserts, caravaneers	Water	
Balam	Leo	12	18	20	21	17	208	13	23	2	3	Sleight of hand, agility	Active magic	

Name of power	Astrological controller	Combat level	Intelligence	Endurance	Agility	Physique	Mana	Magic level	Faith	Resistance to appeals	Rank in host	Areas of interest and patronage	Areas of disfavor	Special characteristics and notes
Allocen	Sagittarius	13	17	20	22	21	108	13	22	2	3	Weapons, especially bows	Air magic	} Up to 5,000 of each alternative form
Incubus	—	13	15	17	18	18	192	12	21	3	2	—		10,000
Succubus	—	13	15	17	22	14	192	12	21	4	2	—		
Demon warrior	—	15	12	15	15	16	176	11	20	5	1	—		
Hellhound	—	17	4	17	14	17	176	11	20	7	1	—		Up to 5,000
Gargoyle	—	11	4	17	13	17	176	11	20	7	1	—		Up to 5,000
Imp	—	7	3	12	19	12	176	11	19	7	1	—		Up to 5,000

to the power and the spells he carries out. An entry in the first column will benefit the appeal (or intercession) twice: lowering the power's "resistance to appeal" and also the Degree of Difficulty of help asked for. An entry in the second column similarly worsens your chances, accordingly. Apply the same procedure in altering the Degree of Difficulty of the spell in the active calculation. Alterations are ±1 unless otherwise stated in the table.

Patron of. This defines the groups within human society with whom the power has a special relationship. Members of those groups appealing to the patron do so at an advantage; the power, however, has no corresponding advantage in carrying out the spell.

Astrological controller. Like everything else in the universe, the Higher powers are intimately involved in astrological workings. Appeals to a power made in a situation or place influenced by his astrological sign, or from a man born under that sign will carry an advantage. The astrological controller also brings ± factors in the active calculation of the spell, as usual.

Mana. Higher powers will not stake mana in advance to increase the likelihood of a spell leading on from an appeal. They may do so when conducting magic in their own interest.

Religious experience

Religious experience is gained through appeals to the powers, the carrying out of (or attendance at) religious ceremonies, the exercise of delegated clerical powers, resistance to temptation and other examples of correct behavior. The figures below are (as with magical experience) only rough guidelines; GMs must consider the circumstances within which the person was working, to achieve a sensible increase.

Appeals. Record the percentage probability of success (with and without piety loss) in the appeals calculation. Subtract from 100 for experience points (if the appeal was successful). No experience is gained by unsuccessful appeals.

Religious ceremonies/delegated clerical powers. Provisional experience figures are given in the section on ceremonies and powers. These figures are for the cleric performing the ceremony or power only, or for the subject of the ceremony (in certain cases). They also need adjustment for the religious level of the person. Level 0-1: as factors. Level 2-3: reduce by ¼. Level 4-5: reduce by ½. Level 6-8: reduce by ¾. Level 9 +: reduce by ⅞. Round down in all cases (even when creating zero experience!).

Attendance at a religious ceremony or being present at the exercise of a clerical power will bring laymen 1 experience point, whatever their religious level.

Resistance to temptation. Christian clerics and religious Knights only receive 16 experience points (reduced by the factors given above) for successfully resisting a temptation test. Other Christian characters with PB2 or above receive 8 points, with the same reductions.

Correct behavior. Everybody in PB2 or above receives 1 experience point per 3 piety points (round up) total gain over the day. For example, a man with piety of 90 gains 34 PP in the day but loses 18 PP for sins. Net gain of piety = 34—18 = 16, which equals 6 experience points. Devil worshippers only receive corresponding experience for "advances" beyond (PB)3. Retreats towards PB 0 bring no loss in experience.

Religion rules section five:

The Norse religion

Teutonic religion operates on the same general principles as Christian/Diabolic: appeal to Higher powers, one's standing with whom depends on piety, which in turn is affected by sins and virtues, performance of certain ceremonies, and the powers' own interests. But there are crucial departures from the Christian pattern in ethos, ceremonial and the structure of the Ethereal hierarchy that require slightly different treatment. We discuss these in turn, and append a list of the main Norse Higher powers; in the cases where an Anglo-Saxon form of a deity's name is known, it is given in the notes following the table, but in other respects the Norse system is assumed to apply for Anglo-Saxon worship as well, for simplicity's sake.

The Asgardian hierarchy

Although the Norse pantheon has none of the clear-cut divisions of rank observed in the Christian, there is an observable aristocratic graduation in the celestial orders. Not all the gods are *Aesir* (Asgardians); the high-ranking *Vanir* come from a different Ethereal strain, while others do not reside in Asgard at all, and some even originated as mortals. The equivalent table to the Christian/Diabolic hierarchy looks like this:

Rank	Gods	Goddesses
9	Odin	
8	*Chief sons of Odin:* Thor, Balder, Tyr	Frigg
7	*Vanir:* Njord, Frey	Freya
6	Bragi, Loki, Heimdall	Hel
5	*Other Asgardians:* Aegir, Hoder, Hoenir, Ull	Idun, Ran
4	*Lesser sons of Odin:* Hermod, Vali, Vidar	*Wives of gods:* Gerd, Nanna, Sif, Sigyn, Skadi
3	*Sons of other gods:* Forseti, Magni, Modi, Nari	*Minor goddesses:* Eir, Gefion, Hlin, Lofn, Saga, Sjofn, Snotra, Syn, Var
2	*Servant gods:* Skirnir and others	*Servant goddesses:* Gna, Fulla
1	Ancestors and other divinized men	Fylgjur, Valkyries

Promotion. Within the ranks works just as in the Christian hierarchy, with the additional complication that the ranks have particular roles assigned in the Asgardian family. If you are a Valkyrie, for example, and wish to rise, you must find yourself a position in service to a goddess of rank 6 or above (generally by displacing an existing servant); having served this "apprenticeship" faithfully, you may then rise to rank 7 by dislodging a rather feeble goddess like Snotra, who will then take over your former position; and if you want to rise still further, you'll need to find an eligible god of rank 5 or over to marry you, if necessary throwing over his existing wife (who then sinks accordingly in rank). If you're male, you'll need to be adopted to rise above level 8.

Intercession. Also depends on going through the proper channels. Spouses, offspring and siblings can all intercede with one another, as can servants of the power interceded with, and one or two special cases specified in the notes to the table of powers below. All other intercession attempts carry a —1, and —2 if the two powers are of different sexes. Some gods don't get on at all; it would be a gross tactical blunder, for instance, to ask Heimdall to intercede with Loki.

Piety, sin and death

The Teutonic religion is not bipolar; there are, strictly speaking, no "Lower powers" to come cadging souls that aren't doing very well with the Higher ones. Norse gods weren't even particularly jealous of other religions; their polytheistic cult readily accommodated foreign deities—even Christ—alongside native ones, and so long as the first comers weren't actually denied or neglected they saw neither Jehovah nor (at least in principle) Satan as enemies. In practice, of course, the Devil couldn't be worshipped syncretistically with Thor and Frey, because while God expects very broadly similar conduct from his worshippers as the Viking gods, Satan's stipulations are simply incompatible with proper Teutonic piety. A comparison of the catalogues of sins and virtues below with the Christian ones above will bring this out.

Thus, a Norseman's divine favor is graded in much the same way as a Christian's. His piety band is assessed from the viewpoint of the collective Asgardian interest, regardless of any special divine loyalties he may display in his personal observance; though if he *offends* any Asgardian by blasphemy (see below), enmity to a particular god's votary, or violent infringement of a deity's special interests, he may incur a *personal* grudge. He is held in contempt by the Christian God, but so long as he commits no viler sin than heathenism he has a chance of salvation through conversion. Below Norse PB0, however, things get more interesting; the Devil will take an interest regardless of whether the worshipper acknowledges him, and will start keeping his own tally of the man's diabolic "virtues" (the sins listed in the *Christian* system), and these will increase his favor with the Devil willy-nilly. At the same time the Norse gods will be making things uncomfortable for their fallen servant by withdrawing their favor; so that an approach by the Devil at this stage may hold considerable attractions. At any rate, for a character below PB0 to perform or attend a sacrifice, enter a temple or other sacred site, or to swear in the names of Higher powers, is now a Class 3 sin.

Piety *calculations* are the same as for Christian and Diabolic worshippers, but the Norse ethic, with its distinctive emphasis on personal honor and martial prowess, employs a somewhat different list of sins and virtues. Among the chief differences are that the practice of magic is *not* a sin; drunkenness and gluttony bring their own punishment where needed; and manslaughter in battle is not a sin unless one's opponent is the sort of person it's beneath one's dignity to kill. The seven classes of sin are:

Class 1: murder, desecration (see notes);

Class 2: breach of oath, treachery, sexual perversion (incest, homosexuality, etc.);

Class 3: grievous bodily harm, rape, adultery, blasphemy;

Class 4: theft, breach of word, lying, cowardice, greed, usury;

Class 5: assault, fornication, neglect of gods (thanksgiving, etc.);

Class 6: sloth, selfishness, manslaughter of weaker opponent;

Class 7: undignified conduct, obstinacy, anger.

Note that piety loss is wholly independent of whether or not material compensation such as weregild is made to the injured mortal party. The heading of "blasphemy" is slightly wider than its Christian equivalent, incorporating all forms of denial or taking in vain of divine honor except desecration of religious sites (on which see below) and breach of oath. There are three different grades of killing with different penalties: murder by guile carries a far greater piety loss and social stigma than manslaughter in fair combat, but this too has to be confessed at once to the dead man's kin (where available), else it counts as murder anyway. Manslaughter in battle or of a sworn enemy is not a sin but may of course entail certain secular reprisals.

The classes of virtue are:

Class 1: heroism, sustaining honorable injury in the service of others;

Class 2: opposing blasphemy, honoring oaths when inconvenient;

Class 3: performing sacrifice, generosity to friends and gods, endangering self for others;

Class 4: attendance at sacrifice, prayer, selflessness, overcoming superior opposition in combat;

Class 5: bravery (general), loyalty, magnanimity;

Class 6: obedience to authority, forgiveness of wrongs done you;

Class 7: initiative, activity, leadership.

The daily bonus of 30 piety points applies to Norsemen as well as Christians.

The Norse *Afterlife* is variously compartmented, but has no equivalent to Purgatory; the fate of your soul depends entirely on your conduct in life and the circumstances of your death, barring decisive appeals from your relatives. Most people go to Niflheim, which is gloomy but not as bad as Hell; it will take intercession by a major deity (Rank 6 or over) directly with Hel to get you out, and in point of fact this has never been known to work. Similarly, (female) virgins go automatically to the halls of Gefion, and those drowned at sea to the halls of Aegir and Ran; these groups get a fairly comfy time of it. But the most desirable fate is naturally entry to Valhalla or even admission to divinity, and for these you have to be fortunate, virtuous and mighty.

Anyone who dies in battle or as a result of wounds sustained in honorable combat goes straight to Valhalla, and this applies to women as well as men (at least in our system!). Otherwise, the following calculation applies:

Add piety band of character at death plus—
Circumstances of death (cumulative):
   Character killed by accident/treachery, +1.
   Character killed in execution of oath, +2.
   Character killed in service of others, +1.
Social class 14-17: +1; 18 or over: +2.
Luck (in the usual way).
Combat or religious experience level (whichever is higher).
Character has a personal divine patron of Rank 5 or above: +1.
Character is interred in barrow: +1.
Character gets ship-burial: +2.

A total of 10 or over will secure admission to Valhalla. To find out whether a character becomes a god, apply this calculation:
Add piety band of character at death plus—
Character goes to Valhalla: +4.
Social Class 18 or over: +2.
Faith 8 or below: −1; 14 or over: +1; 18 or over: +2.
Luck (in the usual way).
Magical or religious experience level (whichever is higher).
Character has a personal divine patron of Rank 3 or above: +1.

A male character will become a god if he scores 15 or over; a female character will become a Valkyrie with a score of 12 or over. Lady warriors who have conserved their virtue can choose whether to go to Valhalla or the halls of Gefion, but for the purposes of the deification calculation it is assumed they all go to Valhalla.

Temples, priesthood and sacraments

Religious objects and places carry plus factors in sacrifices and appeals in the same way as their Christian and Diabolic equivalents, and with the same sort of range: a rock consecrated to Frey in the middle of nowhere might carry +1, the high temple at Uppsala +5. There are no Norse equivalents to Christian relics in the strict sense, though amulets and other symbols may carry +1 or +2; all divine statues are housed in temples and their plus factor is included in that of the temple. *Desecration* means something rather different in Norse religion, though: it refers to wilful defilement of a holy site or object by a mortal, rather than to occupation by enemy powers (the only example of which would be Christian reconsecration of pagan sites, a common missionary practice which would simply count as another form of defilement of the site). Mere desecration in this sense (which covers destruction in or of the site, defacement of cult images, prohibited behavior—including all sins of Class 5 and over—on sacred ground) does not affect the place's link with the power, but may reduce the CMF of ceremonies performed there by up to full value until the damage, spiritual or physical, is repaired.

Norse religion does not observe the Christian/Diabolic functional distinction between clergy and laity, though there is a professional priesthood attached to specific gods and cult sites. All free men and women may also perform sacrifices, however, and if aristocratic they may actually outrank the professional priesthood. This means that everyone except the unfree holds by automatic right an equivalent rank to unordained clergy, and that promotion within the hierarchy depends simply on social rank unless you happen to be a professional priest (in which case you're unlikely to be wandering around having adventures, as Norse priests were simply temple officials and never itinerant). The parallel ranks to the Christian/Diabolic ones tabulated earlier go like this:

Rank	Priesthood	Laity
1		All free men and women
2		Elders and heroes
3	Priests of minor sites	Heads of families
4	Lesser priests (mainly female) of major temples	
5	Godhar (High Priests)	Princes and kinglets
6		Kings and Queens

There are no parallels to the Christian ranks 7–10.

Ceremonies. Nearly always consist of, or at least include, some form of *sacrifice.* The basic ceremony may be performed by anyone of social class 10 or above, and will last from 5 minutes to 1½ hours depending on rank of celebrant and number of victims (and how easy it proves to hold the beggars still!). The sacrifice may be followed by an uninhibited ceremonial *feast* on the flesh of the victim (animals only), which may continue from 1-3 hours and generate further mana. Dedication of a slain enemy's soul before or after combat counts as a privately celebrated human sacrifice; prisoners of war may be publicly sacrificed as normal. The divine recipient(s) of the sacrifice *must* be specified in advance; if more than one jointly, then total mana is distributed evenly among them all regardless of Ethereal rank. All sacrifice has CMF of +1 and mana of ½ point per worshipper, with additional CMF +2 and mana 2 points per worshipper if followed with a feast. Mana from the victim varies: 9 points for human victims, 6 for horses, 5 for boars and cattle, 4 for sheep, goats and domestic swine, 2 for fowl. Experience: points to celebrant equal to mana points from victim (but no accumulation for multiple victims), or "top" victim if different species, plus one point per victim of whatever species. Feast confers 5 experience points on each worshipper. Sacrifice may also constitute an optional addition to all other ceremonies.

Baptism lasts 30 minutes and is celebrated by the highest-ranking secular official present; only infants can be baptized in Norse society. CMF of +1 on parents and kin; 6 points experience for celebrant. At baptism a child may be dedicated to a particular god (in which case he will usually be given a name incorporating that of the god); 20 mana points to the god in this event, otherwise no mana in the ceremony.

Marriage lasts 1 hour, and will normally be followed by a feast of 1-3 hours. Factors as for Christian marriage.

Funeral rites. Take two forms: interment in a barrow for the majority, ship-burial for important chieftains. Ordinary burial takes 1 hour, and is celebrated by male kin if possible; factors as for Christian burial, except for effect on soul of deceased (see previous section). Ship-burial takes 2 hours, plus optional sacrifice and feast, with 30 piety points for relatives, 12 experience points for celebrant, and extra resistance to conjuration of +3 for the departed soul.

Oaths. Are sworn in the name of one or more gods, and may be specific commitments to men or gods or more general pledges of loyalty and trust (blood brotherhood, etc.). They may be reinforced in a number of ways: by sacrifice and/or feasting, by the invocation of additional gods, or simply by pledging piety points to the oath's being kept. An oath held to against one's own interests is a Class 2 Virtue, and so long as an oath in a particular god's name is kept the contractor(s) will score +1 to +3 in appeals to that god (depending on severity of the oath). Oathbreaking, however, carries serious penalties (see below, under *appeals*). Any number of piety points may be pledged at the time of swearing as security for the oath; these are instantly forfeit if the oathmaker breaks trust.

On *seidhr*, see the next section.

Appeals, morale and inspiration

Appeals to Norse Higher powers operate in precisely the same way as Christian/Diabolic appeals, with the exception of a different catalogue of "proofs of serious intent" in the calculation:

Instant appeal: mental only, −1; spoken 0.

Appeal supported by prayer/meditation: +1 for each 60 minutes to max +2.

Appeal supported by oath of service: +1 to +3 according to severity of commitment.

Appeal supported by sacrifice: animals +2; humans +3 (regardless of number).

Appeal supported by promise of sacrifice: animals +½; humans +1 to +3 (see later note).

Oaths of service and promise of sacrifice. A worshipper may assist his appeal with promises of future sacrifices or services. Promised sacrifice will be more effective for being guaranteed near in the future and within a definite period rather than "as soon as I can" or somesuch. The oath of service need not be so immediate, but the more binding it is to the swearer and the more profitable to the god, the more acceptable it will be. Possible oaths would include a primary or exclusive share of all sacrifices, the dedication of enemy souls, service in the god's area of special interest, and so on, and may be definite or indefinite in its span and quota. An oath to a god carried out will also add half its appeal value (rounded up) to the next appeal to the same god; but failure to comply with either an oath or a promised sacrifice is a Class 2 sin, and will result in 3 points subtracted from *all* future appeals to that god unless placated by a major proof of serious intent totalling 10 or more.

Morale and inspiration. Use the same calculations as in the Christian section above, with the following additional circumstance factors for spontaneous inspiration: pitched battle, +3; danger from superior opposition, +2; drunkenness, +2; provocation by enemies, +1; subjection to stirring poetry, +1.

Norsemen become spontaneously inspired much more freely than Christians, and anyone with intelligence 9 or under has a permanent +1, 6 or under +2 on their calculation. All Vikings hold their drink extremely well compared to other peoples, and tend to be stimulated rather than enfeebled by indulgence; the gods hold drunkenness no crime, but conversely do hold men fully accountable for actions or oaths undertaken while under the influence.

One specialized form of ceremonial appeal is the *seidhr,* or shamanic divination (and occasionally also Active magical) procedure, in which a specialist magician, normally female, sits on a high seat or platform and sings ecstatic spells, sometimes with the audience joining in. This is treated as an appeal for knowledge to Freya (for DDs see earlier), and carries CMF +1, or +3 if the audience joins in the chant. Duration is 20 minutes to 1 hour, mana accumulated as for ululation. Experience: 12 for diviner.

Notes

See also the notes to the Christian/Diabolic Higher powers tables. All Norse gods have greed, selfishness, lust of 8, piety band 7, charisma and bravery 14 unless otherwise specified in the following notes, which offer brief supplementary descriptions, kinship information and personal allegiances on such gods as require it.

Aegir. Is husband of Ran and generally paired with her; they share an undersea hall lit by luminous gold, wherein they entertain the spirits of the drowned. Their weapon and symbol is the net. Genial gods, on the whole.

Balder. Is Odin's legitimate, second son (by Frigg); he has the form of a handsome young man, and his body is suffused with light. He's husband to Nanna, and their son is Forseti. Charisma 16.

Bragi. Is one of the least warlike gods, possibly originally a mortal who has worked his way up the ethereal hierarchy. His wife is Idun. Bravery 10.

Forseti. Is Balder's son by Nanna; the axe is his symbol rather than an object of patronage.

Frey. Is Njord's son, Freya's brother, and husband to Gerd; his appearance is strong and handsome, though his statues tend to be ithyphallic and his rites erotic. His symbol and preferred sacrifice is the horse, and weapons were forbidden in his temples. A popular, widely worshipped god. Charisma 15, lust 14.

Freya. Frey's sister, is the chief love goddess, as well as patron of the shamanic *seidhr*. Often she takes a bird shape and travels abroad in Midgard; in cult art, she rides in a carriage drawn by cats. Lust 16, charisma 18.

Frigg. Odin's legitimate wife, is mother of Balder, to whom she is devoted, and served by Gna and Fulla. In appearance she is a mature, matronly female. Anglo-Saxon *Frig*.

Fulla. Is one of Frigg's numerous servant goddesses.

Fylgjur. (Singular *Fylgja*) are an undifferentiated class of female personal tutelary deities, who can convey information or warning to men. Everyone has one, and if one's Fylgja dies its owner follows; often a man will see his Fylgja, usually in an animal form (bears, wolves, eagles, snakes, etc.) before death or in times of extreme peril. Sometimes they take human shape, as rather Valkyriesque armed women.

Gerd. Is Frey's hard-won wife, one of the most beautiful of all goddesses.

Gna. Is another servant, messenger and confidante of Frigg.

Heimdall. Is Asgard's watchman, and has prophetic knowledge. He is the direct father of the human race, and an unrelenting foe to Loki. His symbol is the (blowing) horn. Bravery 16.

Hel. Is Loki's daughter and guardian of the underworld Niflheim, sometimes called after her. She has custody of the souls of the dead who don't go to Valhalla or other specialist abodes.

Hermod. Is a rather obscure son of Odin who can intercede with Hel over the souls in her custody.

Hoenir. Is a slow-witted, inoffensive god; of no use whatever in combat appeals, but popular with other gods and consequently helpful in intercession (no minus factor). Bravery 10.

Idun. Is a powerful goddess, charged with the apples of immortality which keep the gods young (or in *FW* terms the guardian of the mana level required to maintain Asgard). Rarely invoked by mortals or concerned with their affairs, she is married to Bragi.

Loki. Is the most wilful of the gods, and will readily betray both his votaries and the other gods on little more than caprice. Morally flexible, he is nevertheless beguilingly handsome, and extraordinarily powerful in magical matters. His wife is Sigyn, their son Nari; by other unions he is father of the goddess Hel, the Midgard Serpent and the Fenris Wolf, and mother (!) of Odin's eight-legged steed Sleipnir. Greed, selfishness, lust 14, charisma 15.

Magni and *Modi.* Are Thor's two sons by Sif, and each inherits a complementary facet of his father's personality (strength and temper respectively).

Nanna. Is Balder's wife, mother to Forseti.

Nari. Is Loki's son, himself a considerable magician, but more good-natured and dependable.

Njord. Father of Frey and Freya, is a powerful elemental god; his wife Skadi (not, incidentally, the mother of his children) left

NORSE HIGHER POWERS

Name	Astrological controller	Combat level	Intelligence	Endurance	Agility	Physique	Mana	Magic level	Faith	Resistance to appeals	Rank in host	Areas of patronage and special interest
Aegir	Scorpio	14	28	35	35	32	224	14	24	5	5	Sea and sailing, winds, weather
Balder	Cancer	12	35	24	28	24	256	16	26	8	8	Light, peace, happiness, protection in battle
Bragi	Aquarius	10	35	27	29	24	256	16	25	6	6	Poetry, oaths
Divinised ancestors	(various)	14*	25*	22*	22*	22*	208	13	21	1	1	Family and local interests
Eir	Taurus	2	26	22	22	21	240	15	24	3	3	Healing (especially women)
Forseti	Libra	10	30	30	29	29	224	14	23	3	3	Peace, settling arguments, axes
Frey	Taurus	14	33	30	30	24	256	16	25	6	7	Fertility, horses, burial mounds, fields, peace; protection
Freya	Virgo	5	38	24	32	24	304	19	28	6	7	Love, promiscuity, witchcraft and divination, sea, birds
Frigg	Libra	5	30	23	25	23	240	15	25	8	8	Wifehood, motherhood, childbirth
Fulla	Taurus	3	24	24	23	21	224	14	23	2	2	Messages, abundance
Fylgjiur	Sagittarius	6	21	24	21	21	224	14	25	1	1	Personal protection
Gefion	Libra	3	24	24	21	24	208	13	22	3	3	Virginity, fields and farming
Gerd	Virgo	4	28	22	24	23	240	15	23	5	4	Courtship, seduction, unmanliness
Gna	Gemini	3	25	22	28	22	224	14	24	2	2	Travel, communication, flight, swiftness
Heimdall	Leo	17	36	38	36	35	272	17	26	7	6	Vigil, passive strength, sight and hearing, depths of sea
Hel	Capricorn	15	34	35	28	28	272	17	27	10	6	Death and underworld
Hermod	Aquarius	11	32	30	36	32	224	14	26	6	4	Swiftness, travel, horsemanship
Hlin	Libra	4	22	22	22	24	208	13	22	1	3	Protection
Hoder	Capricorn	12	30	28	28	28	240	15	28	9	5	Blindness, darkness, death
Hoenir	Taurus	10	22	23	24	25	240	15	27	7	5	Silence
Idun	Gemini	5	26	24	24	24	272	17	27	9	5	Life, fertility, immortality of gods
Lofn	Virgo	2	23	21	21	21	208	13	21	1	3	Marriage, overcoming obstacles to love
Loki	Aquarius	15	38	35	36	33	288	18	28	10	6	Magic, guile, fire

Name	Astrological controller	Combat level	Intelligence	Endurance	Agility	Physique	Mana	Magic level	Faith	Resistance to appeals	Rank in host	Areas of patronage and special interest
Magni	Aries	16	23	30	29	34	224	14	24	4	3	Individual feats of strength
Modi	Scorpio	16	23	30	34	28	224	14	24	4	3	Anger, impetuous strength
Nanna	Capricorn	4	26	24	22	23	240	15	25	4	4	Loyalty, mourning
Nari	Pisces	15	30	24	27	24	224	14	25	4	3	Magic
Njord	Pisces	14	30	38	36	34	240	15	24	6	7	Sea, ships, wind, fishing
Odin	Gemini	18	40	30	35	30	320	20	30	7	9	Battle, magic, wisdom, authority, inspiration and madness, poetry
Ran	Cancer	8	29	28	34	30	240	15	25	5	5	Sea and sailing, souls of drowned
Saga	Pisces	1	26	21	22	22	208	13	23	2	3	Fresh water, wisdom
Sif	Leo	4	23	23	24	23	224	14	23	4	4	Fertility
Sigyn	Cancer	4	26	23	25	22	240	15	25	5	4	Mercy, pity
Skadi	Aries	3	25	26	26	25	224	14	24	5	4	Mountains
Sjofn	Virgo	2	26	23	24	21	208	14	23	3	3	Love
Skirnir	Aquarius	12	30	32	32	30	240	15	27	3	2	Light, guile, persuasion
Snotra	Cancer	1	21	21	21	21	208	13	21	1	3	Prudence, moderation, virtue
Syn	Leo	2	21	24	22	23	208	13	22	1	3	Doors, protection of home
Thor	Sagittarius	20	21	40	36	40	240	15	26	4	8	Combat, weapons, thunder, fire, forests, feasting, sea voyages
Tyr	Aries	18	35	35	35	35	240	15	24	8	8	Justice, law, battle.combat
Ull	Sagittarius	13	30	34	34	34	240	15	25	5	5	Winter, hunting, shields
Vali	Scorpio	11	30	33	35	34	240	15	25	5	4	Vengeance, purpose
Valkyries	Aries	15	23	28	28	26	208	13	22	2	1	War, individual combat
Var	Leo	2	25	22	23	22	208	13	25	3	3	Oaths between sexes, marriage
Vidar	Gemini	10	28	35	30	33	224	14	25	5	4	Forests, passive strength

* These figures represent upper limits.

him for Odin, leaving him less than well-disposed towards the Father of All. Njord and his family are not of the Aesir (Odin's race, the native Asgardians), but the immigrant Vanir, so they are always a bit apart from the other Asgardians.

Odin. Is the supreme god and the most widely-travelled, frequently seen among men as a long-bearded stranger, one-eyed, with a wide-brimmed blue hat partly obscuring his face, who may offer advice or warning, or even actual weapons and magic items. Particular forms of sacrifice he favors are hanging, burning and spear killing; occasionally strangulation. He is the main battle god, ready to turn the tide of battle by manipulation of a host's morale; altered states of consciousness are a particular specialty, and berserks are under his particular aegis. His symbols include spears, wolves and ravens. By and large, the other gods have to kowtow to his policy decisions, though the Brynhild story recalls that even a mere Valkyrie *could* defy him. His favored sons are Thor, Tyr and Balder; others are Hermod, Vali and Vidar. Frigg is his legal Mrs., but he has a roving eye at the best of times. Lust 13, charisma 15. Anglo-Saxon *Woden.*

Ran. See *Aegir.*

Sif. Is Thor's wife, and mother to Ull as well as to Thor's sons Modi and Magni; like most gods' wives, her beauty is surpassing, particularly her famous golden hair. Charisma 16.

Sigyn. See *Loki.*

Skadi. Fell out with her husband Njord, partly because of incompatible preferences in landscape and partly because she only married him in the first place because she thought he was Balder. A later attachment with Odin was impermanent, and she no longer dwells in Asgard much. A wayward goddess. Selfishness 10, lust 12.

Thor. Is the most trusted and worshipped Asgardian, as important to individual combat as Odin is to large-scale, and invoked in nearly all aspects of human living, including birth, marriage and burial. He is a large figure with a huge red beard and a famous hammer (T-shaped, shortish handle, thong in the end), which symbol is worn as an amulet (usually of bone, sometimes of precious metals) by worshippers in a manner not distant from the Christian cross. In temple art he stands in a chariot drawn by a pair of goats, and temples often housed an arm-sized "ring of Thor" in gold or silver on which especially powerful oaths were sworn. He was often associated with oak trees and pillars. Odin is his father, Sif his wife, Modi and Magni his sons. Bravery 18. Anglo-Saxon *Thunor*.

Tyr. Is a rather serious god, son to Odin and the major patron of law and order in Viking society, though he is also, like his sire, a giver of victory. Anglo-Saxon *Tiw*.

Ull. Is Sif's son by an unnamed sire, and is a handsome, widely-worshipped character whose special symbol is a snowshoe.

Vali and *Vidar*. Are minor sons of Odin. Vali is a friend of Balder and may intercede with him; he is an enemy of Hoder and Loki.

Valkyries. Are closely related to Fylgjur, but serve in Asgard rather than on Earth, the exception being their role as monitors of battle. They waitress in Valhalla and, under Odin's authority, convey thither the select souls of dead heroes. They appear as helmeted and armored young women with spears and shield, mounted on flying steeds, and easily form favorites among the living warriors, though this is built up by the warrior's own displayed prowess rather than his worshipping a particular Valkyrie (which you can't do). Their numbers fluctuate, and the number attendant at any battle will depend on its scale, importance and mortality rate. *Grimnismal* lists a few of their names: Geirronul, Goll, Hild, Hlok, Hrist, Mist, Randgrid, Rathgrid, Reginleif, Skeggjold, Skogul, Thrud. Anglo-Saxon *Waelcyrgean* (singular *Waelcyrge*).

Monsters, magical beings, and general fauna

The following pages give brief descriptions and playing characteristics for some 60 monsters, spirit beings and magical races, followed by a similar table of characteristics for a few useful species of mundane animal. A few of the factors require a brief word of explanation first.

Size. There are five size grades, which generally get assigned according to head-to-toe length (what would be relative height if all the creatures stood erect). In the case of serpents and one or two other non-conformers where this index is not a very good one, we have interpreted size in terms of overall bulk. In a few instances more specific details are given for matters like length of horns. The approximate range of each grade is as follows: Tiny, about or less than the size of a domestic cat; Small, dog-sized up to about goats, pigs and wolves; Medium, man-sized or thereabouts; Large, on a scale with the bigger domestic beasts (horses, cattle, hippos, etc.); Huge, anything from a baby elephant upwards. A couple of monsters that seem to run off any reasonable scale are designated Bloody Huge!

Speed. Once again, five grades roughly centered around man. The factor refers to a range of possible speeds rather than a single typical one, on the reasonable assumption that most creatures conserve the same ratio between comfortable and maximum speeds of movement. Thus a monster of *average* speed will normally move at human walking pace, but under exertion (in combat, pursuit, etc.) will travel at the same rate as a running human. For simplicity's sake it is assumed that travelling rate (covering ground) is directly related to other speed factors like reaction time, moving limbs, and that modifications on the basis of agility (which describes the organism's control of its movements) apply to all these equally.

Society. This factor is intended to give a guide to how many of the particular monsters are likely to be found in any single encounter. *Solitary* monsters never collect into groups of any sort, and will always be encountered singly; *unique* specimens will also naturally make only one appearance in any adventure (or one series of repeated appearances, of course!). *Lairs* and *nests* mean that the creature's social unit is a family one of up to half a dozen, but that the full unit is unlikely to be encountered unless you stumble on its home base. *Packs* indicates that the creature moves freely about in groups of up to 15, though many smaller groups than the full pack can also turn up. *Herds* means that the animal habitually associates with others of the species in groups of 10 to 50; many herding animals can also appear individually, especially if the adventure country is not their wonted habitat, and most of the monsters will only rarely turn up in full herds. In one or two places *flocks* is used synonymously with *herds* for familiarity's sake. *Swarms* means that the creature can appear in social groups of 50-200, and even when not in its group (scouting, raiding, what have you) will rarely appear solo.

Source. This gives a general pointer to the tradition from which the particular monster derives (see chapter three), and doubles as a guideline only, if you want one, to the period and geographical area you might be most likely to encounter it. Creatures from a culture-bound source (like Anglo-Saxon, Irish, general Teutonic) will be most likely to feature in the relevant home zone, unless of course the Gaming Master chooses otherwise; this doesn't, of course, mean that they require characters of the appropriate background in order to appear! When a monster turns up in the Dark Ages or High Middle Ages only, this is indicated in the note of source; once again, this is only meant as a suggestion, and shouldn't be allowed to clog your fun.

Other factors. All monsters are assumed to have intelligence 2, greed and selfishness 14, lust 0 and bravery 12 except as specified below; these factors apply equally to the separate table of ordinary animals. Only sentient beings have faith and charisma, and *no* magical races have piety because none of them have souls. Five per cent of all monster species (those that grow) are infants, and 5 per cent are senile; for the former subtract ½, for the latter ¼, from physical factors (physique, agility, endurance, combat factor, size, speed, but *not* armor class). Where the species has two sexes, intra-species lust is assumed to be 11, except where specified.

Alphyn

A nasty piece of work, like a lion but with pointed snout, four- or five-inch horns, and viciously wide jaws and sharp teeth. The hindlegs terminate in large claws, the forelegs in even sharper talons. The tail has a complicated knot in it, which doesn't affect its mobility; doubtless there's something marvellous to be found inside if you untie it, but we leave this to GM's ingenuity as nobody is on record as having got close enough to succeed.

Physique: 18; Agility: 16; Endurance: 15; Combat factor: 14; Size: medium; Speed: fast; Society: packs; Armor class: 2; Method of attack: tooth and claw; Source: heraldry (High Middle Ages only).

Amphiptere

Small winged serpent, highly maneuverable, with venom that will reduce victim's endurance by one point every quarter-hour until cured; lost endurance points are not recoverable. As there is no known medical cure, magic and prayer are all that will serve.

Physique: 1; Agility: 17; Endurance: 4; Combat factor: 1 (excluding venom); Size: tiny; Speed: fast; Society: nests; Armor class: 0; Method of attack: fangs; Source: heraldry.

Amphisbaena

Viper-like serpent with a head at each end, both fanged with an *instantly* fatal poison. It moves freely in either direction, and has a trick of holding one head in the mouth of the other and bowling along like a hoop, by which means it can reach surprisingly high speeds. Fortunately, its eyesight is extremely poor (focus up to 10 ft only; detect movement up to 25), and each head can only administer one poison bite per day.

Physique: 2; Agility: 16; Endurance: 5; Combat factor: 2 (excluding venom); Size: tiny; Speed: fast, (hooped) very fast; Society: nests; Armor class: 0; Method of attack: fangs; Source: bestiaries.

Animated corpse

A dead body inhabited and reanimated by its, or a, Conjured spirit or Demon. For all corpses over one month dead, determine physical factors by 3D6 and roll 1D6 to ascertain state of decay, as follows: 6 Corpse is virtually intact; no alteration to factors; 5 Smells a bit, with squidgy spots; 20 per cent off endurance; 4 40 per cent off endurance; 5 per cent chance of spontaneous disintegration when struck; 3 60 per cent off endurance; 10 per cent chance of spontaneous disintegration when struck; 2 80 per cent off endurance; 20 per cent chance of spontaneous disintegration when struck; 1 Corpse cannot hold together (but other factors, including physique, remain constant!).

For psychological characteristics see *ghosts* below. Animated corpses have no intrinsic ability to *frighten*.

Animated skeleton

All characteristics as for *animated corpses,* but with addition of *frighten* effect; see under *ghosts,* below.

Antelops (sic)

The antelope of the bestiaries was a rather more fearsome specimen than the modern equivalent, being considerably more ferocious and sharper in the horn. Like its smaller relative the *Calopus,* it had problems with its horns in undergrowth.

Physique: 12; Agility: 18; Endurance: 11; Combat factor: 10; Size: medium; Speed: very fast; Society: herds; Armor class: 1; Method of attack: horns; Source: bestiaries.

Barrow-wight

See chapter three. Barrow-wights look like warriors, but with their bodies in varying stages of decay, and all the attendant reek that implies. Treat as *animated corpses.* Insubstantial Barrow-wights are just *ghosts,* and have the power to frighten; for calculation see under *ghosts.*

Basilisk (or Cockatrice)

The Basilisk and Cockatrice are assumed to be identical in *FW.* It is a species of serpent hatched from a cock's egg and incubated by a serpent or toad, and has the cock's head and wings and feet on a serpentine body, with white-streaked feathers over its back and sides. Timid and physically harmless, the Basilisk has the unfortunate property of magically slaying (not turning to stone) any creature it looks on. It is also a rabies carrier, and emits a powerful and noxious odor which will poison anyone who inhales it within 10 ft for over two minutes, at a loss of one physique point per half minute (recoverable). It has to be slain when fleeing, for obvious reasons, and weasels are particularly good Basilisk killers, being resistant to the smell and able to pursue the creature down its readily identifiable hole.

Physique: 6; Agility: 15; Endurance: 5; Combat factor: 2; Size: tiny; Speed: average; Society: solitary; Armor class: 1; Method of attack: beak, claws; Source: bestiaries, heraldry (High Middle Ages only); Other: bravery 4.

Black Men

Not humans, but soulless sentient giants (up to 8 ft tall) with tough black skin and the arms of a warrior. They behave much like Celtic *giants,* and are usually non-magical but tricky.

Physique: 20; Agility: 17; Endurance: 20; Combat factor: 13; Size: large; Speed: fast; Society: solitary; Intelligence: 7; Faith: 8; Charisma: 8; Magic level: 1; Greed: 12; Selfishness: 16; Lust: 12; Bravery: 18; Armor class: 2 (skin); Method of attack: armed or unarmed combat; Source: Celtic, Arthurian.

Black Oppressor

A one-eyed *black man* who lives in a hall with his three (attractive, white) daughters. He lost his other eye to the *Black Worm of the Barrow,* and such is his shame that he kills any man who refers to the incident or his disfigurement, however indirectly. As it happens, he kills all visitors anyway, though sometimes he lets them stay the night first, and will allow them arms for a fair fight.

Physique: 22; Agility: 18; Endurance: 20; Combat factor: 14; Size: large; Speed: fast; Selfishness: 16; Lust: 10; Bravery: 18; Society: unique; Intelligence: 10; Faith: 10; Charisma: 8; Magic level: 3; Greed: 12; Armor class: 2 (skin), 4 (armed); Method of attack: armed or unarmed combat; Source: Welsh-Arthurian.

Black Worm of the Barrow

"There is a mound that is called the Dolorous Mound, and in the mound there is a barrow, and in the barrow there is a Worm, and in the Worm's tail there is a stone, and the virtues of the stone are that whosoever should have it in the one hand, what he would desire of gold he should have in his other hand." The mound is surrounded by a camp of pavilions, each housing a knight who has gone there to slay the Worm but hasn't the nerve, and anyone thinking to enter the barrow has to overthrow this jealous mob or slip past them.

Physique: 25; Agility: 20; Endurance: 24; Combat factor: 15; Size: large; Speed: fast; Society: unique; Armor class: 3; Method of attack: fangs, crushing, lashing; no venom; Source: Welsh-Arthurian.

Bonnacon

A horse-like creature with a bull's head and extraordinary inward-curling horns that are consequently quite harmless. The Bonnacon is extremely timorous and will turn tail and run at the first sniff of trouble. Paradoxically, this is when he is most dangerous, for as the Cambridge Bestiarist tells us "when he turns to run away he emits a fart with the contents of his large intestine which covers three acres. And any tree that it reaches catches fire."

Physique: 5; Agility: 13; Endurance: 8; Combat factor: 3; Size: medium; Speed: fast; Society: herds; Armor class: 1; Method of attack: butting with horns, kicking with hind legs; Source: bestiaries, heraldry; Other: bravery 2.

Boreyne

A very rare, fearsome-looking beast with a basically leonine body and head, but with in-curving horns like a Bonnacon's, enormous taloned eagle feet, and a strange spiny fin at the root of the tail. Its tongue is forked, its breath caustic (emerging as a 15° cone, range 6 ft; will burn exposed flesh, rot clothing, rust metal).

Physique: 17; Agility: 13; Endurance: 18; Combat factor: 12; Size: medium; Speed: average; Society: solitary; Armor class: 2; Method of attack: talons; Source: heraldry.

Calopus

Wolf-sized, but like a cat in face, tail and form of feet, with vicious razor horns a foot or so long, serrated on the back and curved slightly backwards, ending in a sharp point. The one relief is that the Calopus is a denizen of woodlands and brush, with the result that its horns get continually trapped in thickets and can

only be extricated by sawing laboriously through the branches
with the exceptionally sharp, tough rear edge.

Physique: 12; Agility: 12; Endurance: 10; Combat factor: 12;
Size: small; Speed: fast; Society: packs; Armor class: 1; Method
of attack: horns, tooth and claw; Source: bestiaries, heraldry.

Calygreyhound

This bizarre chimerical specimen has a lion-like body, feline face
and enormous (up to 3-ft) reindeer-like horns. The forelegs end
in long, cruel talons, and the creature can rear on its leonine
hindlegs for brief periods (up to 1½ minutes) to fight with them.

Physique: 11; Agility: 14; Endurance: 14; Combat factor: 8;
Size: medium; Speed: very fast; Society: packs; Armor class: 1;
Method of attack: horns, talons; Source: heraldry.

Caretyne

The Caretyne has the body of a white lion, with cloven hoofs and
the hind legs of a goat. Its head is pointed in a snout, with short
(5 in or so), sharp horns; it has upward-pointing tusks of about
the same size, and a gold mane, gold spots all over the body, and
shaggy gold tufts on the chest, bum, thighs and tip of tail. It emits
flames not only from its mouth but from its ears as well; all three

sources may be separately deployed, emitting a single jet up to 3 ft long.

Physique: 16; Agility: 13; Endurance: 20; Combat factor: 10; Size: medium; Speed: fast; Society: lairs; Armor class: 1; Method of attack: horns (plus flame); Source: heraldry (High Middle Ages only).

Catoblepas

Gnu-like beast with a hard, scaly hide and a shaggy mane that falls into its eyes. Its natural posture is with its head fixedly staring at the ground in front of it; good thing too, as anyone who does meet its gaze eye to eye dies on the spot.

Physique: 17; Agility: 10; Endurance: 18; Combat factor: 7; Size: medium; Speed: slow; Society: herds; Armor class: 3; Method of attack: kicking with hind legs; Source: bestiaries.

Chimera

There are two varieties of this celebrated classical bogey by the time of the High Middle Ages, though both are extremely uncommon. One has a lion's body and head with a goat's head and neck emerging from the middle of the back and a tail going into the neck and head of a Dragon; the second, less common yet, has all three heads at the front. The lion's head breathes flame (in a 20° cone, range 10 ft), the serpent's has poisonous breath (10 points off physique instantly; recoverable at one point per ten minutes).

Physique: 20; Agility: 12; Endurance: 22; Combat factor: 15; Size: large; Speed: average; Society: solitary; Armor class: 1; Method of attack: goat's horns, lion's jaws (plus flame), dragon's fangs (plus breath); Source: heraldry.

Dragons, Celtic

The typical Celtic Dragon is a giant, wingless serpent generally dwelling in or near fresh water, in pools or caves or underground lairs. In the High Middle Ages most of the younger worms have a bit of Germanic blood in them and consequently sport those magnificent reptilian wings. For those with poisonous breath, adversaries will lose one physique point per combat round (recoverable at normal rate).

Physique: 24; Agility: 20; Endurance: 25; Combat factor: 16;

Size: large-huge; Speed: fast; Society: solitary; Armor class: 4; Method of attack: fangs, crushing, lashing; Source: general Celtic.

Dragons, Teutonic

Teutonic Dragons are generally golden, fire-breathing, and sometimes but not always winged, and live in underground or mountain caves with their hoard. They have bulkier, less sinuous bodies than their British counterparts, and four feet with razor claws, as well as a distinct tail, usually with a spike, that is highly mobile and deadly. Fire is emitted in a jet from the mouth up to 10 ft long, or in twin jets from the nostrils up to 6 ft long. Armor is very tough; go for the mouth, eyes or underbelly.

Physique: 25; Agility: 19; Endurance: 25; Combat factor: 17; Size: huge; Speed: fast; Society: solitary; Armor class: 5; Method of attack: claws, tail (and breath); Source: general Teutonic; Other: greed and selfishness 20; (if sentient) intelligence and faith 8, charisma 15, magic level 4.

Dwarfs, Dark Ages

Physique: 11; Agility: 13; Endurance: 14; Combat factor: 8; Size: small; Speed: average; Society: kingdoms; Intelligence: 13; Faith: 18; Charisma: 7; Magic level: 10; Greed: 18; Selfishness: 15; Lust: 11 (mortal women); Bravery: 13; Armor class: (skin) 0; Method of attack: armed combat; Source: general Teutonic.

Dwarfs, High Middle Ages

Physique: 5; Agility: 15; Endurance: 7; Combat factor: 2; Size: tiny; Speed: average; Society: kingdoms; Intelligence: 10; Faith: 16; Charisma: 5; Magic level: 3; Greed: 18; Selfishness: 15; Lust: 9 (mortal women); Bravery: 6; Armor class: 0 (skin); Method of attack: petty and furtive (hair-pulling, sticking with pins, etc.); Source: general Teutonic.

Elementals

The physical characteristics of Elementals depend on the size of their appearance circle, but their manifest form remains constant: Air as a miniature whirlwind, Earth as a protean mass of rock,

Fire as a pillar of flame, Water as a dancing wave, and Ether (of course) invisible. In addition to their magical properties of attack, they have physical properties that can be brought into play if the Elemental can attain physical contact with the victim: smothering (all), crushing (Earth), violent agitation (Air, Water), burning (Fire). For these purposes their speed is assumed to be very fast, and their physique and agility 10 points per foot diameter of circle to a maximum of 35. Elementals cannot, of course, be injured in any way, though they may give up on their vengeance and retire to the Ethereal plane (or back to the Conjurer, if he's not the same as their immediate victim!) in disgust.

Elves/fairies (Courtly)

See earlier. Roll for characteristics if you prefer.

Physique: 15; Agility: 16; Endurance: 12; Combat factor: 8; Size: medium; Speed: average; Society: kingdoms; Intelligence: 18; Faith: 24; Charisma: 20; Magic level: 12; Greed: 12; Selfishness: 11; Lust: 15 (own species and mortals alike); Bravery: 12; Armor class: (skin) 0; Method of attack: armed combat; Source: all over Western Europe before about 1350.

Elves/fairies (Diminutive)

Physique: 8; Agility: 16; Endurance: 10; Combat factor: 4; Size: small; Speed: average; Society: kingdoms; Intelligence: 12; Faith: 20; Charisma: 16; Magic level: 7; Greed: 13; Selfishness: 13; Lust: 12; Bravery: 7; Armor class: 0; Method of attack: weapons; Source: general European, later High Middle Ages only.

Fenris Wolf

Under normal circumstances, this gigantic supernatural wolf will remain bound till Ragnarok, the doom of the gods; to release it would take a magic of DD12, and once free it would destroy first Tyr, then the rest of the gods, then everyone else. A monster for GMs with a taste for the apocalyptic.

Physique: 38; Agility: 30; Endurance: 40; Combat factor: 20; Size: huge; Speed: very fast; Society: unique; Intelligence: 9;

Faith: 26; Charisma: 5; Magic level: 14; Greed: 18; Selfishness: 20; Lust: 3; Bravery: 18; Armor class: 3; Method of attack: jaws, claws, and sheer weight; Source: Norse.

Ghosts

A dead spirit that returns, conjured by a Necromancer or by itself, to the Earthly plane has magic level and faith 1½ times what it had when it was alive. If they are not known, level = 2D6, faith = 3D6 + 12. An insubstantial ghost cannot move physical objects, with the exception of its own physical remains, by other than magical means; and all use of magic necessarily diminishes its own being while it is away from the Ethereal plane. Ghosts may assume whatever physical form they wish (but DD2 to present an appearance of *substantiality* for five minutes, increasing by one DD every five minutes thereafter). Unless otherwise known, ghosts are assumed to have their operating level of mana (calculate from magic level) when they first appear from the Ether, and if this falls below half they are automatically recalled there to recharge, at a rate of 2 minutes per mana point. If they choose, they can hold further mana up to their maximum (again calculated from magic level), but no matter what their initial mana level on emergence from the Ethereal plane, they will be automatically returned when it falls below half. Intelligence and other mental factors are as when alive, or 3D6. All ghosts have a chance, independent of any magical assistance they give it, of *frightening* a mortal who perceives them, for which apply the following calculation:

Faith, intelligence, charisma, bravery: for each factor under 7, +1; 8-10, +2; 11-14, +3; 15-17, +4; 18+, +5; character is forewarned, +2; character has seen ghosts before, +2.

Result: 11+, no effect; 8-10, character's bravery is halved, recoverable at 1 point per 2 hours; 6-7, madness; 4-5, instant death.

Giant ants

Typical Celtic oversized monsters: carnivorous ants the size of foals, with clawed feet and knife-edged mandibles.

Physique: 11; Agility: 13; Endurance: 10; Combat factor: 8;

Size: average; Speed: average; Society: swarms; Armor class: 4; Method of attack: claws, mandibles; Source: Irish; Other: selfishness 4.

Giant boars

A common Celtic monster, usually encountered in forests and sometimes deliberately sought out by heroes as a prestigious kill. For famous individual specimens see *Twrch Trwyth* and *Ysgithyrwyn Chief Boar*.

Physique: 20; Agility: 12; Endurance: 24; Combat factor: 15; Size: large-huge; Speed: fast; Society: lairs; Armor class: 2; Method of attack: tusks (impaling and tossing); Source: general Celtic.

Giants, Celtic

See earlier. Roll for characteristics if you prefer.

Physique: 22; Agility: 16; Endurance: 21; Combat factor: 15; Size: large-huge; Speed: average; Society: solitary; Intelligence: 6; Faith: 15; Charisma: 8; Magic level: 3-12; Greed: 12; Selfishness: 17; Lust: 15 (mortal women only); Bravery: 13; Armor class: 1 (skin); Method of attack: armed or unarmed combat; Source: general Celtic, Arthurian.

Giants, Norse

See earlier. Roll for characteristics if you prefer.

Physique: 36; Agility: 27; Endurance: 37; Combat factor: 18; Size: large-bloody huge; Speed: fast; Society: various (solitary, families, castles, kingdoms); Intelligence: 10; Faith: 24; Charisma: 9; Magic level: 15; Greed: 19; Selfishness: 20; Lust: 18 (indiscriminate); Bravery: 16; Armor class: 2 (skin); Method of attack: armed or unarmed combat; Source: Norse and general Teutonic (mainly Dark Ages).

Giolla Dacker

A Fomor, or ugly, bad-tempered, magic-using giant; his name means approximately "Lazy Bugger." "He had a large, thick body, bloated and swollen out to a great size; clumsy, crooked legs; and broad, flat feet, turned inwards. His hands and arms and shoul-

ders were bony and thick and very strong-looking; his neck was
long and thin; he had thick lips, and long, crooked teeth; and his
face was covered all over with bushy hair. He was fully armed;
but all his weapons were rusty and soiled and slovenly looking. A
broad shield of a dirty, sooty color, rough and battered hung
over his back; he had a long, heavy, straight sword at his left hip;
and he held in his left hand two thick-handled, broad-headed
spears, old and rusty, and seeming as if they had not been
handled for years. In his right hand he held an iron club." The
Giolla Dacker wanders the land with his enormous horse (see
below) looking for employment, but complains so much that he
rarely gets any. Formidable if angered.

Physique: 20; Agility: 10; Endurance: 21; Combat factor: 12;
Size: large; Speed: fast; Society: unique; Intelligence: 7; Faith:
14; Charisma: 3; Magic level: 8; Greed: 16; Selfishness: 18;
Lust: 9; Bravery: 12; Armor class: 1 (skin); Method of attack:
armed combat; Source: Irish.

Giolla Dacker's horse

"Even larger in proportion than the giant himself, and quite as
ugly. His great carcase was covered all over with tangled, scraggy
hair, of a sooty black; you could count his ribs, and all the points
of his big bones through his hide; his legs were crooked and
knotty; his neck was twisted; and as for his jaws, they were so
long and heavy that they made his head look twice too large for
his body." The horse can seat 15 heroes and travel at extraordinary speed, which may be turned to good or ill depending on
how the Giolla Dacker's feeling.

Physique: 23; Agility: 19; Endurance: 24; Combat factor: 9;
Size: huge; Speed: very fast; Society: unique; Armor class: 2;
Method of attack: striking out with hoofs; Source: Irish.

Grendel

One of the mightiest of the *Hafgygr* race: a shaggy, man-shaped
anthropophage dwelling in a mere who emerges at night to trap
solitary men and kill and eat them in swift silence.

Physique: 22; Agility: 16; Endurance: 22; Combat factor: 13;
Size: large; Speed: fast; Society: unique; Armor class: 1; Method
of attack: unarmed combat; Source: Anglo-Saxon (Dark Ages
only).

Griffin

One of the most ferocious of medieval monsters, the Griffin has a lion's body and hindlegs and tail, with an eagle's wings and head (only on an appropriate scale to the rest of the body). The forelegs are those of an eagle, terminating in nasty talons; the beak is curved, razor-sharp. Griffins are bad-tempered and rapacious, as well as enormously strong; they frequently carry off cattle, and are nesting carnivores. As well as one of the most powerful of legendary beasts ("a weedy Griffin with spindly legs is unthinkable," says Rodney Dennys in *The Heraldic Imagination*), Griffins are fairly common, though hard to catch as they nest on mountaintops and descend generally only to snatch prey. A close relative is the *Opinicus*, which has a lion's forefeet and only a short tail.

Physique: 26; Agility: 15; Endurance: 20; Combat factor: 16; Size: large; Speed: very fast; Society: nests; Armor class: 2; Method of attack: claws, beak; Source: bestiaries, heraldry.

Hafgygr

The type of monster of which Grendel and his mother are the most famous specimens: amphibious man-eating lake monsters, secretive and hard to catch on land. They have humanoid shape, tough hides, cold blood and thick matted body hair, and lots of big teeth. Light and heat are odious to them and sufficient to drive them away.

Physique: 20; Agility: 14; Endurance: 21; Combat factor: 12; Size: medium; Speed: fast; Society: lairs; Armor class: 1; Method of attack: unarmed combat, wrestling, teeth; Source: Anglo-Saxon (Dark Ages only).

Kraken

A vast sea monster never glimpsed in its entirety, but thought to be whale-like in form. It habitually floats just under the surface of the sea, and its upper hide is hard and coarse enough to pass for smooth rock, so that the Kraken can be mistaken for an uncharted island. It's also rather insensitive, so that it generally won't notice people tramping all over it unless they start trying to beach ships on it or hold axe-throwing competitions. But it rolls over or otherwise adjusts position to water its drying-out top surface on average once an hour. If it's in a good mood it spouts: 60 ft from an inconspicuous blowhole.

Physique: 30; Agility: 5; Endurance: 35; Combat factor: 18; Size: bloody huge; Speed: very slow; Society: solitary; Armor class: 5; Method of attack: spouting, lashing tail and fins, swallowing, causing whirlpools; Source: Scandinavian.

Lamia

A kind of female relative of the Manticore, with a panther-like body and a beautiful woman's face and breasts. In spite of its beguiling looks, it's a rapacious, non-sentient man-eater, with needle-sharp teeth lurking just behind those kissable lips, and a fondness for drinking fresh blood. The body is covered in armored scales.

Physique: 17; Agility: 16; Endurance: 16; Combat factor: 11; Size: medium; Speed: fast; Society: solitary; Armor class: 3; Method of attack: tooth and claw; Source: bestiaries.

Lions

Though not native to Europe in the Middle Ages, lions appear frequently in romance, and are sufficiently literary creatures to class as monsters. Celtic lions differ from real-life ones in being solitary, variable in color, and not tied down to any particular sort of habitat. They're man eaters, but not always vicious; many are more hostile to evil monsters than to man. Heraldry offers two more eccentric flavors: see below.

Physique: 20; Agility: 17; Endurance: 16; Combat factor: 12; Size: medium; Speed: fast; Society: solitary; Armor class: 0; Method of attack: tooth and claw; Source: Welsh, Arthurian, heraldry.

Lions, two-headed

These fight with the added combat asset of an extra set of jaws; each head can manage the body independently if its partner is killed, so you either have to take out both or go for the body instead.

Physique: 20; Agility: 18; Endurance: 18; Combat factor: 14; Size: medium; Speed: fast; Society: solitary; Armor class: 0; Method of attack: tooth and claw; Source: heraldry.

Lions, two-bodied

Double-bodied lions have a single head and a bifurcating neck; enormously clumsy, their combat advantage is limited to a further clutch of limbs and a lot more body to incapacitate. Each body can function autonomously (though not without the head!); if one is slain, however, the other will have to drag it around, being unable to get the head round to chew it off. Should be a bit of a pushover, as it spends most of its time posing for shields . . .

Physique: 20; Agility: 4; Endurance: 18; Combat factor: 10; Size: medium (twice); Speed: slow; Society: solitary; Armor class: 0; Method of attack: claw and tooth; Source: heraldry.

Manticore

One of the most fearsome of medieval beasts: a lion's body with a convincingly human head save for the evil red eyes and rather a lot of facial hair, and an instantly lethal sting in the tip of the tail. The manticore has three rows of razor-edge teeth that interlace as the jaws clamp shut. It is extraordinarily strong in the hind limbs and capable of 15-ft leaps, and its favorite food is human flesh. In spite of the face, it is not sentient.

Physique: 25; Agility: 15; Endurance: 17; Combat factor: 16; Size: medium; Speed: fast; Society: packs; Armor class: 1; Method of attack: sting, tooth and claw; Source: bestiaries; Other: greed 20.

Midgard Serpent

The largest monster in the universe; unlikely to be aroused before Ragnarok, however. The World Serpent encircles the earth be-

neath the surface of the ocean and will only emerge at the end of
the world (though Thor has done a couple of rounds with it in
his time). Its tail is in its mouth, and no matter where you sail to
the edge of the world you have an 80 per cent chance of encoun-
tering its head if you disturb it. Another apocalyptic monster.

Physique: 40; Agility: 8; Endurance: 40; Combat factor: 20;
Size: bloody huge; Speed: very slow; Society: unique; Armor
class: 4; Method of attack: jaws, and sheer bulk; Source: Norse.

Monoceros

The Monoceros of the Cambridge Bestiary is evidently a degenerate, belligerent strain of *Unicorn:* "a monster with a horrible
howl, with a horse-like body, with feet like an elephant, and with
a tail like a stag's." The horn protrudes 4 ft from the forehead
and is extremely sharp and tough; and the Monoceros, unlike the
Unicorn, is aggressive and will charge with the horn. In other respects, the horn is like that of the Unicorn: elegant, and valuable.

Physique: 14; Agility: 20; Endurance: 11; Combat factor: 12;
Size: medium; Speed: fast; Society: solitary; Armor class: 1;
Method of attack: horn, hoofs; Source: bestiaries.

Nicor

A pervasive type of amphibious sea and freshwater monster
whose true shape has never been seen, such is its elusive speed
and suddenness. But it has limbs or tentacles, and lairs on land in
damp, rocky caves, only emerging at night or under cover of mist.
It preys on warm-blooded creatures by preference, though cold-
blooded itself.

Physique: 15; Agility: 18; Endurance: 14; Combat factor: 10;
Size: medium; Speed: fast; Society: lairs; Armor class: 1;
Method of attack: wrestling, drowning, strangulation; Source:
Anglo-Saxon (Dark Ages only).

Nightmare

A spirit monster that torments the sleeping, either by entering
their dreams and trapping them in a nightmare from which they
cannot awake, or by riding the body of the sleeper until he
suffocates or dies of fright. The Nightmare can take the form of a
human female (beautiful or haggish) or of an animal; she can be

driven out by a command from the sleeper or another, and if discovered at work has a 50 per cent chance of deserting the sleeper on the spot. Characters of PB2 and above cannot be ridden by Nightmares, nor can anyone who has said their prayers to an appropriate Higher power before retiring. A Nightmare presents a substantial appearance but is in fact only physically palpable to her victim, to whom she appears to have physique 18, agility 12, endurance 20, size medium, speed slow. Otherwise, blows from without will not connect and cannot dislodge her, although if the sleeper is magically awakened (by a counterspell to the Nightmare's sleep spell) she will instantly vanish. Anglo-Saxon *Mara,* German *Mahr.*

Opinicus

A close relative of the *Griffin,* the Opinicus has lion's forepaws instead of eagle's talons, and a short, harmless tail a bit like a camel's.

Physique: 22; Agility: 15; Endurance: 20; Combat factor: 14; Size: large; Speed: very fast; Society: nests; Armor class: 2; Method of attack: beak, claws; Source: heraldry (High Middle Ages only).

Parandrus

A timid stag-like creature with the deep shaggy coat of a bear, and the peculiar property of being able to blend chameleon-like with its background, a property which is instantaneous when the creature is frightened or trying to hide. Its normal color is a rather neutral brown. If cornered, it will fight with its horns, but given the least opportunity it will prefer flight. A useful beast to kill, though; its hide is warm to wear and versatile, its meat delicious, and even its fat makes rather a good grease.

Physique: 12; Agility: 15; Endurance: 9; Combat factor: 6; Size: large; Speed: fast; Society: herds; Armor class: 1; Method of attack: horns, kicking with hind legs; Source: bestiaries; Other: bravery 4.

Sharvan the Surly

Another of the Irish Fomor, or ugly magic-using Giants (see *Giolla Dacker*): "burly and strong, with heavy bones, large thick nose, crooked teeth, and one broad, red, fiery eye in the middle of his black forehead. And he had a great club tied by a chain to an iron girdle which was round his body. He was, moreover, so skilled in magic that fire could not burn him, water could not drown him, and weapons could not wound him; and there was no way to kill him but by giving him three blows of his own club. By day he sat at the foot of his tree, watching; and at night he slept in a hut he had made for himself, high up among the branches."

Physique: 20; Agility: 15; Endurance: 22; Combat factor: 15; Size: large; Speed: average; Society: unique; Intelligence: 8; Faith: 17; Charisma: 7; Magic level: 11; Greed: 12; Selfishness: 18; Lust: 9; Bravery: 14; Armor class: 5 (magically sustained); Method of attack: armed combat; Source: Irish.

Singing bone

A human bone inhabited and animated by the spirit of its owner, another Undead, or a Demon. It may fly freely around the place, and will have a 40 per cent chance of remaining possessed if the bone is shattered (in which case the fragments take on independent existence under the spirit's control). Psychological and magical factors as for *ghosts,* without ability to frighten.

Physique: 10; Agility: 18; Endurance: 8; Combat factor: 5; Size: tiny; Speed: very fast; Method of attack: percussion.

Trolls

See earlier. Roll for characteristics if you prefer.

Physique: 20; Agility: 8; Endurance: 22; Combat factor: 14; Size: large; Speed: slow; Society: solitary; Intelligence: 8; Faith: 19; Charisma: 3; Magic level: 6; Greed: 18; Selfishness: 20; Lust: 12 (mortal women); Bravery: 7; Armor class: 2 (skin); Method of attack: armed or unarmed combat; Source: Norse.

Twrch Trwyth

A sentient *giant boar,* accompanied by his seven whelps, also sentient; all are capable of speech.

Physique: 22 (whelps 10); Agility: 14 (whelps 14); Endurance: 23 (whelps 10); Combat factor: 15 (whelps 9); Size: huge (whelps medium); Speed: fast (whelps average); Intelligence: 9 (whelps 7); Faith: 10; Charisma: 12; Magic level: 4 (whelps 1);

Greed: 14; Selfishness: 14; Lust: 8 (lady boars); Bravery: 15; Armor class: 2 (whelps 1); Method of attack: tusks; Source: Welsh-Arthurian.

Unicorn

The true Unicorn is smaller than the Monoceros and much more docile, though it too can put up a fight if cornered. It is goat-sized, with a white spiralled horn 15-30 inches long (depending on age and size), and a goat's beard. The approved method of capture is to entice it to put its head in the lap of a young virgin; later tradition piously teaches that this is because it is attracted by her purity, and will placidly fall asleep in her lap, whereupon the harsh hunters may emerge and capture or slay it. Physiologus, however, informs us that, far from nodding off, the unicorn will begin to suck at her breasts and "conduct himself familiarly" with her, at which point she must seize his horn and hold him fast for the hunters. What would happen if the Unicorn were allowed to proceed further can only be conjectured; why not game it and find out? Unicorn horns have no intrinsic magical properties (though they can always be Enchanted), but are highly prized and readily distinguishable from narwhal horns . . .

Physique: 10; Agility: 21; Endurance: 11; Combat factor: 10; Size: small; Speed: very fast; Society: herds (very rare); Armor class: 0; Method of attack: horn, hoofs; Source: bestiaries, heraldry.

Vampyre

The medieval Vampyre is a spirit monster, not the undead human shape shifter of later tradition, though it is nocturnal and does take human form by preference. Other common shapes are dog, frog, flea, cat, toad or spider, and the size of bite and amount of blood drunk will vary according to the creature's size; but the painfulness of the bite will vary *inversely* with the size, and physique points are lost on an absolute basis (one immediately upon the bite, five minutes for the next, ten for the next, and so forth). A Vampyre may attack a victim in sleep and cast a magical command on him not to awaken. Vampyres have substance *only* when feeding and for 60 minutes thereafter.

Physique: 13; Agility: 11; Endurance: 8; Combat factor: 5;

Size: medium; Speed: average; Society: solitary; Intelligence: 9; Faith: 20; Charisma: 10; Magic level: 13; Greed: 20; Selfishness: 16; Lust: 15; Bravery: 10; Armor class: 0; Method of attack: various; Source: East European (High Middle Ages only).

Venomous sheep

One of the more bizarre Celtic monsters, they look like perfectly ordinary sheep but for a wicked glint in their eyes and an unnerving habit of baring their jagged, pointy teeth. But they move faster than their everyday cousins, and will knock ten physique points off anyone they scratch with their poison fangs (a second bite won't make any difference). Recovery takes three hours per point, though anyone who's recovered from the poison once will be immune to it thereafter. Venomous sheep eat carrion and are usually found in flocks.

Physique: 9; Agility: 12; Endurance: 8; Combat factor: 7; Size: small; Speed: fast; Society: flocks; Armor class: 1; Method of attack: teeth; Source: Irish.

Werewolf

Physical characteristics as ordinary wolves (for which see below), mental as Mage's own characteristics in human form.

Wild Men

Wood-dwelling shaggy barbarians, with their own peculiar language (they don't understand any other), stone implements, and clothing of animal hide and leaves. Any metal weapons they may wield have been captured from civilized men. A furtive, withdrawn people, wary of outsiders and reluctant to make themselves known; they'll stay out of your way unless you seem a real threat, in which case they'll lay ambush or subtle traps.

Physique: 16; Agility: 17; Endurance: 14; Combat factor: 9; Size: medium; Speed: average; Society: rough camps, up to 25; Intelligence: 7; Faith: 6; Charisma: 6; Magic level: 2; Greed: 9; Selfishness: 12; Lust: 12; Bravery: 8; Armor class: 2 (if wearing any); Method of attack: various; Source: Anglo-Saxon (Dark Ages), general European (High Middle Ages).

Winged bulls

The wings emerge from the shoulders; in other respects they resemble earth-bound bulls except for a limited ability to stand erect on their hind legs (no more than a minute at a time, with a 5-point drop in agility while bipedal and speed slow). Flight is relatively short-range, limited to about ten minutes aloft at a time.

Physique: 20; Agility: 12; Endurance: 14; Combat factor: 10; Size: large; Speed: fast; Society: herds; Armor class: 1; Method of attack: horns, hoofs; Source: heraldry.

Wrnach

One of the most formidable of Celtic *giants*. He lives in a vast fort of mortared stone with unusually gigantic *black men* as his attendants, and can only be killed with his own sword, which has to be won from him by trickery, but will add 3 points to any mortal's CF if he only has physique 16+ and agility 14+ to wield it.

Physique: 24; Agility: 15; Endurance: 22; Combat factor: 16; Size: large; Speed: average; Society: unique; Intelligence: 9; Faith: 15; Charisma: 10; Magic level: 5; Greed: 15; Selfishness: 15; Lust: 12; Bravery: 18; Armor class: 3; Method of attack: armed combat; Source: Welsh-Arthurian.

Yale

A black, horse-like beast with a boarish head fitted with two long (3-4 ft) horns, which are sharp, slim and graceful and can be independently rotated through a full circle in combat.

Physique: 12; Agility: 16; Endurance: 10; Combat factor: 10; Size: large; Speed: fast; Society: herds; Armor class: 1; Method of attack: tips of horns; Source: bestiaries, heraldry.

Ysbaddaden Penkawr

Penkawr means "Chief Giant," and of the Celtic giants Ysbaddaden is undoubtedly the mightiest. He dwells in a fort with nine gates each with a mighty gateman and a mighty mastiff, and requires forks to prop up his eyelids. He keeps by his hand at all times three poisoned stone-headed spears, which will cause instant death to anyone they pierce but only local pain and difficulty to Ysbaddaden even if they pierce him through the middle. He has a daughter called Olwen, most beautiful of all maidens on earth: "clothed in a robe of flame-colored silk, and about her neck was a collar of ruddy gold, on which were precious emeralds and rubies. More yellow was her head than the flower of the broom, and her skin was whiter than the foam of the wave, and fairer were her hands and her fingers than the blossoms of the wood anemone amidst the spray of the meadow fountain. The eye of the trained hawk, the glance of the three-mewed falcon was not brighter than hers. Her bosom was more snowy than the breast of the white swan, her cheek was redder than the reddest roses. Whoso beheld her was filled with love. Four white trefoils sprung up wherever she trod." Unfortunately, anyone who asks Ysbaddaden for her hand gets a stone spear back by instant reply. If he misses with all three he might be satisfied with setting impossible tasks instead. But God help you if you take the lass without his permission . . .

Physique: 28; Agility: 25; Endurance: 28; Combat factor: 17; Size: huge; Speed: slow; Society: unique; Intelligence: 10; Faith: 13; Charisma: 10; Magic level: 9; Greed: 12; Selfishness: 13; Lust: 5; Bravery: 14; Armor class: 3 (skin); Method of attack: armed combat, preferably sedentary; Source: Welsh-Arthurian.

Ysgithyrwyn chief boar

Greatest of the Celtic *giant boars;* his only vulnerable spot is the center of his forehead, where a blow from a heavy axe should kill him instantly.

Physique: 24; Agility: 15; Endurance: 25; Combat factor: 16; Size: huge; Speed: average; Society: unique; Armor class: 4; Method of attack: tusks; Source: Welsh-Arthurian.

ANIMAL CHARACTERISTICS

	Physique	Agility	Endurance	Combat factor	Size	Speed	Armour class	Method of attack	Society	Bravery
Bears	16	10	18	10	Medium	Slow	1	tooth and claw	Lairs	10
Boars	14	12	14	9	Small	Average	1	tusks	Lairs	13
Cattle	20	7	14	10*	Large	Average	0	horns, hoofs	Herds	12*
Dogs	8	13	10	6	Small	Fast	0	teeth	(Packs)	9
Eagles	8	16	6	9	Small	Very fast	0	beak, claws	Nests	16*
Goats	9	13	10	9	Small	Fast	1	horns	Herds	14*
Horses	19	10	14	8	Large	Fast	1	hoofs	(Herds)	11
Ravens	3	15	4	3	Tiny	Very fast	0	beaks	Nests	10
Sheep	9	6	10	6*	Small	Slow	1	hoofs, (horns)	Flocks	8*
Wolves	12	12	10	9	Small	Fast	1	teeth	Packs	10

* Halve for females.

Index to Tables

Index

A

O

P

R

S